My Silver Lining

Thank You !!

Sept. 22. 2024

My Silver Lining

From Survival to Perseverance

A MEMOIR

———————————

Adel Ben-Harhara

———————————

Volume Three — US and Canada

Cover design: Jana Rade

ISBN print: 978-1-7776000-1-3

ISBN e-book: 978-1-7776000-0-6

ISBN audiobook: 978-1-7780381-0-5

Disclaimer

Although I have made every effort to ensure that the information in this book was correct at the time of publication, I do not assume and hereby disclaim any liability to any party for any loss, damage, or disruption caused by errors or omissions, whether such errors or omissions result from negligence, accident, or any other cause.

I have tried to recreate events, locales, and conversations from my memories. To protect privacy, in some instances I have changed the names of individuals and places and some identifying characteristics and details such as dates, physical properties, occupations, and places of residence.

This book is not to be used as a religious, historical, geographical, or political reference text. The information, opinions, and details about religion, history, politics, and geography presented in this book are included for the purpose of enhancing my story only, not to teach.

The terms "South Arabian," "Arabian Peninsula," "Arabs," "Arabians," "Arab," and "Arabic" refer only to Yemenis and the country of Yemen.

The term "Yemen" refers to the country after the unification of North and South Yemen in 1990.

Dedication

To my daughters, **Lina** and **Summer**, for giving me a reason to live.

To the six mothers who raised me: **Weinishet**, **Rukia**, **Emebet**, **Maryam**, **Zeinab**, and **Fatuma**. And the American mother who "adopted" me, **Norma**.

To my main supporters during my time in the US: **Kathleen Warner** and **Dennis Meier**.

And to those who play a role in adding so much positivity to my current life in Calgary, who are listed in the **Acknowledgments** section.

Contents

Foreword

Only fools and practiced liars look you in the eye and give simple responses to complicated questions. Reality is not simple.

The preceding quote is not attributable to any person that I know of. I made it up for a story I am writing, which has been years in the crafting and is only twenty-one words long. I am still not sure I have it right. It may change.

What will not change is that Adel Ben-Harhara is one of the people who inspired the quote.

Born and raised in South Texas when public schools were still segregated and little white boys like me wore gray Johnny Reb caps while playing Civil War soldiers, I was taught to "look a man in the eye and give an honest answer" when responding to questions. I guess I did that. Sometimes I still do. Later, it would occur to me that while this show of certainty can be good, there are occasions when a more measured response is needed. I blame my education in nuclear engineering for this change in perspective. Nuclear physics is ruled by probability rather than simple cause and effect. Once my brain began thinking in probabilities rather than binary determinism, I began to question the worth of simplistic answers altogether. I started noticing that the people who looked me in the eye and guaranteed something were wrong at least as often as they were right. I concluded that a person who doesn't look away before answering a question for which there is no simple answer either (a) doesn't know what they are talking about or (b) is lying.

Years later, I was in Boise, Idaho, managing an information technology project for Scientech Inc., a consulting company that would soon make it onto the Inc. 500 list. We had a contract to write and maintain software used by the National Park Service's wildland firefighting program, a part of the National Interagency Fire Center, located in Boise. I met Adel Ben-Harhara. The details of this meeting have fled my memory, but two key impressions jump out. The first is that Adel was a soft-spoken young man whose physiognomy reminded me of someone I knew only in pictures: Haile Selassie, the former Emperor of Ethiopia. My second impression was that before answering a question that required thought, Adel looked away for a moment. Instead of parroting some hackneyed cliché and hiding behind it in hopes of sounding erudite, Adel Ben-Harhara lowered his gaze, thought, synthesized a response, and only then spoke. I was not used to such behavior, but I knew what it was, and I liked it.

I struggle to recall how long Adel worked for me. In *My Silver Lining*, he says eighteen months, and that number strikes me as probable. My brain is just not built for recording such details.

After his time with Scientech, Adel went on to work at the Idaho State Library. We remained in contact. I met Richard Wilson, who was Adel's boss at the library, and I would, in time, learn of the problems Adel was having with the US Immigration and Naturalization Service (INS). I vaguely remember that there were limits on his student visa. I also remember something about marriage. The details have abandoned me, but I remember being upset with what I saw as a bureaucratic effort to deport the kind of thoughtful person that America needs more of. As a second-generation descendant of German immigrant farmers, I have great respect for those brave souls who come here to start a new life in this country.

I remember writing a check and sending it to an attorney who was representing Adel. It was for naught; Adel left, but he would later return to North America, choosing Canada, the United States' more civil northern neighbor, as his home. When we reconnected, he was [and still is] living in Calgary, Alberta. Somewhere along the line, we became friends on Facebook, and I have watched the thoughtful young man I knew raise a family, build a successful career, travel the globe, and, like me, lose his hair.

I thought I would have made a trip to Calgary to visit Adel by now. But life has a way of intruding. Between raising a son, taking care of elderly parents, dealing with cancer, enduring a pandemic, and (now) taking care of elderly pets, time has slipped away. And yet, if I were to meet Adel Ben-Harhara again, I predict that I would come away with three impressions—one more than last time! My first impression will be that this mature man who mysteriously replaced young Adel still reminds me a bit of Haile Selassie but with less hair. My second impression will be that he still thinks before he speaks, looking away now and then as thoughtful people do. And my third impression? That I was fortunate to meet Adel Ben-Harhara, one of those unique humans who will never give simple answers to complicated questions.

— Dennis Meier, Boise, Idaho, May 2022

Preamble

As you're embarking on reading the last volume of my three-volume memoir, I felt it is necessary to debrief you on my early life. After separating from my Ethiopian mother as a toddler, I was essentially orphaned at the age of five when my father died. I went to live with an uncle, who squandered my portion of my father's inheritance and then disappeared, leaving me a homeless eight-year-old boy. As my mother was unable to provide support, I lived on the streets for three years until my Aunt Emebet, my mother's sister, took me in.

As an adolescent in Marxist Ethiopia, I was imprisoned for taking part in a communist party youth movement. I barely avoided the death squad's bullets before moving to my father's ancestors' land: Yemen. I was sixteen when I left Ethiopia for Yemen.

My struggles continued in North Yemen, where I suffered from prejudice, discrimination, and the effects of civil wars. I was constantly fighting for equal rights and citizenship. From age sixteen to twenty-two was a period when I endured harsh treatment because I wore dark skin, was born in East Africa, and was unable to assimilate into an underdeveloped society living according to primitive cultural traditions. As a young man of twenty-two, I decided to move to the US to pursue a university degree and my dream of a better life.

Introduction

Despite the setbacks and misfortunes one faces, it is human nature to be hopeful. I suppose there's a silver lining to losing my father when I was five, disconnecting from my mother, and facing challenging times in Ethiopia, Yemen, and the US. I'm fortunate to be in Canada living a stable life and raising my children. I can focus on the positive aspects of life by developing gratitude and continuing to be curious about nature. I'm a happy man because I'm grateful. I choose to have an attitude of gratitude! That gratitude allows me to be happy.

US Supreme Court judge Oliver Wendell Holmes Jr. once said, "The great thing in this world is not so much where you stand as in what direction you are moving." When I was a teenager, I decided to move toward the West, both literally and figuratively. I didn't believe the West was better than the East, but I focused on the better opportunities the West offered me—education and fundamental human rights. Living in North America hasn't erased my formidable memories and values from my youth, but it has reshaped my personality and perspectives. Without a doubt, the West has become my silver lining!

As I write this book, I am a sixty-two-year-old professional nearing retirement. At this phase of my life, I would say there is a positive side to every struggle, and it's a little tricky at times to get the silver to shine. It is also true that there will be no silver lining without the haze. Therefore, I might add that survival has defined my past, but perseverance continues to shape my tomorrow. I completely agree with author James Allen, who said, "Your circumstances may be uncongenial, but they shall not long remain so if you only perceive an ideal and strive to reach it. You cannot travel within and stand still without."[1] Every misfortune presents a precious clue as to what will come.

Major Life Events

Volume One

1962   Born in Addis Ababa, Ethiopia.
1964   Separated from my mother and started to live with my stepmother and father.
1967   My father died of cirrhosis.
1967   Began studying Judaism and Islam.
1970   My uncle squandered my father's estate and disappeared. Abandoned. Left for two years without a home or a parent.
1971   Rescued by and lived with my aunt until 1978.
1972   Attended an evangelical Bible school until 1974.
1976   Arrested and detained three times throughout 1976 and 1977 for being a member of a communist party (youth branch).
1978   Moved to North Yemen.

Volume Two[2]

1978   Completed high school in Ta'izz, North Yemen, and then lived in Hodeidah, North Yemen.
1981   Moved to Sana'a, North Yemen, and started to work for US Aid Development Agency (USAID).
1981   Made frequent trips to communist South Yemen over the next three years to visit relatives.
1983   Made the Umrah pilgrimage to Mecca, Saudi Arabia.
1984   Moved to the US to study computer science and engineering.

1992   Returned to Yemen (North and South were united by this time).

1994   Survived the Yemen Civil War.

1995   Married a woman from South Yemen.

Volume Three

1985   Married an American woman to obtain US resident status. Shortly after, detained by the Immigration and Naturalization Service (INS) and lost US resident and student status. (Marriage was soon annulled.)

1987   Embroiled in a six-year-long legal quagmire in a quest for political asylum in the US.

1996   Moved to Canada.

1996   My first daughter was born.

2003   My second daughter was born.

2006   Earned an MBA.

2010   Ended a fifteen-year-long marriage; reunited with biological mother.

2014   Ran my first marathon in Calgary, followed by thirty more since then, including the six Majors: Boston, Chicago, Berlin, London, New York, and Tokyo.

2017   Climbed Mount Kilimanjaro.

2020   Visited the hottest and one of the lowest points on the planet: Danakil Depression, Dallol.

2022   Published my first two books: *To Have Nothing* and *Hope in the Sky.*

2024   Completed the Six Majors.

2024   Published my third book: *My Silver Lining.*

Part One

I

In Transition

The American dream. Those three short, simple words encompass the hopes and aspirations of all the peoples on Earth. The words are not only short and simple. They are also fragile.

— Ross Perot, American businessman and former presidential candidate

When I was a teenager, the foundation of my American dream was built on freedom—freedom of religion, language, and cultural practices; freedom to choose whether I wanted to learn or obey religious rules rather than having them imposed on me; freedom from being confined by certain cultural values, some of which were unacceptable to me. The West was where I thought individualism flourished as opposed to the communal lifestyle I had lived in Ethiopia and Yemen, where society imposed everything on me.

The American dream also meant opportunities for advanced education and varied career choices. I thought the majority of educational institutes would be available to me, and I would have countless programs to choose from. But when I left Yemen to pursue my university studies in the US, self-doubt crept in.

University in a second language? Or a third language in my case?

I've dreamed of this my whole life, and now it's happening. But what if I fail? What if my English isn't good enough to complete my courses?

How can I afford this? I only have enough money for two years. I won't be able to complete my university degree unless I find a way to pay for the second half of my studies. What if I have to return to Yemen after only two years because I can't pay for the rest of my degree?

What if my ESL [English as a Second Language] teacher in Yemen was right? What if the US isn't the land of hopes and dreams for immigrants I've always envisioned? What if the racism I experienced in North Yemen these past several years was only minor compared to how Americans will treat me?

Have I overestimated my ability to live in Idaho? What do I really know about the US and Idaho?

What if I hate the food? Food is essential for survival. What if I can't find anything I like to eat?

And what about the climate? I've never seen snow before. I know Americans, Canadians, and Europeans all survive cold winters, but maybe my body won't be able to adapt.

*

In my later adult years, I heard a quote by rock singer Billy Idol: "If your world doesn't allow you to dream, move to one where you can." The worlds I lived in during my first twenty-two years—Ethiopia and Yemen—didn't allow me to dream, so I moved where I can.

US Bound

On July 5, 1984, at the age of twenty-two, I boarded an airplane to the US via Italy (Rome) and Germany (Bonn). I was emotionally shaken by my sister Muna breaking down at Sana'a International Airport. Until then, no one in my family or circle of friends knew my destination was the US and that I had no intention of returning to North Yemen. Only a few of my American colleagues knew my plans. The Yemeni government was recruiting men for the military, so they were not allowing youth to leave the country. I made all of my arrangements in secret other than enlisting the help of some of my American colleagues.

Muna became aware of my reality when she dropped me off for my flight. She had driven me to the airport, thinking she was seeing me off to Ethiopia for a visit. She broke down crying when I told her my final destination was the US. She sobbed as if I had died. At that moment, she realized that I didn't intend to return to Yemen. Her wailing caught the attention of airport officials.

"What is the problem?" they asked Muna.

"She is missing her mother and is unable to fly with me to Ethiopia to visit her," I told them. They accepted my explanation and let me go.

The stops in Rome and Bonn were due to the need to visit two friends. During the early 1980s, I met two men who used North Yemen as a haven before being granted political asylum in Europe: a lawyer from Somalia named Abdi and Berhane, an engineer from Eritrea. I needed to see how these men were functioning, as I hardly knew how to live within Western society and wanted to learn from their perspectives and experiences.

After its independence from Italy, between 1942 and 1990, Eritrea was annexed as part of Ethiopia. Berhane, the first person I interacted with at my workplace, United States Agency for International Development (USAID), was living in the same apartment complex I was living in. During those days, there was an active struggle to free Eritrea from Ethiopia, and many freedom fighters were operating in the neighboring countries, including North Yemen. Berhane, who had abruptly left Ethiopia for Yemen in 1979 due to the conflict, was a civil engineer and was a refugee in Yemen. About six months before I left for the US, he migrated to Bonn, Germany.

While living in North Yemen, he and his wife often invited me to their house. His wife didn't speak Amharic or Arabic, but we had mutual respect and appreciation. Even though I'm half Arab and also half Ethiopian, born in the country they wanted to flee from, they welcomed me as a friend without any reservations or prejudices.

Abdi was a practicing lawyer in his homeland (Somalia) and was trained and certified to practice law in the UK and Italy. Mark Hansen, my English teacher and friend in North Yemen, introduced me to Abdi, who was also living in Yemen as a refugee. He, like Berhane, was funded by the United Nations High Commissioner for Refugees (UNHCR) and was approved to emigrate to Rome, Italy.

Berhane and Abdi always reminded me of those who were struggling against the communist military government and were jailed with me in Ethiopia for my political activism during the revolution in the 1970s. Both men had worldly outlooks and were versed in the English and Italian languages. They were intellectual individuals with an in-depth understanding of global events and issues. Watching and listening to Mark, Abdi, and Berhane's debates was like watching the best live music of a political symphony.

After a week in Germany and Italy, I was off to Boise, Idaho. Mark had suggested I go to university in Boise because he could connect me to friends there and the cost was lower than other universities, so I took his advice. I thought the flight from Sana'a to Rome (about six hours) and the connection to Bonn (roughly another two hours) were long, but the flight from Bonn to Los Angeles was about twelve hours. However, it didn't feel like a long flight. Nestled on the Pan Am airplane, I enjoyed in-flight entertainment for the first time. During that flight, I watched three shows: *Endless Love,* starring Brooke Shields and Martin Hewitt; a musical named *Islands in the Stream* with Dolly Parton and Kenny Rogers; and a third that I don't remember.

I had previously seen *Endless Love* in North Yemen; however, watching it on the airplane I noticed it was totally different. The version I had seen in Yemen was heavily censored, and restrictions were applied to the sexually explicit scenes, which conflicted with Islamic culture and religion. Although I don't recall reading anything on the topic in the Qur'an as a child, there was a human-made law prohibiting content that negatively impacted public order, religious values, public morals, and privacy, which could include content that promotes drug use, pornography, and gambling.

During the show on the plane, even though I wanted to use the washroom badly, I had to hold it so that I didn't miss any intimate parts of the movie, like kissing and sexual acts. Forcefully prohibiting something will eventually result in a greater desire or urge to seek it.

II

University in a New Country

Education is the passport to the future, for tomorrow belongs to those who prepare for it today.

— Malcolm X

Before departing North Yemen, I received three acceptance letters, one each from the University of Arizona in Tucson (UofA), Oregon State University (OSU), and Boise State University (BSU). Arizona's landscape and weather conditions were like Yemen's, making it appealing. Oregon was the greenest and perhaps the most beautiful coastal state with lush greenery. Boise was the smallest and the most attractive when it came to easily adjusting to the American system. The cost of tuition and accommodation in Idaho was also lower than in the other two.

Initially, I wanted to spend one semester at each campus to understand the different environments. Then I started worrying about expenses and that my courses may not transfer over to other universities. Americans I knew from my work connected me to some Yemeni students in the US, but I could only find information on the University of Arizona

19

from those students; I didn't know anyone at the other two institutions. The North Yemeni students who went to Tucson on scholarship told me all good things. However, I became concerned about being part of a large cluster of Arab students around campus, as the primary goal of not all but most students who came from the Middle East was to party ... I was fully aware of the wealthy Arab children's actions and behaviors when they found their freedom. I worried that I wouldn't sleep or study, so I quickly eliminated Arizona.

I was left to choose between Boise (Idaho) and Corvallis (Oregon). OSU was well-known for its agriculture engineering program, which wasn't interesting to me. But I didn't like the idea of Boise, as it was in the middle of nowhere and very cold.

Mark Hansen, my English language instructor in North Yemen, who had also lived in Oregon, had taught in an ESL program at BSU long before he went to Yemen. He assured me that the computer science program at BSU was reputable. He recommended I start with BSU and, if I didn't like it, move to a different city. That way, I would not be wasting lots of money or time. Moreover, he told me he had a couple of friends who would assist me upon my arrival in Boise. Half-heartedly, I chose Boise.

One other American expat who worked at USAID Yemen, a Mormon fellow, had family in Boise. He wrote a letter to introduce me to them and urged them to assist me if I needed help upon landing in Boise. As a result, the Mormon family came to pick me up from the airport.

My plane landed around 1:15 a.m. After clearing customs, I wasn't in the mood to talk. I was grateful for them welcoming me at such an hour, but I was exhausted so I fell asleep immediately upon getting to their house and being shown my room. I woke up early the following day, around 5:30, and I was hungry. The family got up at around 6:30 to embark on their daily school and work life.

"Good morning! Have you taken a shower?" the mother, Norma, greeted me.

"No."

"Here you go." She handed me a set of towels and pointed to the nearest washroom.

I was impressed by the size and cleanliness of the bathroom, and I was mesmerized by the showerhead and the water pressure. Out of excitement, I kept turning it on and off; it simply wasn't something I had ever experienced. I had only had showers in Yemen, not baths, but I had never experienced such instant and powerful water pressure.

Norma had one of the most welcoming smiles I'd ever seen. She led me to the kitchen table, where her children were having breakfast. She introduced me to Kevin (twelve), Steve (ten), and Marta (six). Norma was a single mother and would have been in her mid-forties at the time.

The children were happy and proper. They ate a lot but did so quietly, and the only conversation around the kitchen table consisted of polite requests: "Can you please pass me the jam?" or butter or milk jar. This was in stark contrast to family meals in Yemen, where we ate on the floor, talking loudly over dinner sessions (a token of love and excitement). We often had the TV playing, and the children were running around the room with their mouths full or carrying meals in their hands. In Yemen, we didn't eat much and were always in a hurry when we ate. I thought the amount of food one of

21

these boys consumed for breakfast alone could feed an entire family of five in Yemen.

Norma said, "I will drop the children off at school, and then I will take you to the university campus."

She knew that I wanted to stay in the campus dormitory so that I would get acquainted with the environment.

She glanced at the glass of milk she had poured for me and noticed it wasn't touched. Then she asked me politely, "Are you allergic to milk, or do you have a dietary restriction?"

"I'm okay. I am not used to drinking cold milk," I responded.

In Yemen, we drank powdered milk at night before bed, and hardly anyone drank milk during breakfast, let alone a cold glass.

I asked, "Where can I find coffee or tea to make one for myself, too, as I don't want to make you late?"

She quickly picked up the glass of milk and put it in a square metallic box with a glass window.

She looked at me and said, "I am sure you have never heard of Mormons in your country. I can tell you more about it later. In short, we don't drink alcohol, coffee, or soda, and we don't smoke cigarettes."

She returned to the microwave, removed the milk, and handed it to me. The milk was hot, and I was taken aback by the speed of the machine and how it was able to warm up the milk in a short span.

She said, "It's called a microwave."

I thought the microwave was a mini fridge, as I had never seen anything like it. That was a revelation, and I started to think about how I would describe it to my friends in Yemen when writing my first letter.

While Norma dropped the children off at their school, I wandered around the house admiring the size of it, the furniture, and the vaulted ceilings. Over half an hour passed, and while I was looking at the landscape and the backyard through a huge bay window, I heard a voice say, "I'm home. Are you ready?"

"That was quick," I said.

"Only forty minutes in total," she told me.

To me, it had felt like only five minutes.

Looking out the back window, I asked, "Are those horses yours?"

She confirmed that they were.

I wasn't used to seeing horses in someone's yard. In Yemen, I had rarely seen horses; I was more accustomed to seeing goats and camels. And the horses I had seen were only in the countryside.

I quickly returned to the room where I had slept and dragged out my luggage. We loaded my bags into the car, and she drove me to the university admissions office. As she dropped me off by the entrance, she wrote her home number on the back of her office business card.

"Give me a ring if you need anything," she told me as she handed me the card.

"Thank you," I replied and headed to the office, pulling my two 50-pound (22-kilogram) suitcases. *I learned a new phrase today—give me a ring. I bet it means, "Give me a call."*

I completed the necessary paperwork at the admissions office, obtained my student ID, and headed to the dormitory building. It was mid-July, and the campus was empty. The girl working at the front desk of the dorm checked me in and gave me my room key.

"The cost will be around nine dollars per day," she informed me. "Once the school semester starts, you will have a roommate. You're lucky to be here first. You can choose the lower or upper deck now," she said, smiling, referring to the bunk beds.

I settled into the designated room and emptied and put away my suitcases. The room had a large rectangular window, and I was able to see the library and the Broncos' football stadium from my bed. There was so much to observe and see, as just about everything was new to me.

In looking at the landscape and how they cut and trimmed the grass, I thought, *It seems smoother than the carpets in my apartment in North Yemen.* The trees were fascinating. There were so many of them, and they were huge. They cast shade everywhere, and the houses looked like they were being swallowed by the trees. The branches were reaching out and connecting to each other from across the street. Compared to the rocky, dusty desert in North Yemen, the greenery in Boise astonished me. I stood there, taking in everything.

Around noon, I went to the main floor to ask the girl at the front desk a few more questions. She was so polite. For a moment, not knowing most people were kind and friendly, I thought she liked me—she was just doing her job, but her friendliness, too, was new for me.

When I was living in North Yemen, I found that the majority of men viewed women as sex objects. Girls in North Yemen never smiled at strangers or engaged in conversation with them. Most North Yemeni girls tended to be abrupt and combative in an unknown environment to deflect unwanted advances, not wanting to mislead a man.

I had hardly ever seen North Yemeni girls smiling because their faces were always covered. It's human nature to want what you can't have, and so the fact that women in North Yemen were covered and untouchable meant that men were even more curious about them. Women were the forbidden fruit. For a young North Yemeni man conditioned to respect women but not interact with them, the friendliness and assertiveness of an American woman can be confusing and can lead to misunderstandings.

I soon learned that women in the US are friendly and make direct eye contact with men. I laughed at myself and how foolish I was to think this girl liked me without knowing me simply because she was smiling and friendly.

I wanted to know where the nearest bank was, and I also asked her to recommend a place to get something to eat.

"The nearest bank is called Idaho First, about 300 yards [275 meters] past the stadium, but you have to cross the traffic light. It's Friday, and they should be open now. As for something to eat, there are two places you could grab sandwiches, and the closest is Bronco Burger, about 150 yards past the bank. They sell burgers and hot dogs."

I thanked her. *Hot dog?*

I asked her, "Did you say 'hot dog'?"

She said, "Yes."

"Thanks," I replied and walked away.

How far is 300 yards? I only knew measurements in metric, like 300 meters. *I will figure it out. However, what is this "hot dog" business? I never knew Americans ate dogs.*

I found the bank, opened an account, and deposited the US$4,000 I was carrying from Yemen. That was a considerable amount of money to have around campus, and I didn't want to lose it.

Later, I discovered hot dogs weren't quite what I was thinking of.

III

Settling In

One's destination is never a place but a new way of seeing things.

— Henry Miller, novelist

T he university admin office gathered all international students for an orientation session a week before school started. I showed up wearing a suit and tie, thinking I should present myself as Sidney Poitier would. Poitier was the first Black person I had watched on screen. I was particularly stricken by the strength and integrity of his character in the movie *Guess Who's Coming to Dinner.* I wanted to be like him intellectually, physically, and even in manner of dress.

Around 105 students were at the orientation, and nearly two-thirds were Asian (Chinese, Taiwanese, Hong Kongers, South Koreans, and Japanese). The rest were roughly equal numbers of Europeans from Germany, Scotland, Holland, Italy, the Czech Republic, etc., and South Americans from Brazil, Argentina, Chile, Paraguay, and Uruguay. There were no Arabs or Africans, but I noticed a couple of Persian students from Iran.

The orientation schedule included a time slot for electing a new president, as the former International Student Association president was returning to his home country of Malaysia after completing his degree. After the orientation, everyone was asked to introduce themselves by stating their full name, both in English and their native languages, and their majors. The order was set alphabetically, so I was the first to introduce myself—A (Adel).

I stood up, stated my name, and said, "I am a product of a mixed racial background from Arab and Ethiopian ethnicities. I was born in Ethiopia and raised in Yemen. I have a Christian mother, and my father's side of the family is Muslim. I speak both Amharic and Arabic."

I continued, "Clearly, no African students are here today, or any Arabs for that matter. Therefore, I'm more than happy to represent the two geographical regions, Africa and the Middle East, with due respect to my fellow Iranians in the room." And I sat down. Everyone laughed. They wanted to ask questions, but I told them, "Perhaps after, as we have 100 remaining students to introduce themselves, and we need to dedicate time to everyone."

We then needed to elect the international students' president. The decision didn't involve rounds, discussions, or panels; they all said, "Adel." I was overwhelmed. They asked me to stand up and give an acceptance speech. I was sweating like a horse. I didn't have the same voice or courage this time.

I said, "Thank you for trusting me to lead the group. It will be our association. I will lead it, but we will work together to promote individual countries' culture, food, and dance to the people of Boise, Idaho."

New Digs

During those first few weeks in Boise, I was stunned by the university and its surroundings. I consistently compared it with Sana'a University, where I had spent a few semesters. However, there was nothing similar between the two of them. My new home was a completely different planet than where I had come from. The BSU campus was surrounded by residential neighborhoods and small businesses catering to the student population.

I used to go and sit inside the empty Broncos football stadium, which had a 37,000-person capacity. Sitting down in the empty stadium gave me a sense of calm; those were reflective moments. Even so, I was worried that whoever saw me might think that I was foolish to keep coming to the same site day in and day out; perhaps they would think that I was there with the hope that a game would start any time.

Within two weeks, I purchased a bike and used it to start to explore the city. Boise appeared to be flat for the most part, making it easier for me to roam around (at least the university and downtown area were).

There was no ethnic food, and I had trouble eating cold sandwiches. In Yemen, we never ate cold meals. I wasn't used to eating cold food.

The food was not only cold but also tasteless. I love spicy food, but none of the food I could get my hands on was spicy. My favorite place to eat was the Bronco Burger place, owned and operated by a family and located across from the stadium and campus. I had to satisfy my curiosity and try a hot dog one day, but eating hot dogs was a short-lived part of my US experience. In 1986, I had one from a street vendor at 3 a.m.

when I went to a club with friends. I ended up getting food poisoning and had to be hospitalized!

I wasn't happy living on campus. I was twenty-two, and the dormitory was full of eighteen-year-olds who had left their parents' homes and were living on their own for the first time. They drank and partied all night, and the dorm was noisy. I wanted to focus on my studies. The other struggle I had was with mealtimes. Because the university cafeteria closed at 6 p.m., I had to eat before then. In Yemen, my dinner used to be between 8 and 9 p.m. so I was never hungry at 5 or 6 p.m. I was unable to eat before 6 and I kept getting hungry around 9 p.m. I decided to move out so I would have more personal space and be able to eat a meal when I wanted without being confined to dorm rules.

One afternoon, as I was exploring on my bike, I saw a "Room for Rent" sign. The address was only a block from the university library. I went to the house and rang the doorbell to inquire about the rental fees and conditions.

An elderly white lady with gray hair approached the door. Her hair and dress were tidy and proper. She was wearing a watch and had pristine, clean teeth. She was limping slightly, so I assumed she had a bit of a knee or hip problem. Her height was almost the same as mine, and she looked well-to-do.

"I'm here to inquire about the room for rent."

Before I finished my sentence, she said, "The room is no longer available."

"Oh, I see. I'm sorry to have bothered you." I added, "Perhaps it is best to remove the rental sign so that other people won't bother you."

Immediately, she asked, "What did you say?"

I repeated my last statement.

The main door was already open, but the sliding screen door was closed, allowing fresh air to come into the house.

She opened the sliding door and said, "I heard an accent."

"Yes, I have an accent, as English is my third language."

"Holy cow! Your English is good. You just sound different from us. Where are you from? Are you a student?"

"I'm from Yemen but was born in Ethiopia. Yes, I'm enrolled in a computer science program and perhaps will be doing a double major in computer science and engineering this fall. I will be a freshman, proudly."

"Would you care to come in and see the room?" she asked me.

I was flustered. "I thought you said the room is no longer available, didn't you?"

"Oh, well. A long story. Come on in."

I was a bit frightened and befuddled. Nevertheless, I stepped into the house. She noticed my hesitation and said, "Come on," pointing me to an armchair in her living room.

It was a smaller room than the Mormon family's house but was neatly kept. I sat down, looking at the exit in case I had to run away.

"My name is Margaret, and I'm from the South. My husband was a minister at a Baptist church. We moved to Idaho during the civil rights movement in the 1960s because my late husband didn't approve of the integration of our children with Black Americans. We thought this was a good place to raise our children. It's best to keep our children with their kind."

She continued, "When I saw you from my kitchen, I thought you were one of our Black people. I am always frightened by them. But you are not one of our Negroes."

I had read plenty of books about the Black civil rights movement, particularly Malcolm X's speeches. Nothing had prepared me for this type of conversation, though, and I didn't know how to respond.

As she spoke to me, I couldn't help but picture her as one of the young white ladies I had seen on video clips who were shouting at a little Black child who was escorted to school or at Black students entering the universities in the South.

*

In Yemen, I heard a lot of stories about how Americans treated Black people. I heard examples of white mothers saying to Black children, "We don't want you, nigger!"[3] I saw documentaries portraying these actions. A few years before I was born, on November 14, 1960, six-year-old Ruby Bridges was escorted to school by four white US marshals sent by J. F. Kennedy to ensure her safe entrance on her first day of school in New Orleans. As they approached the school, crowds gathered, throwing items and shouting, "Two-four-six-eight. We don't want to integrate!" in protest as this young Black girl walked up the steps to begin school. The crowds doubled the following day, shouting threats of poisoning and hanging in protest of Ruby attending school.

The white parents who came to protest Ruby's plan to attend an elementary school and the comments they were making to her and the media were very difficult for me to unsee or forget. All the child wanted was to attend school, but the community's reaction was terrifying.

As a teenager, I was dumbfounded and petrified seeing how violently a person opposed someone attending school simply because of their skin color. Even though I experienced and witnessed discrimination in Yemen, it wasn't violent. The images I saw as a teenager frightened me; I took these images with me to the US. After the conversation I had with Margaret, I was unable to avoid imagining this lady's face among those protestors who were shouting.

*

Margaret said, "Our country went through some shameful periods. I don't feel good about it. Our children grew up, finished university here in Boise, and moved on to bigger cities. My husband passed away, and I missed the South where I grew up. I still miss it."

She gave me a glass of lemonade, and I sensed both guilt and sorrow in her voice.

The room she offered to rent was where her boys had slept.

"There were two twin beds in the room when the boys were growing up, but I replaced them with one double-size bed and added a desk for a student like you to sleep and study in the privacy of your own space. The rent is $150 monthly, all-inclusive—water, electricity, and heat. However, if you cut the grass and shovel the snow year-round, I could reduce the rent to $125 monthly." She added, "You have a private shower," and suggested I could use her kitchen to cook.

I told her, "I don't know how to cook. I'm capable of burning water."

She laughed and said, "For someone who speaks English as a third language, you are managing to add humor!"

I finished my lemonade, thanked her, and left her house with a plan to think about the room.

*

When I was a young man in Yemen, the negative printed material I had read of the lives of Black Americans, as well as a documentary on Ruby Bridges, made me feel uncomfortable. I started to compare the predicament of Black Americans to the Jews in the European lands. The more I read about modern American history, the more I started to feel Americans are uncompromisingly the most racist nation in the world. I started to compare the level of hate Hitler had for Jews to white Americans' attitudes toward Black people. I concluded that before the Nazis came to power in Germany, the life of Jewish people wasn't as difficult as it was for Black Americans. But the Jewish people became political victims, and their lives were forever changed. Black American life was never changed; it was always based on suppression, racism, and suffering beyond measure.

In Yemen, perhaps in other places, too, the media continually shared footage to generate emotional reactions. Most people create an image of a society or a country based on the messages propagated by the images they see in the media. While living in Yemen, I knew almost nothing about

Martin Luther King Jr. (MLK), but I had read plenty of materials about Malcolm X. Why? Because Malcolm X was Muslim? Were the government and media showing materials so that society would take sides and develop a mistrust toward Americans? That was a complete contrast to what I was exposed to in Ethiopia as a child. At that time, during the imperial days, the movies, most books, and the trends of the youth were to mimic the American lifestyle. I hardly heard of anyone in Ethiopia speaking about the mistreatment of Black Americans. Everything I learned about the US civil rights movement was in Yemen.

My encounter with Margaret triggered several memories for me. I started to think of my lengthy conversations with Mark Hansen, who was a product of the 1960s. In his words, the repressive US war abroad (Vietnam) and the state of poverty at home completely affected him. He thought the US invented a war in Vietnam. He thought the US foreign policies were messed up, and what the US did to other countries was unacceptable according to his standards. He never had a good opinion of his home country. He vividly recalled and explained to me the Stand in the Schoolhouse Door at the University of Alabama on June 11, 1963, when George Wallace, the white Governor of Alabama, stood at the door of Foster Auditorium at the university and attempted to block two African American students from entering. I was only a year old when Wallace spoke the symbolic words, "Segregation now, segregation tomorrow, segregation forever." Still, those words felt current and real when Mark told me about them twenty years later in 1983.

Even then, when I referenced the summary of Kennedy's speech, "This nation was founded by men of many nations and backgrounds. It was founded on the principle that all men are created equal and that the rights of every man are diminished when the rights of one man are threatened,"[4] Mark brushed me off, saying, "That was just the rich boy talking, halfheartedly calling it a moral issue." I never considered myself to be American when I was living in the US, nor was segregation ever a factor in my life, so the notion of preventing Black students from attending university was something I was unable to comprehend. Because of the discrimination I endured in Yemen, I can understand people not wanting to invite a person from another race to their homes, not socializing together in a public place, or disapproving of interracial marriage. I saw and experienced discrimination in Yemen but not segregation in schools. Preventing students from attending the same school was bizarre to me.

The Vietnam War had ended less than ten years prior to my moving to the US. Many individuals who witnessed or took part in that war were still alive. The memory of this conflict was real for those of us who saw the reports live on TV. The war was fresh in our minds. In contrast, the images of WWI and WWII came to us in textbooks or other readings, and people who fought in those wars are mostly dead now. How much change took place from the 1960s until I enrolled in university in early 1984?

After my conversation with Margaret, I concluded society hadn't progressed, and self-imposed fear consumed me.

*

I didn't rent Margaret's room, but I found a one-bedroom apartment for $200. It was a little further from campus than Margaret's house and an additional $50, but I valued my freedom more than the money. I would have my own space. I could stay up late, listen to music of all kinds (including Arabic and Ethiopian songs), and have friends over at will. Due to my upbringing, I tended to respect elders, so I felt slightly guilty for potentially disappointing Margaret. I also thought I wouldn't be too happy living at her place, feeling trapped, as if I always had to watch myself so I didn't offend or upset her. I made sure she knew my decision so she could rent it to another individual.

Neighbors

The apartment I rented was in a fourplex, and I had a corner unit plus two parking spaces. My next-door neighbor was a nurse who worked in a dentist's office. Next to her was a man who worked in a government office at the Boise Capitol. The last apartment on the other corner was rented by a young man who never seemed to have a day's work. Whenever I went to school or returned, I passed by his door, and he was always looking at me from his kitchen window. He often came out of his apartment to watch me walk to the university until I was out of his sight. He never responded to my greetings, and I eventually stopped saying hello. After about two months, he broke his silence and asked me a couple of questions one day.

"What's yer name, dude? Where are ya from? Whatcha takin' at the university?" and so on.

I shared with him that much information, and he didn't talk to me again. I didn't bother with him either. I wondered why he would be interested to know a few details about me and never want to speak to me again. Now and then, I saw a couple of white friends coming and going to his place, and they all had shaved heads.

One day that fall, as I was hurrying to get to campus for a midterm exam, I heard someone yelling, "Hey, dude!" I kept marching as I was about to be late for class. The voice repeated, "Hey, dude!" I had to turn to see who the person was and if he was yelling at me. It was the weird guy, my neighbor, and he rushed to me and asked if I could join him and his friends for a barbecue the next day. He told me his name was Steve. Then he apologized for not remembering my name. I said, "Sure, can we talk about it later," and ran toward the math and science building.

Later that day, I spoke to Steve to get the details about his party. When I first arrived in the US, I was invited to a barbecue and was told it was BYO. I didn't know what BYO meant, so I went to the party empty-handed. I quickly learned that BYO was supposed to be Bring Your Own whatever you want to eat or drink. In Yemen and Ethiopia, it's insulting or even shameful to the host to bring your own food or drinks to social gatherings. However, this time, I was well-prepared, and I asked Steve what I should bring. He said, "Whatever ya want, man."

I knew hot dogs weren't dog meat by this time, but I never liked or wanted anything to do with pork, such as ham or bacon. I wasn't sure what to bring. To be safe, I ate supper at my place and visited Steve and his friends with a couple of cans of 7Up. He greeted me at the door.

Five guys and three girls were at the party, including the host. A couple were outside the apartment, tending to something they were cooking. The rest were spread between the kitchen and the living room.

Steve introduced me to the group as "a computer science and computer engineering student." He told them that I was a cool dude and that I came from Yemen but was born in Ethiopia.

"English is his third language. Isn't that cool? Hehehehe."

He was bragging, but I thought the way he talked was foolish and kiddish. Reflecting on it now, he sounded like the TV character Bart Simpson.

One of the others approached me and said, "We don't like niggers, but we like you!" A second person joined us, and he asked me if I was bothered by the word "nigger."

I told him, "I don't have the history of slavery in me, and that word doesn't bother me at all. I take pride in being born in Ethiopia and having an Ethiopian mother. Europeans never colonized her country. If I recall, Ethiopia was the first African nation to defeat one of the European powerhouses. Moreover, in Upper Yafa, where my father's ancestors came from, no European ever landed in the area. Apart from my skin color, I never thought I would be any less of any man I know, whether Black, yellow, or white. Perhaps I am naive, rash, and uninformed, but that is how I think." I concluded by saying, "The name 'Ethiopia' is mentioned in the Bible numerous times [thirty-seven times in the King James version] and is in many ways considered a holy place."

They both went silent, and I stopped talking.

There was a flag that I always saw covering the kitchen window facing the street, and I didn't know what it symbolized.

I asked one of the two guys, "What is that flag, and what does it represent?"

He gave me an extended explanation concluding with, "The Confederate flag was used by the seceded Southern states during the American Civil War." He added, "It's Southern pride!"

I didn't understand why "Southern pride" was relevant in Idaho.

Fast forward to today: I have seen the Confederate flag flown on homes and in trucks here in Canada, where we have no history with the American South, but obviously, some people share the ideology.

He seemed to be passionate and animated when he spoke about the flag. His parents came from the Lexington, Kentucky, area.

A few of the others clustered around the kitchen counter, where beer cans were piled up. One of them yelled, "To kill every nigger until the last Jew dies!" They high-fived each other.

I was standing alone and somewhat confused.

After replenishing their beers, the same two guys approached me again. They noticed I was drinking only soda and asked me, "Why not beer?"

I told them, "My father was an alcoholic, and I vowed not to be a man like him."

One of them gave me a high-five and said, "That's cool, dude. I respect that."

I learned from them that they were skinheads and members of the Aryan Nation, the Idaho chapter. They told me about a training camp in Northern Idaho near Hayden Lake. Most of the stuff they said didn't register with me, as I didn't have the background or context. I remained polite and kept socializing.

*

There were a lot of Black jokes that night, and of course, they were all derogatory. However, I wasn't offended by these jokes because they weren't about me. Rather, I was puzzled and curious about these people's mindsets and attitudes.

Even as someone who is half Ethiopian, during my time in the US, I struggled to identify with Black Americans. I disassociated myself from being Black even though I am dark-skinned and half-African. From my understanding, Ethiopians see themselves as Ethiopian (brown), not Black.

Why do we Ethiopians struggle to identify ourselves with Black Americans? And why do dark-skinned Indians, Sri Lankans, etc., consider themselves different than Black Americans? Even today, I ponder these questions.

At one point during my studies in Idaho, a communications course instructor brought a VHS tape to class showing MLK's "I Have a Dream" speech. After we viewed it, one of the students commented that people should be judged by character rather than skin color. An East Indian student commented, saying that he was disappointed by the MLK speech for not including "brown" children. Clearly, he didn't think he was Black and needed brown kids recognized as such. I was taken aback when the instructor replied to him, "Son, in America unless you are white, you are Black."

My experiences with these comments and attitudes took me back to what Mark Hansen had told me before I left Yemen: "Unless you know your history, you don't know who you are. You'll never be respected if you don't know your history."

*

After that gathering, Steve and I kept saying hello to each other in passing. He never came to my apartment, but one time, he did ask if I could assist him in boosting his truck, as the battery had died. He showed me his big hunting gun mounted in the back of his truck. Occasionally, he shared with me salmon and other fish he caught every time he went to the Boise River and elsewhere on fishing trips. I never saw him speaking to the other two neighbors, though. The guy who worked at the Capitol told me once that he found it "very strange that Steve has no communication with us, but he speaks to you. Do you know why?" I wonder even today why Steve befriended me yet never talked to the white neighbors.

IV

Girls, Girls, Girls

But I learned that there's a certain character that can be built from embarrassing yourself endlessly. If you can sit happy with embarrassment, there's not much else that can really get to you.

— Christian Bale, American actor

Vacuum Cleaner

When I moved out of the dormitory and into my apartment at the beginning of my first semester of university, on the day I took the apartment complex key, I noticed the place smelled funny. When I pointed out the smell to the property manager, he informed me that the previous tenant had had a dog and shared his plans to have the carpets cleaned shortly after.

The following day, a lady knocked on my door. She was the first person to ever arrive at my doorstep, and I quickly opened the door to see who was there.

A beautiful blonde lady about my height was standing at my door, holding a vacuum cleaner in one hand. I guessed her age to be late twenties or early thirties. She was slim and looked elegant in her dress pants and nice shirt. She spoke faster than other people I had met in Idaho by then and started telling me things too quickly. I was a bit taken by her looks and completely stopped listening to her words. That's not to say my English was bad; if I'd paid attention to what she was saying, I would have understood what she was telling me. But for a young man who had hardly seen a woman's face in Yemen, to have such a beautiful lady showing up at his door unannounced was totally out of the norm. I assumed the property manager had sent her to clean the carpet.

While staring at this lady's looks, I quickly opened the door and let her into the living room. I had been in the apartment for a couple of days, so I didn't know where the electrical plugs were. I was amazed at how quickly she found one to plug the vacuum cleaner into the wall. I was perplexed as to why such a good-looking lady with a nice outfit worked as a cleaner.

She kept talking while pushing the vacuum back and forth. Not only was I unable to hear what she was saying due to the noise, but she spoke too fast. I looked at her like a starved dog the entire time, standing still and admiring her posture. She stopped the machine to demonstrate to me how much dust the machine could gather. She then showed me how to change the dust bag and how other features of the machine worked. I was so impressed with what she could do in a short span.

Then, she pulled out some paperwork and asked me to sign it. When I read it, I saw it was a purchase order for $357. She asked me if I would be interested in paying the total amount at once or making four equal installments.

I paused. The entire time, she explained payment options and asked if I would be interested in purchasing a vacuum cleaner. I kept saying, "Yes, I agree," smiling and nodding, not grasping the conversation's topic. She thought that I had agreed to buy the vacuum.

I told her that there was a misunderstanding.

"I was expecting the property manager to send you to clean the place due to the smell of dog pee in the unit."

She said, "Honey, no. I'm a sales agent."

That was a disappointment.

The cost of the vacuum was equivalent to almost two months' rent. I could not say no to her because she was cute, and I wanted her to sweet-talk me more.

I signed up for a contract and purchased the vacuum, which I hardly needed.

Little did I know then that in those days, companies knew who to put up front to sell products and services; sending attractive women door-to-door was one of their sales ploys. I quickly realized that growing up in Yemen with limited interaction with women exposed my male weak spots. Charming looks and sexy voices fooled me into buying appliances that were not in my budget or on my list of needs

Avon Lady

About five weeks into being in the US and over a month at my new place, I heard the doorbell ring again. Since the vacuum cleaner lady and the person who came to shampoo my carpet, no one else had come to my place. I eagerly jumped up to open the door.

This time, it was another good-looking lady, similar to the one who had appeared with the vacuum cleaner but a few years older, maybe around thirty-five. But the vacuum cleaner lady was natural looking; this lady looked much more proper. She was well-groomed with lots of makeup and nicely done wavy blonde hair. She smelled fresh and was wearing perfume. The vacuum cleaner lady smiled when she needed to but was focused. By contrast, this lady was very friendly and had a somewhat seductive or cunning voice. I kind of felt she was trying to look like Marilyn Monroe.

I knew I shouldn't be fooled again and planned to put my guard up right away and not accept any offers. The second lady's approach was much different.

The first question she asked me was, "Is your wife home?"

"No. I'm not married."

Her response was very deceiving and cunning.

"That is fine. Even better."

At least, I thought that was what I heard her saying.

"I would like to show you some of my products."

She motioned to the bag she was carrying, and I thought, *What is her product?*

In Yemen, if a lady or a girl looks at a boy for a split second, we assume she is romantically interested, and our imagination travels faster than the speed of light. Hearing such a beautiful voice in a personalized way coming from a pretty woman with an unforgettable smile melted me on the spot. I was sure the lady was proposing that I sleep with her. I began to think that the American dream encompassed much more than I had initially thought it did!

Instead of listening to what she was saying, my mind was thinking about how much she would charge me and how long it would last. At twenty-two years old, I had never been sexually intimate with a woman and thought it would now be my opportunity to do so with an American woman. I assumed that day would be my luckiest day in the US. While my second brain was operating and controlling my blood flow, my primary brain wasn't functioning. I was consumed, and I barely heard a word this lady said.

The only words I heard were, "Be right back. Let me get something from my vehicle."

I left the door open for her, and I rushed to take a shower. I finished my shower in a heartbeat and came out to the living room with a towel wrapped around me. The lady was sitting comfortably on the couch, and she gave me a beaming smile.

"I was wondering what happened to you when I came in, and I heard the shower was running. You must have taken a shower. That was quick," she said.

"I took a shower in the morning, but I did it again for you," I told her.

She continued to smile but looked a bit confused.

I went back to my bedroom and put on lots of cologne that I had brought from Yemen. Wearing an expensive cologne was what Arab men do, and I smelled like I had bathed with it.

By the time I returned to the living room, the lady had put a bunch of products for both men and women on the coffee table. I didn't know why or what they were for. I remembered reading a book somewhere about body massage, and I thought these products could be for a body rub before sex. I caught a glimpse of myself in the sliding door reflection; with my towel on and just out of the shower, I looked like Gandhi or the Dalai

Lama. While covering a certain portion of my body, I quickly sat next to her on the couch. That was an awkward moment, as she was focusing on the lotion, shampoo, and other beauty products.

I put my arm around her shoulder.

She swiftly removed it and, with a firm voice, informed me, "I'm here to demonstrate to you my Avon products for you and possibly for your future girlfriend."

Everything went cold and shrank. I was swamped with massive embarrassment. I was unable to look at her. I was confused.

She kept talking.

I thought about getting up and going to my bedroom to put on pants and a shirt. She kept talking.

Once I gathered myself, I noticed about four men's hygiene products and about seven others for females. She kept saying that it was a good idea to purchase those female products for my girlfriend.

I told her, "I don't have one."

She said, "You will. You're an attractive man. Who could resist you with those smiles!"

The embarrassment was unbearable. I just wanted her to leave the room right away. I told her, "I will take all the male products and half of the female products that are on the table."

She asked, "Which ones?"

I said, "I don't care. Just split it into two halves."

I asked how much I owed her.

She asked why I was in such a hurry.

I said, "I don't know …."

I didn't want to tell her how embarrassed I was about my misunderstanding and assumptions. I went to my bedroom, put some clothes on, and returned to the room with $50.

She said, "That is plenty."

She packed the remainder of her stuff and left.

Yes, this was the second humiliation in only a few weeks of being in America.

I sat down on the floor to reflect on and reassess those incidents, my actions, and the final outcomes. I was operating with the mindset of a Yemeni man who was unfamiliar with the basic protocol needed to interact with women. I decided to write this episode in my journal, which served as a refuge and a secret space to confess and speak to a ghost friend.

Playboy and *Penthouse*

During my first few months in the US, one of the first things I did was subscribe to *Playboy* and *Penthouse* magazines. Such magazines were prohibited in Yemen, and punishment was severe if one was caught possessing one. My subscriptions were more of a token of freedom and perhaps the result of my assumption that all forbidden fruits taste better.

As the copies of magazines arrived, I ripped out the middle pages and put the centerfolds on the bedroom wall. Girls who ventured into my bedroom expressed their disapproval in various forms. As a typical young adult male, I didn't care about their perspectives of the matter or their opinion about me. The ability and the freedom to put a naked woman's picture on my wall was immensely empowering.

Amanda was a nineteen-year-old first-year student I met at BSU. We dated for a few weeks, and she ended up seeing those images on the wall. By this time, I had no less than ten images on the wall from the two magazines. Unlike a few girls before her, she took the time to look carefully at every one of those nude pictures. She was looking at them as if she was in an art gallery. I was taken by her reaction; she didn't judge or belittle me. She was factual and unbiased. Other girls I had brought to my apartment had made me feel like I was a dirty man for having those pictures, but she didn't. I stood by her while she gazed at the figures.

Once she finished looking at all the images, she turned to me and asked, "Which one is your favorite?"

It didn't take me more than a split second to respond, "Miss April?"

There were two Miss Aprils—one from *Penthouse* and one from *Playboy*—but I preferred one over the other. I was eager to point my finger at my favorite image.

She said, "Ah-ha. I see."

Then she requested I stand on the opposite wall. I complied without asking why.

"Now," she said, "I would like you to close your eyes and position your head where the picture is. As if you're looking at the picture, but your eyes should remain closed."

Since I had seen those pictures so many times, I knew exactly the spot and fixed my little head exactly where it should be.

Amanda instructed me to open my eyes only after she counted to three. I agreed. While my eyes were closed and my face was still pointed to the picture's location, she told me to open my eyes and respond to her question immediately. I agreed.

She counted, "One-two-three," and when I opened my eyes, she said, "Imagine that is your mom or one of your sisters."

I was stunned. I could never view that picture, or any of them, again. After she left, I removed all the images from the wall. Future magazines were put in the garbage.

Amanda rescued me from a very skewed view of women and from objectifying women as sex objects. With that one comment, she cured me of watching and procuring pornography. I would thank her if I found her today, as she taught me a valuable lifelong lesson.

Three's Company

I really liked one of my classmates, but she never cared about me. In spite of her indifference, I always tried to impress her with my grades. She never gave me space or a chance to discuss my feelings with her, but one day, when my soccer team came back from a different city where we had been playing, we went to Chi-Chi's restaurant, where she was a server. I told one of the guys I had a crush on this girl, and that guy told another player, who told another one, who told another one, who told the coach.

When she came to serve us, the coach looked at her and said, "You see that guy—the little one?"

"Yeah."

"He has a crush on you. Promise me you'll go out with him one day."

"Yeah, I know he's a nerdy boy. He was my classmate."

(I didn't yet know the meaning of the word "nerd.")

She agreed to go out with me and gave me her phone number.

A few days later, I took her to dinner. I don't remember the restaurant's name, but we ate lobster. After dinner, when I took her to my apartment and we were sitting and talking, she asked me, "Do you have any grass?"

I said, "Yes, I do, but the landlord is taking care of it."

She said, "No, I mean a joint."

I had no clue what a joint was, and after a bit more back and forth, she finally got frustrated and said, "Marijuana."

"Oh, no. I don't have one."

"What kind of nigger are you who doesn't have a joint?" she asked.

I wanted to impress this girl, and I knew one of the college guys who was selling drugs, so I phoned him and explained the situation.

"I have $37. Give me some marijuana for one person," I told him.

He laughed because he measured the marijuana by ounces or some other measurement, not per person. He knew I was not experienced in buying drugs, anyway.

He said, "Yeah, so you have the chick with you?"

"Yeah, she is here."

"Hey, I'll get some," he assured me.

I gave him the address, and he came by shortly after that. Like a hotel room, my apartment had a chain on my door. I opened the door with the chain in place and put $37 out. I stuck out my hands to get the marijuana, and he laughed and said, "Open the door."

I said, "No, just take the money and give me the stuff— enough for one person."

He started intimidating me with gestures, posturing his body, and deepening and raising his voice. We started arguing. At that, the girl came to the door and stood behind me.

She was taller than me. As she came up behind me, she said, "What's going on here?"

She unchained, opened the door, and saw who was on the other side.

"Hey, Tyree!" she said, and they high-fived each other.

"You know each other?" I asked.

"Yeah. His name's Tyree." She looked at me.

The guy was about 5'8" or 5'9".

"Dude," he lowered his voice to me. "You don't have to pay. Just let me get some meat."

"She's my girlfriend," I told him.

"Relax," he said, pushing his way into my apartment. He didn't take the money I was still holding out.

I followed him to my couch, where the three of us sat down, me, the short one, in the middle. They started smoking the joint, passing it between the two of them in front of me. My eyes followed the joint back and forth as if my gaze were following the ball during a tennis game. I didn't partake, but the second-hand smoke was blowing directly into my face.

That's not the last I remember, but it's the end of what I will say about this event ….

V

Developing Relationships

Some people think football [soccer] is a matter of life and death. I don't like that attitude. I can assure them it is much more serious than that.

— Bill Shankly, Scottish soccer player

Boise was where I started hiking, and I participated in organized sports like soccer, playing for both BSU and local clubs. Even though I initially didn't make the university soccer team due to my petite stature, I was eventually chosen and then proudly co-captained and played for the team. The hilarious part was that when I heard the university gave partial scholarships to the athletics department, I went to the department to ask when the football team tryouts would occur. Someone told me they were taking place then and said, "You'd better hurry," so I did.

When I arrived on the field, I told the assistant coach I was there for the tryout. He looked at me with some amusement and asked, "What did you say?"

"I'm here for the football tryouts," I repeated.

He yelled at the head coach, "This little man is saying he wants to try out."

I was insulted by his adjective. The head coach approached and asked me what I was looking for. From my accent, he suspected I was referring to a different sport.

He said, "You meant soccer."

I had said football, but I quickly realized it is called soccer in the US. I knew I was at the wrong tryout. I thanked him and left the field.

*

A significant aspect of my adjustment to the US was being alone and lonely. I had sat in on qat-chewing sessions[5] on occasion in Yemen and had a sizable circle of friends. As much as I hated living in Yemen, I started to miss Yemen and Yemenis. I began to feel homesick and miserable. Often, I drifted into depression, even though I didn't know what mental health and depression meant at the time. During my first year in Boise, the holiday seasons were the hardest to deal with; most university students went home, and the city and the campus looked deserted. I defaulted to isolation, withdrawal, and writing in my journals. I started to wonder if it had even been worth coming to the US.

The excitement of seeing and being in a clean city like Boise, with its infrastructure, landscape, and natural beauty, started to fade away. To earn and keep friendships, I began to dish out the souvenirs I had brought from Yemen to random temporary friends I met. Most of those individuals asked me why I was giving away items with such sentimental value. I quickly realized people in Boise gave away things they didn't want. In Yemen, we gave to an individual something significant to us. My generous approach, which most Arabs are proud of, didn't buy me friends. Some distanced themselves from me as they were worried about taking advantage of me. That aspect of thinking also informed me— that in Yemen, if most people find you generous and kind, they take advantage of you. In North America, I found the party on the receiving end was worried about taking too much. Various people flat out told me I shouldn't buy something or give something to sustain friendships.

Over time, I did make a lot of friends. Despite what others may think of Boise, Idaho, viewing it as a redneck state and knowing the presence of the Aryan Nation, I found that the purest, friendliest, and most honest people I have ever known were from Idaho. Yes, they didn't know much about the outside world, and perhaps that is true for many Americans, but most people from Idaho were decent and good. After my first year, I never had to worry about Christmas or Thanksgiving, as plenty of families were ready and happy to host me. Often, I had dinner at one family's home and dessert at another's.

Even now, after over thirty-eight years, I am in touch with many people I met in Idaho. Sharese Munson and Conrad Johnston were the most significant people I connected to because of soccer. Conrad was a Scottish guy who had married an American girl and settled in Boise. He co-captained the university and international soccer teams with me for several years. Our recreational team was named the Internationals as all players were from different countries except for two Americans. We spoke other languages, came from various continents, and practiced different religions, but we shared one language and one religion: soccer.

For me, soccer wasn't only a sport that boys and girls played around the globe. I quickly learned how the international students on campus shared a similar feeling. We quickly bonded over our common sport. But this sport brought more to my life in Boise and positioned me to build additional human networks. Besides receiving a partial scholarship in soccer to supplement my school fees, I found that regular exercise gave me an enormous sense of well-being. I felt more energetic throughout the day, slept better at night, had sharper memories, and felt more relaxed and positive about myself and my life. The exercise helped me combat the stress from cultural adjustments and academic challenges. It had a profound positive impact on my depression, anxiety, and the lasting effects of my painful past.

Before arriving in Idaho, and through the history courses I took, I learned that Idaho had formerly been a territory in the Northwest that was larger than Texas. But following the creation of Montana and Wyoming, the size of Idaho shrank.

In the early 1980s, the population of Boise was around 120,000. It was a much smaller city than Addis Ababa (1.2 million!) or Sana'a (500 thousand), where I had lived before arriving in Boise. The first year or so, I hardly saw any ethnic person outside the university campus. All were white! The downtown area was clean and quiet compared to the dusty, noisy, crowded areas of Sana'a's downtown. Back then, Addis Ababa wasn't much better but was a greener city than Sana'a. All I was doing was comparing what I saw with where I came from.

In Boise, Julia Davis Park took my breath away. Arriving from the grimy city of Sana'a, with few well-maintained public parks, discovering this park within a few weeks of my arrival was a surprise. The park gave me access to the Boise River

Greenbelt, a trail along the banks of the Boise River that is great for walking or cycling. The tree-lined pathway followed the river through the city's heart and provided scenic views and wildlife habitat. At that time, I wondered why access to such a park was free. I thought perhaps I had missed paying for a day pass somehow. My apartment was about four blocks away from Julia Davis Park.

Like Mocha Port in Yemen, Julia Davis Park was where I could sit and process my thoughts. I often went there to carve out my plans for what to do with my life. It was the first place I picked up a basketball to throw into a net. My first times playing bocce and horseshoes were in this park, which provided me with my first opportunity to see someone catching fish as a form of recreation. (Fishing is a business and lifeline in Yemen.) I played with my soccer ball and biked in the area. And in later years, I often took my dates to walk, sit, and talk with me in the park.

During my first three weeks in Idaho, I spent nearly half a day circling the Idaho State Capitol building on bicycle. It was the most majestic structure I had seen to date. There was also a theater named The Egyptian Theatre, and I wondered why it was called that. I asked myself if Egyptian shows played or what, but I soon learned it was just a name.

Improbable Ally

And I learned more about the skinhead culture in Idaho. The training compound was established in 1974 when Richard Butler came from California and bought twenty acres of land near Hayden Lake. The FBI was always hovering around that area.

*

In my second semester, during the spring season, a brown Toyota Celica sports car passed by my apartment one day around 4 p.m. I was sitting on the step in front of my door. The music in the car was so loud one could hear it from a block away.

After driving about 90 meters (100 yards) past my apartment, the car stopped. Moments later, the car was driven backward and stopped in front of my unit. There were two young Black men in the car, aged between twenty and twenty-two, whom I had never seen before. They got out and approached my place. I thought they were perhaps wanting to ask me for directions or something. Looking to my left, I saw Steve watching us from his doorstep.

One of the Black guys started talking to me. He talked fast. It was English, but I was unable to understand a single word. I thought I heard, "Whassss up." The rest flew over my head.

I was so excited to be able to meet these two Black American men! I had never met one in person. Before coming to the US, I had only seen pictures and movies about Black Americans. I vividly recalled the story of Kunta Kinte in the movie *Roots*, but what I had at this moment was a real live experience with Black Americans. *It is a wonderful opportunity!*

I stood up and asked, "Can I help you?"

They paused and looked at me as if something was wrong with me.

"Dude, chill. We stopped by to say hi," one of them said.

The more they talked, the less I understood. As this was my first encounter with real Black Americans, I was humiliated and bashful for being unable to say anything because I didn't understand the words they were saying. I sensed they wanted to come to visit. I tried to shake hands, but they had their own greeting style, which I had never practiced.

They pushed their way into my apartment; I followed them. They glanced at my living room wall, where I had several little things from back home: giant posters of Ethiopian women and pictures of mountains in North Yemen. I asked if I could make them coffee or tea, but they didn't respond. They proceeded to my kitchen and opened my fridge. Where I came from, that was the most inappropriate thing to do. You didn't go and open the fridge of someone you didn't know. I had never even opened my sisters' fridges. I would ask my sisters for something, and they gave me whatever I needed. These men's behavior was bizarre and confusing.

They found nothing in my fridge.

One of them said, "This little shit has nothing to eat. No wonder he is as skinny as those starving Ethiopians."

Clearly, they don't know that I'm partially Ethiopian, I thought.

One of them asked me, "Are ya from North Carolina?"

"No, why?"

"You kinda have an accent like them."

They didn't give me an opportunity to introduce myself. They scouted my place, including the bedroom and washroom, before leaving. They were big boys, perhaps 185 centimeters (at least six 6 feet) tall, with massive muscles. I felt minuscule standing next to them.

About an hour after they left, I returned to my desk to finish my school assignment. I noticed my HP-41C calculator was missing. It was a calculator one of the American expats had purchased and brought to North Yemen for me, costing me $250. That was a considerable amount of money at the time. Without it, I was unable to complete my homework.

The following day, I shared my predicament with Reza, a classmate from Iran. He told me, "There are only fifteen Black students at the BSU campus, and they're under basketball and football scholarships. If you go to the gym, you could find them all there. You might be able to get your calculator back."

I walked to the Bronco gym for the first time. As I glanced through the facility looking for a Black person, I kept smelling the pungent odor of Bengay. On a campus where 99 percent of the population was white, it wasn't difficult to spot a Black person working out. I identified two around the weightlifting area and kept looking at them to be sure at least one was part of the group that came to my apartment. Yes, the two of them were there. I started to think about what to say to them. I worried that I might say the wrong thing—that I would make them angry.

As I approached the bench where they were working out, one of them said, "Look who the fuck is here, Jermaine. The skinny little shit is here."

They both looked at me. Before I even uttered a word, one of them said, "What the fuck are ya doin' here?"

Clearing my throat, I said, "I was thinking to ask …."

"Ask what?" one of them said.

The other repeated, "Ask what?"

They already got pissed. What are they going to do if I ask about my calculator?

I asserted myself and said, "I could not find my HP-41C calculator after you visited my apartment. It is an expensive calculator, and I need it for my schooling."

One of them slowly approached me. My face was barely above his belly button.

"If you ever come back again looking for a fucken calculator, I'll break your skinny neck. Ya got that? Get the fuck outta here before I beat the shit outta ya."

I went straight back to my apartment. As I was passing by Steve's entrance, he jumped out of his apartment and said, "What were those niggers doing to your apartment yesterday?"

I said, "Nothing."

He knew that I always wore a smile when I greeted people, and he noticed something was wrong because of the absence of my usual smile. I looked sad and out of sorts. He quickly changed the topic from asking about the Black men's visit to my situation and asked if I was okay. I told him I had lost an expensive calculator.

It didn't take him much to figure things out, and he quickly said, "Those niggers snatched it from your apartment yesterday."

"I don't really know. It could have been them as I used it before they came, and it was gone after they left."

I kept saying, "That is okay. I will buy another one," fearing I would ignite a civil war.

He just turned and walked back to his apartment.

A couple of days later, I heard my doorbell ring. When I opened the door, it was Steve with his buddies. There were five of them … with baseball bats.

I noticed Steve had a calculator in his hand.

He said, "Does this calculator look like yours?"

I took it from his hand and said, "It is mine. I know the last four digits of the serial number."

Later, I found out that they had stormed the gym and threatened to crack the heads of those two Black boys with baseball bats if they didn't hand over my calculator. The Black boys were outnumbered five to two, and they handed over the calculator without a fight.

*

Did Steve and his friends recover the stolen calculator to help me or because they felt bad for me? I'm not so sure. I wonder if it was more likely because they had a deep-rooted hatred toward Black Americans. Perhaps such an incident was a good excuse for them to initiate a fight with the local Blacks. As for me, I didn't care whatever social and political issues they may have had; I was happy to have my calculator back.

Reflecting on that incident, I always say that most people don't dislike how another person looks. Instead, people judge others primarily by the way they conduct themselves. Every time I tell this story to friends, they can't believe that Aryan

Nation members and skinheads defended their African and Arabian neighbor and repatriated a stolen calculator for me. Moreover, even though I'm Black, I've never thought of myself as Black. Instead, I view myself as an Arab and an Ethiopian. I'm not sure if I felt superior to Black Americans, but I didn't think I was less than a white man, either. I had too huge of an ego to think of myself as less!

One of my role models since I was young has been Sidney Poitier. I have often pondered over the moment in *Guess Who's Coming to Dinner* when Poitier's character's (John Prentice) father said Prentice shouldn't marry a white woman. In response, Prentice's main message was this: "Dad, I love and respect you. I appreciate everything you've done for me, but the fundamental difference between us is you think you're a colored man, but I think I am a man."

My real-life mentor, Mark Hansen, always used to say to me, "You're the man." He instilled in me the desire to make sure I saw myself as a man, not a colored man.

In another Poitier film, *In the Heat of the Night*, when a white man hits Poitier's character (Virgil Tibbs) in the face, Tibbs's response was a first in US movie history—it was the first time a Black man hit a white person on screen. Poitier refused to take the role unless the retaliation was included.

Likewise, Mark ensured I didn't adopt the "turn the other cheek" mentality. He knew I tended to be submissive, bowing down to others and walking away from a conflict. He encouraged and inspired me to be assertive and to develop a strong personality. Knowing the racial tensions in the US, and in particular, knowing the presence of the Aryan Nation in Idaho, he wanted me to come to the US with complete confidence. He worked hard to bring the likes of Malcolm X and Sidney Poitier to my life as examples. He thought I would be better off staying in Yemen since I came from a strong tribe, but knowing I had my mind set on going to the US for a Western education, he wanted to make sure I wasn't crushed in the US. Mark worked to build a character within me that I didn't possess when he met me.

Underdog

After I had been in the US for a few years, one of my friends decided to transfer to Pocatello, Idaho, to continue his education at Idaho State University. One weekend, his girlfriend came to Boise to visit her distant relatives. My friend asked if I would take her downtown to show her around.

I took her to a club where most university students hung around. It was a Saturday evening during the summer of 1989. We were dancing to songs like "Girl You Know It's True" by Milli Vanilli and "Straight Up" by Paula Abdul, having a good time.

A tall, burly man approached our table and asked to purchase a round of drinks for us. Neither the girl nor I consumed alcohol and, therefore, thanked him and told him we were not interested. He walked away.

I noticed he was circling the area where our table was. He waited another fifteen minutes or so, and then he came to ask me if it was okay if he danced with my lady. I told him he should ask the lady if that was okay with her, which he did, and she told him he should ask me for permission. He returned to me asking again. I said, "Just one song," and they proceeded to the dance floor.

The next song was slow, and he kept her against her wishes for another dance when it was over. After they danced together, he brought her back to our table. He suspected we were not a couple, and he asked me if she was my girlfriend. I told him she was not, but she was my good friend's girlfriend. He wanted to ask the girl to go home that night, which wasn't acceptable to me or her. The music was loud, and the guy directed his comments into my ear, so the girl didn't fully know what was happening. In hindsight, perhaps I should have said she was my girlfriend, which would have ended the story there.

When they had returned to the table, she told me she was uncomfortable with this man and suggested we leave. I agreed to do that after one or two more songs.

By this time, he had already pulled up a chair and decided to join us. Instead of sitting, he leaned on the chair and stood there, hovering over us. We told him he was not welcome at our table and we were leaving. He wasn't happy and started to flex his muscles and stand up straighter, towering over us to try and intimidate us. His posturing didn't bother me, and I firmly asked him to leave. After a few seconds of leaning on the table, he left. As he walked away, he kept staring at me, seemingly surprised that I was unfazed but still trying to exert himself.

We sensed that he wanted to fight and perhaps turn her nice evening into an ugly one. He also had one too many drinks, and we thought it was best to avoid him. We agreed that she would pretend to go to the washroom, leave the club through the back, drive my car away, and meet me at the gas station about a mile and a half from the club.

She left, and I waited another fifteen minutes or so, and then I decided to leave the club. During those fifteen minutes, the guy wandered around, wondering where the girl went. He kept coming and asking me where she was. I tried to tell him she had a boyfriend and that he should find another girl rather than wasting his time on her. He didn't like my response and seemed somewhat obsessed. Perhaps the rejection was what triggered him.

I left the club's central area, which was in the basement, and when I reached the top of the stairs, I ran into a pair of long, thick legs blocking my way. When I looked up, I realized the legs belonged to the same guy who was hovering around, trying to make his move on my friend's girlfriend. He again asked me where the girl was. And once again, I told him he'd better find someone else, as she was taken. He picked me up by my shirt.

"Where is she?" he demanded to know as my legs dangled in the air.

I politely asked him to let go. I could smell the alcohol on his breath, and he seemed determined to get to her at any cost.

As he lowered me, my instincts told me he was about to throw me to the ground or against the concrete wall.

Within a split second, I sprang up like a goat and smashed his face with my forehead, head-butting him in the same manner I had done to a soccer ball millions of times prior. I heard a colossal roaring yell as he started falling. He let go of me and held his face, not knowing what had hit him.

I took off and met the girl at the gas station.

Later on, I heard that he was taken to hospital with a broken jaw. No one knew who did it. He was probably too ashamed to admit that a 167-centimeter (5'5"), 54-kilogram (120-pound) man had knocked down a six-foot-tall man with an unorthodox head butt.

VI

Fraudulent Marriage

Do not oppress a foreigner; you yourselves know how it feels to be foreigners, because you were foreigners in Egypt.

— Exodus 23:9

From the day I departed North Yemen, I had my mind made up never to return. I also knew the saved funds would not be enough to get me through the four-year university degree program. I considered permanently migrating and staying in the US. The student visa I was given was only valid for four years and could have been extended for one more after graduation to gain work experience in a practicum placement. To maintain my legal status in the US, I had to be enrolled in a US university and carry a minimum course load of twelve credits (three courses). My chance of employment while studying was limited to minimum-wage jobs in the university cafeteria, library, computer labs, or other departments for no more than twenty hours a week. The minimum wage at the time was $3.35.

It was deeply engrained in me that I had to become a permanent US resident to legally work off-campus and reduce my university tuition costs (international students paid threefold compared to US citizens and residents). Even though I had a shot at becoming a resident after finishing university, I needed to find an employer to keep me on their payroll for six consecutive years and maintain no criminal record for the entire duration I lived in the US.

However, after the first two years, I knew I would be short of cash. Room and board plus tuition during the mid-1980s in Boise was $12,500 per year, and that didn't include additional expenses such as owning a car, traveling anywhere, and other leisure expenses.

Mark Hansen had convinced me that I was likable and could find any girl to marry me. The notion was appealing to me, but it was a complicated matter on my part. When I arrived in the US, I was still in love with my Yemeni-Hadhrami fiancée back home. Even though I had ended the relationship, my feelings for her remained. I also wasn't sure if I was ready to be married to an American girl.

But in my second semester, I dated a few more girls, and I focused on finding someone to marry me right away. Most girls who attended university were between eighteen and twenty-two and were only interested in dating to gain experience. Frequently, I felt that I was a slice of exotic meat to try, as there were fewer than thirty Black students on campus. Early on, I started to wonder if that is the way women feel when a man approaches them only for sex. That is the most degrading feeling I felt—was I only suitable for tryout sex?

Within my first few months in Boise, I became acquainted with two brothers. They were from West Africa, and one was a BSU student. The youngest brother was sent to me by the university admissions office to orient him, as he was enrolled in the university and new from Africa. As president of the International Student Association, I was the person most first-year students came to for guidance. The oldest brother had been in the US for several years but lived in a different state before moving to Boise. He didn't attend school, and I wasn't even sure what he did for a living.

The youngest brother started to play soccer for the university, and we became further acquainted. Shortly after we met, he found a girlfriend and married her. He had only been in Boise a few months by then. She was a white American girl. I attended their wedding ceremony. After getting married, he obtained temporary resident status and could work off-campus in one of the restaurant chains, earning well and working more hours. The thought of marrying someone like he had motivated me to continue my search.

His wife, a twenty-four-year-old single mom with a child of eighteen months, worked as a cashier at a local grocery store. That kind of arrangement or partner of choice didn't appeal to me, as I had a standard of my own. *How would I introduce a cashier with a child to my sisters?* I didn't have respect for that kind of woman at the time. I felt the woman I married should be an engineer, accountant, or other type of professional. I looked down on people like her at the time— a single mother with a child. How ironic and hypocritical of me! Coming from a developing country and looking down on someone earning an honest living, working hard as a cashier.

And I wondered who would take care of her baby while she was working. I viewed my friend's situation as a headache and a huge financial responsibility. Marrying someone who had a child and was not likely to be educated beyond high school did not interest me.

After one of the university soccer games, Malik, the older brother, who was a womanizer and had a habit of flipping girlfriends like McDonald's burgers, asked me if I ever had any plans to be a resident of the US. I didn't know how to respond to his question because I was worried about what he would do or say based on my answer. I told him, "Maybe someday, but it's not on my radar now." I casually brushed him off even though that wasn't the truth.

He said, "I have some ideas."

Although I wanted to marry and become a US resident, dealing with this man or following his suggestion was worrisome. I just didn't get a good feeling from him. I didn't know what held me back, but I felt uneasy.

I told him, "I'll connect with you if I pursue that route."

Later the same year, in the first week of December, I broke down and went to Malik's apartment to ask for suggestions on getting married to an American girl. This was the second time I had come to his place, the first being his brother's wedding day.

As I approached the door, just before I rang the bell, a lady opened the door and left his place. She appeared to be in a hurry. She didn't acknowledge me standing by the door but quickly departed, leaving the door open for me.

As I walked into the house, I smelled smoke—a mix of both cigarettes and joints. I always suspected either he sold drugs or at least used them, as he seemed to have plenty of friends and drove a fancy car. He wasn't even attending school or working. I didn't say anything about the smell.

He asked me, "What are you up to?" and asked if I wanted a drink.

"I don't drink."

"Oh, yeah. I remember. You're a Muslim."

The coffee table was full of alcohol bottles, beer cans, cigarette trash, etc. He apologized to me. "The room is messy."

He offered me a seat and said, "Man, these white girls love black dick."

I didn't respond. The TV was on. He turned it off and said, "It's hard to hear you. You speak so softly."

He continued to talk about how many girls he'd had that week and mentioned that the girl I saw was the third one he had slept with that day. Then he sensed that I wasn't interested in the girl talk, nor did I want to drink. He was also aware I didn't smoke. After some ten minutes of useless talk, I told him I had come to talk about something.

"I would like to become a resident, and is there anything you could do to help me?"

He went silent for a bit and said, "That's easy. You can marry Donna."

I was surprised that he had a solution to my problem instantly. *Perhaps he had a plan in mind already,* I thought. I asked him who Donna was.

"The gal you saw by the door as you came in."

"I thought you said you just slept with her and were also smoking joints with her?"

"Yes, but who cares about that? She is a student like you but a bit older."

"How old is she?" I asked.

"She could be about ten years older than you. I'm sure she would agree to marry you. I think she could be between thirty and thirty-two."

For the duration of my visit, approximately an hour, I asked a bunch of questions about Donna and concluded it would be best if he introduced me to her directly. He agreed but said she probably needed at least five grand to marry me.

"Maybe she wants half of it up front."

I didn't respond.

"If she agrees, I need a couple hundred from you, too."

I said, "We can discuss that," and I stood up to leave.

He promised to contact her and, if she agreed, would pass on my number; the rest would be on me.

A couple of days later, Donna phoned me, and after a twenty-minute chat, she agreed to meet me the following day. She came to my apartment. I made spaghetti, and we talked a lot. Knowing she had already slept with Malik, and with her being a smoker and not as young as the couple of other girls I dated, I wasn't attracted to her.

She quickly gathered I wasn't the street-smart type like the others. "I thought you would be like the other Africans. You're kind of a nerd," she said.

I still didn't know the meaning of the word "nerd."

As the evening wore on, I was getting bored and irritated by her. I wanted her to leave, but she was the only possible avenue to a green card, and I had to be polite. I didn't dare to ask her about the marriage and the money. She left.

I followed up with her the next day over the phone and asked if Malik had spoken to her about why I needed to talk to her.

She said, "I know."

Without even talking about it, she quickly added, "Let's do it."

We also didn't talk about the exchange of money. I assumed the two of them had spoken and the arrangement was done.

She said, "We can do it in Elko, Nevada, if you can find a witness."

"I will try to find one."

*

When I was still in Yemen, Mark had told me about a friend of his—a university English language professor, Kathleen Warner, whom I became close to almost immediately after I landed in Boise. Kathleen was instrumental in giving me insight into university life and her work, and she quickly became a close and supportive friend.

Kathleen taught folklore at BSU for more than thirty years. She earned her Ph.D. at Indiana University and then joined the English faculty at BSU in 1966. She trained her students in both academic research and fieldwork.

Kathleen also took me on several camping trips to Ketcham and Sun Valley, Idaho.

She showed me the house in Ketchum where Ernest Hemingway once lived and where he killed himself. The

Community Library managed it. The home was listed on the National Register of Historic Places, but it remains private property and was not open to visitors then. I first learned about Hemingway from Al-Arasi, my roommate in Yemen, as he was an English literature student and had wider exposure to literature than I did. I read a couple of Hemingway's books but wasn't interested in literature.

I told Kathleen my plan to marry Donna so that I could obtain a green card.

She looked at me and said, "They wouldn't believe me, but I would happily marry you to get your paperwork sorted out. I'm probably almost the same age as your mom, and it would easily catch the attention of the authorities if you and I got married. I hope she's a fine person."

She agreed to travel with Donna and me to Elko, Nevada, to witness the marriage. On January 12, 1985, we drove my car there. I spent the night in a hotel room with the two ladies and a small dog, all in a queen-sized bed, as there were no other rooms we could find that evening. The following day, on January 13, we got the marriage license with the court clerk acting as the second witness. Once that was done, we all drove back to Boise.

Even though it was clear that this was a fixed marriage, Donna never asked for the money, nor did I offer it to her. We arranged to move in together so it would appear to authorities that we were husband and wife living under the same roof. Three weeks later, on February 1, we moved into a two-bedroom house.

On Valentine's Day, I took Donna for supper and told her how grateful I was for her willingness to help me obtain my residency. At the dinner table, I put $2,000 cash in an envelope and pushed it toward her side of the table. She didn't know what it was and asked me to explain.

I said, "The money that we agreed on."

She pushed it back to me and said, "I'm not looking for money anymore. When did I agree to the money aspect?"

I tried to explain, but she told me to put the money away and insisted she didn't do it for the money. I was confused and became speechless. She gave me no choice but to take back the money.

VII

Frivolous Asylum

No one leaves home unless home is the mouth of a shark.

— Warsan Shire, British author and poet,
Teaching My Mother How to Give Birth

Within a month, Donna wrote a letter to the Immigration and Naturalization Service (INS) in Helena, Montana, requesting a work permit for her husband so that I could start working and contributing to the living expenses. She also stated in the letter that she would submit the necessary application to change my status from a student to a permanent US resident. I was not aware of her actions.

Once I received a work permit, I stopped working at the BSU computer lab and started working for Electronic Data Systems (EDS), owned by the former presidential candidate Ross Perot. Donna and I continued to attend university and live together while sharing the living expenses but occupying two bedrooms. I was working from 6 p.m. to 2 a.m. and got up at 9 a.m. to attend my first class at 10:20 a.m.

I remained confused and asked myself why Donna took such an approach—marrying me for no cash reward. When I told Kathleen about Donna's decision not to accept any money, Kathleen suggested Donna might like me and want to help me.

"You're a good soul, Adel," she told me.

I no longer spoke to the African guy who had introduced me to Donna. I didn't think paying Malik for suggesting that I enter into this arrangement was necessary. No transaction ever took place between any parties. Donna never circled back to him either. The matter was complicated, and I didn't even know what to say to him. I never liked Malik to begin with, and I found nothing in common between us. I only knew his younger brother and had much in common with him: we were both students, we played soccer together, and neither the younger brother nor I smoked marijuana. I thought we were on the same path.

It was not clear to me why Donna stopped visiting Malik. But she did speak to me about her desire to quit smoking. I gave her space, and I hardly asked her any personal questions. I always respected her and wanted to keep our situation as a business arrangement. She fetched lunch for me and ensured I ate something before leaving home for work. I cleaned the house and did the dishes, and she cooked. I felt my life was stable, and I started to get good grades.

After six months or so, during the summer, Donna picked up the INS forms, filled in the application, and submitted it to the INS office. Again, she didn't tell me she had done this, so I wasn't aware of the application submission. In the meantime, I phoned Kathleen and asked her when a good time would be to visit her. By then, she wasn't teaching summer courses and told me she could meet anytime, perhaps before or after her visit to her aging parents in Nevada.

We met before she flew to Nevada, and I again talked to her about the situation between Donna and me.

"Donna didn't ask for money and even refused to take some money when I offered it to her. I am a bit concerned, mainly, not knowing what is happening behind the scenes. I'm worried that Donna perhaps has changed her mind about going through this arrangement."

Kathleen quickly phoned Donna to tell her she wanted to meet with her. I ended my visit with Kathleen, and I went home. Donna and Kathleen met that weekend. I received a call from Kathleen the evening after the two of them met.

"Donna is not interested in the money. She likes you and wants to turn this relationship into a real marriage. She found you to be a very good man and spoke about you highly. I recommended that you two find a way to speak about her feelings openly as she didn't know how to express them to you." She added, "I would like to hear good news upon my return from Nevada," and she hung up.

Donna knew I had spoken to Kathleen, and she was also aware that I most likely learned about her feelings toward me from that conversation. For a couple of days, it was an awkward situation for me. I avoided Donna as much as possible, primarily going out to meet friends and locking myself up in my room. After a week had passed, as I was preparing to do laundry, I saw Donna standing beside me. I said hello, and she was happy I spoke to her.

She immediately said, "I made some breakfast. You can have some if you like."

She followed me as I approached the kitchen and she mentioned, "We have an immigration interview with the INS. It will be in October." (It was currently September.)

"What interview?" I asked.

"I applied for you to change your status from a student to a permanent US resident."

That was when I learned that she had sent the application.

"I know you didn't ask for it, but you deserve it. You're a good person. The little I know about you is that you have a wonderful soul."

She came closer to hug me. I hugged her and felt guilty about everything she had done for me.

I told her, "You're a much better person than I expected you to be. I'm now indebted to you. Thank you very much!"

She suggested we talk more later over supper that night. I agreed.

*

At the dinner table, as I sat down to eat that night, Donna started to talk.

"This is very difficult for me to say, but you must know I have feelings for you. I didn't care much about you at the start, and all I needed was money to pay for my addiction. The more I interacted with you and saw your struggles, the more I started to reassess my situation and life. You've become a source of motivation and inspiration for me. I've stopped doing drugs and have been clean now for a few months. I am working on quitting smoking. I'm thirty-two years old, and I should get my act together. Soon, I should be married and have children of my own. I have one more year to finish my degree program, and then I will be a nurse. I wasted my life with some useless people and doing stupid shit." She ended the conversation by saying, "I really want this marriage to be real. Can we work on it together?"

I uttered no words. I could not swallow the food in my mouth let alone finish the meal on my plate. The room was dead silent for about ten minutes. I stood up to clean my dish, and as I walked toward the kitchen, she said, "That is okay, too, if you say no."

I turned and looked at her face.

How can I say no to this woman after what she has done for me? I thought.

At the same time, even though there were no other women in my life since I started to live with Donna, I hadn't developed any romantic feelings for her. I saw tears drop as she struggled to hide her emotions.

Donna was a ticket for a better future for me. However, I didn't want to play with her emotions and go through with a marriage when my heart wasn't in it. To do so was simply morally unacceptable to me. I thought I would damage her more if I pretended to love her.

How would I like it if someone treated my sisters in such a way?

It was a cruel thought, and I went to my room and cried. I was torn between my core principles and my desperate need to be a US resident.

A few days later, I told Donna that I never thought of her romantically. I assured her, however, that I appreciated and liked her kindness toward me and everything she had done for me. I told her it was too soon for me to feel one way or another and requested her to give me time to process the whole situation. She said she understood.

"I intended to make you aware of my feelings and perhaps work slowly toward sharing a life if possible."

I felt better when she said that.

*

We went to the INS office in Boise for an interview about four or five weeks later. The purpose of the interview was to confirm that the marriage was real and that we lived together. It was a Thursday morning in October.

I didn't know the process, but Donna did as she had consulted with her friends. Before the appointment, Donna coached me. She told me they would be asking her about my sleeping habits, toothbrush, mother's middle name, and so on. I would be asked whether I had met her family or not, and I would be expected to remember the names of her brothers, which I had already memorized for the meeting.

When we entered the plaza where INS had an office, Donna told the receptionist who we were. An agent stated the interviews would not be conducted with Donna and me in the same room. Then, the officer led Donna to a room and returned to the front desk to take me to a separate interview room. I was left alone in a room for about forty minutes.

Two INS agents entered and started to set up a tape recorder. A third person joined them and said he was late because he had been escorting the professor, Kathleen, to her vehicle. I was confused about why Kathleen had been called to the INS office.

After clearing his voice, one of the agents asked me if I spoke English. I said yes. He asked me to state my full name, birth month, day, and year. He also asked me my current address. The tape recorder was recording the entire conversation.

Then he told me, "Your marriage to Donna was fraudulent. We know you two don't sleep in the same bed. She and the professor were just trying to help you get residency so you could stay in this country. We spoke to both, and both gave similar statements verifying this. The application filed by Donna has been rejected, as the marriage has been deemed to be fraudulent, and it should be annulled."

I knew the meaning of fraudulent, but I had never heard the words "annulled" or "annulment" before and didn't know what they meant.

He continued, "Your student visa, which was granted to you to stay in this country for the next three years, is no longer valid because the moment Donna applied for permanent status, your student visa was automatically revoked."

I asked, "What is my status now?"

"You have no status, and you will be deported to Yemen next week."

I needed to pee badly.

I had only been in the US for about sixteen months.

I have no university degree and am returning to Yemen in disgrace, I thought.

I said, "I need to pee."

As I stood up, I fainted, and they assisted me back onto the chair. They gave me water and escorted me to the washroom. I vomited into the toilet.

When I returned to the room, I told the agents, "Yes, we may have entered into this marriage with the wrong intentions. However, we didn't exchange money and planned to make this marriage work."

The lead agent responded to me, stating, "That is exactly what Donna was trying to tell us, too. All we know is that you entered the marriage with the purpose of becoming a resident, and that is illegal. The purpose and the intention are what matters. Tomorrow, we'll be booking a flight to Amsterdam and will fly with you. From there, we will put you on a direct flight to Yemen. We will return, and you will go to Yemen."

They all left the room.

The feelings of failure and misfortune were haunting me. The death of my father when I was five, the disappearance of my uncle and being left homeless when I was eight, the imprisonment in Ethiopia for being a member of a communist party when I was a teenager, and the struggles I faced in Yemen later in my teens all came rushing into my mind. Now I was being forced to return to Yemen with unfinished objectives and goals. I sobbed alone in the room.

After about twenty-five minutes, they transferred me to the county jail and kept me in a holding room. They didn't take fingerprints or a mugshot, as I thought they might do; they just locked me up.

After I had been sitting in the holding cell for about an hour, they called my name. As I approached the counter, they told me, "Your lawyer wants to speak to you," and pointed me to a wall where the phone was mounted just across from the officers' desks.

When I picked up the phone, a lawyer introduced himself. He informed me that he had been retained by Donna and that she had posted a bond for me. He further mentioned that he was waiting for the judge to sign the order so that I would be released that night on bond and, therefore, wouldn't be deported the next day. Instead, my case would go to the courts. I was further confused and, at the same time, happy.

Donna was waiting for me outside the county jail and drove me to our home. I was shaking and exhausted.

My lips were dry, and mentally, I was all over the place. I didn't know what to think or say. Most of the day's events felt like a bad dream.

From the time of the interview to my release, nine hours had gone by.

When we got home, Donna called Kathleen and informed her about my status. When she got off the phone, Donna told me, "Kathleen posted a $3,500 bond and wrote another check for $1,500 as a retainer fee for the lawyer."

Before she finished talking, we heard five INS agents by our house, and we opened the door to inquire as to why they were there.

They asked me for my car keys (I had bought a car in December 1984, shortly before marrying Donna), and when I asked why, they told me, "The car was used as the means of transportation to enter a fraudulent marriage and is considered to be accessory to the crime. We have an order from a judge to confiscate it."

They took my car, which was one of the items I was planning to sell to pay back Kathleen the $5,000 she advanced on my behalf. The car was worth a little over $6,500, a considerable asset in those days.

The next day, Donna, Kathleen, and I met to exchange information as to what had happened at the immigration office. Apparently, the INS had an informant who had reported us and details about the marriage, the witnesses, and the living arrangements. And that informant was Malik, the African guy. We knew it had to be him because no one else besides the three of us knew of the arrangement. Donna later heard from others that it was indeed him. He was angry at me for not paying him a finder's fee. I hadn't wanted to pay him as doing so would have been considered evidence of the marriage.

Well, we now knew the source. For not paying the couple hundred dollars we were supposed to give him as a commission on the thousands of dollars I never paid Donna, we ended up in this legal fiasco. Maybe he was also pissed off that Donna wasn't sleeping with him anymore. Who knows? Since Donna didn't ask for or want the money, and therefore, no financial transaction took place, we didn't think we needed to pay him anything. That turned out to be a fatal mistake on our part.

Kathleen argued to INS that it was a matter of principle for her to assist me and to drive with us all the way to Nevada and witness the marriage, even though the purpose of the marriage was to help me with my immigration status. She believed and told them that I was a good person and so was Donna. Based on her conversation with Donna, Kathleen had the assumption the marriage was soon to be authentic. Donna, on the other hand, reported that she loved me, and that was the reason she submitted the application for permanent residency. She emphasized to them that she hadn't accepted a dime from me.

None of that mattered to the INS agents. Their ultimate goal was to ship me to Yemen on the next flight. They had no chance of capturing the millions of illegal aliens living underground in the US and committing crimes; in comparison to those people, I was an easy target because I had a known physical address and was attending university.

My lawyer advised us that the likelihood of fighting and winning the case in court, which would require us to convince the judge that we were in love and working toward the marriage, was nearly impossible.

He said, "The three of you have already admitted the marriage certificate was signed for the purpose of obtaining a permanent residency. What comes after is your business, but from a legal perspective, it is a violation."

He suggested Donna file for annulment.

He also suggested that I apply for political asylum, as my birthplace, Ethiopia, and my home country, South Yemen, both had Marxist regimes. He felt that avenue may give me a better chance at residency.

"Based on your previous involvement in Ethiopia and your imprisonment, your application will most likely be accepted as political asylum."

Finally, he informed me that he was not a specialist when it came to political asylum applications and provided me with the name of the best lawyer in Seattle, Washington.

I liquidated every penny I had to pay back Kathleen. My cousin Ferdows, who was living in Los Angeles at the time, also provided me with $1,500 to pay Kathleen the entire amount I owed.

Donna and I stayed together for the next six months. By then, she had graduated with her nursing degree and was ready to move to Florida, where she had a job waiting for her.

She broke the news to her mom and her brothers that she was falling for this young man from Yemen. The entire family in Montana rejected the notion of her entering into an interracial marriage. She was willing to marry me again, as the first one was annulled, but I told her I would be lying to her if I said I loved her. We were simply two people with little or nothing in common who had come together for a shared goal.

However, I assured her that she was one of the most significant women in my life. The sacrifices she made were so enormous, and I told her that I didn't know how I would ever pay her back.

In addition to what she had done, or at least attempted to do for me, I had been a positive influence on her as well. She had kicked her drug habit and stopped smoking. And the predicament we had been in together brought out the generous, giving side of her.

She quoted John Bunyan, author of *Pilgrim's Progress*, to me: "You have not lived today until you have done something for someone who can never repay you back."

Applying for Asylum

I had hired Dan P. Danilov, who was regarded as one of the top lawyers in the US. He was born in Russia, and his family escaped to China when he was two years old. He later migrated to the US, becoming one of the country's most prominent and well-renowned immigration lawyers. He was regarded as one of the best immigration lawyers in the US and even aided Nikita Khrushchev's son Sergei when he immigrated to the US in 1991. He also wrote several books on immigration law. Because I was told he was the best lawyer money could buy and that he was "godlike," I fully trusted him to look out for my best interests.

Once my file was transferred to a different immigration lawyer, I put together a package outlining the persecution I had faced in Ethiopia due to my political affiliation with the communist party that was opposing the military government. I elaborated on the reasons I was forced to seek haven in North Yemen: fear of future imprisonment and possible execution, as was still happening to millions of Ethiopian youth in the 1970s and '80s.

In addition, I explained the prejudices and discrimination I was facing in North Yemen, primarily due to being born outside Yemen and my ancestry initially being from the communist South Yemen, which was another Marxist state. I stated that I had had to obtain a North Yemen passport to enter the US as well as eliminate using my last name, as it would identify me as being from South Yemen. All of my statements were true, and since they were sincere human rights violations, I pleaded to be granted a stay in the US.

The process took nearly seven years to be heard in court, and I had one immigration hearing in Seattle, Washington. By that time, I had already graduated from university and had been working at various engineering firms in Boise. While working for the Idaho State Library in 1992, I was also looking for another job opportunity and exploring the possibility of entering graduate school in the Seattle area so that I could be close to my lawyer.

At the immigration hearing in 1992, the judge looked at my application and stated, "It seems you were a fifteen- or sixteen-year-old when you were imprisoned in Ethiopia. In addition, you left Ethiopia for Yemen legally from the Addis Ababa International Airport. Even though your application is well written and genuine, I have difficulties believing that you were actively involved in a Marxist-Leninist party and part of the struggle against military rule at that tender age.

"Nearly all the applications I review to make these types of decisions, from the part of the world you came from, are from applicants who fled their homeland on foot to the nearest bordering countries. In your case, you departed both Ethiopia and Yemen legally from the airports, and if the governments officially wanted you to be jailed or executed, you wouldn't have been allowed to leave the countries. As for obtaining a North Yemen ID due to discrimination, the State Department has no record of any human rights violations on North Yemen's citizens or those of the citizens of South Yemen."

He reiterated that he was not saying that no discrimination happened to those born outside Yemen or to me specifically, but he clarified that discrimination alone was not a sufficient reason to be granted asylum.

"Therefore, I didn't find compelling evidence to warrant political or humanitarian asylum of any kind to grant you to stay in the US. Young man," he added, "you seem to be a bright individual, and it is my hope you find an alternative way to remain in this country."

He looked at me, Norma, and Dan Danilov (my lawyer) and asked me if there was anything I would like to share with him that was not mentioned in my application. Before I opened my mouth to speak, Norma, my adopted American mother, stood up to speak. The judge asked who she was and requested that she identify herself for the record and why she was there.

"My name is Norma G. Rice. I consider him to be like my son. I have known Adel since the day he arrived in the US. He also spent considerable time in my house while attending university. My children saw him as their older brother. He is an upstanding individual. He coached soccer to hundreds of children while he was living in Boise, Idaho. He served the Boise State University International Student Association and was never a burden on society. He came to the US with sufficient money for his first two years of university and then worked and supported himself, including paying his own university tuition for all four years. As you saw in his application, the governor of Idaho wrote a letter supporting his claim on humanitarian grounds. [See Appendix One.] His employers and members of my church also endorsed the same sentiment. Please consider his case, as he would be an exemplary US citizen."

My lawyer hadn't uttered a single word but stood the entire time, listening to Norma speak.

The judge glanced at the three of us and stated, "Mom, I do understand all you said is to be true. I appreciate you coming here from Boise, Idaho, in support of this young man, but he simply doesn't have a strong enough case to warrant asylum. I hope he finds an alternative to remaining in this country."

The judge stood up and left the chamber.

My lawyer, Norma, and I spent some time in the parking lot to recap the hearing outcome and discuss the next steps. Dan suggested we file an appeal. In the meantime, he asked Norma if she could "find anyone to marry this young man. Perhaps we can explore the H-1B visa." Norma asked what that was.

Dan said, "It's a professional employment visa. Or we can find ways to get him accepted in Canada. He is a highly skilled individual, and there are plenty of opportunities for him."

He added, "The issue is that the fraudulent marriage is showing on his record, and INS keeps bringing it up." He told Norma, "I'm sure you can find a wife for him from your church, too."

His suggestion didn't make sense to me. Marriage was how I got into this mess; I didn't understand how another marriage would solve it. Perhaps he was thinking that if I had a real marriage, and in particular if I had children, I would have a chance to stay. Regardless, I wasn't interested in going down that road again.

Why must my problems always be resolved through marriage?

VIII

Another Religion

Baptism is an outward expression of an inward faith.

— Watchman Nee, Chinese Christian
church leader

*U*ntil I landed in Boise, Idaho, I had never heard the word "Mormon" let alone learned anything about the religion. The extent of my knowledge and readings of variations of Christianity was initially limited to Orthodox, Catholicism, and Protestantism. Then I came to learn about the Pentecostal, Jehovah's Witnesses, and evangelical denominations. As part of my childhood living arrangement, I spent much time with my Ethiopian Orthodox family. I also briefly attended the evangelical Sunday school in Addis Ababa for nine months, as they were handing out school supplies to local children.

Some children attending the Sunday school in Ethiopia were invited to the missionaries' residences. My aunt didn't mind me attending the weekend Bible classes, about a five-minute walk from our house, but she never allowed me to mingle with anyone before or after Bible study hours.

I slowly decided to move away from religion altogether. Growing up in Ethiopia, I had read the three Holy Books of the Qur'an, Old Testament (Hebrew Bible), and New Testament (Christian Bible) a few times before the age of thirteen. I came to understand the foundations of Judaism, Christianity, and Islam to basically be the same. Clearly, God didn't appear to have a religion and all the dressings, at least in my mind. Moreover, at a young age, I noticed multiple personal flaws and hypocrisies in the religion teachers I had. Primarily, my attention shifted to Marxist ideas when I was a young teenager. Quickly mastering Marxism ideology made me stand out from my friends. Shortly after I began to attend it, I abandoned the Bible school in Addis Ababa, and I ended up being less religious but more of a spiritual person.

In North Yemen, I knew about Islam and all the rituals, but I hardly ever practiced it properly. My roommate and I were not practicing Arab Muslims. To no one's knowledge, we ate during the Ramadan months and pretended to be fasting.

The family who picked me up from the Boise airport and who put me up on my first night in the US—Norma's family—was Mormon. When I moved into my dorm room and then my own apartment, she and her family kept in touch with me, and Norma quickly started introducing me to everyone as her adopted son. She invited me to her family's home for supper once a week. Then Norma would pack leftovers and give them to me so that I could have them in my place for the rest of the week.

After two years in the US, due to the consequences of the fraudulent marriage to Donna and its subsequent annulment, I was on the brink of being homeless, just as I had been when I was between eight and eleven years old. I was destitute.

Norma recommended I move into her basement until I properly sorted things out. I was desperate and had nowhere to go, yet I felt her generosity was too much to take from a family that had already given me so much. Yes, Norma gave more than she could or should have. I was also worried about how I would return the favor. However, with no alternatives in front of me, I moved in with them temporarily.

Norma ordered her sons, who were fifteen and twelve by that time, to help me pack everything in my apartment and bring it to their home. I was late with my rent; she paid the outstanding amount, including the late fees. I moved to her basement, which was bigger than my entire apartment. I was working from 6 p.m. until 2 a.m. at that time, so it was nearly impossible for me to take public transit during the wee hours (during those days, public transit hardly existed in Boise). She let me drive her second car to school and work. In exchange, I often assisted her in driving her children to school.

The family was always clean, organized, and polite, and I knew they did not consume alcohol or caffeine. They prayed before each meal, and they were always thankful to God. Later, I learned most Mormons held similar beliefs to Muslims, except for the tea and coffee part, which was the only problem for me. After all, I came from two countries that both claim to be coffee's origin. I learned that the value system of both religions was essentially the same regarding abstaining from alcohol and sex before marriage, diligence in saying prayers, etc. There were, however, individuals who stopped going to the Mormon temple. These people smoked, had sex before marriage, and got drunk. Everyone called them Jack Mormon, a slang term to refer to an individual who has lapsed in their following of the religion.

Several bookshelves in Norma's basement contained all kinds of books. One shelf had a collection of encyclopedias. I spent many hours reading and glancing at the pictures in the encyclopedias. Those books were my main source of information about the religion. On another of the shelves, I found *The Book of Mormon.*

I was curious about their religion and started reading and asking questions. Norma's family noticed that I regularly took the initiative to spend time reading *The Book of Mormon.* That prompted them to invite me to join them in going to Sunday service. Out of respect for the family who gave me meals, shelter, care, respect, and love, and because of my curiosity, I began to accompany them to their church. I also started to wonder about those children in African and Asian countries wearing shirts bearing Jesus's name; I began to think religion was being used in exchange for food and shelter. I was one of those but living in the US!

The family thought I was interested in being a Mormon, but I didn't read *The Book of Mormon* seeking faith. I wanted to learn about the religion to compare it with Judaism, Islam, and Christianity.

My oldest sister, Hind, who constantly questioned the depth of my Islamic faith, always reminded me to read the holy Qur'an. Despite being influenced by and spending twenty-five years under the South Yemen Marxist system, she thought faith was more important than religion. I didn't know the difference between a faithful man and a religious one. All she had at her disposal to give me was the Qur'an, so that's what she encouraged me to read and follow. Even though I never intended to read it, out of respect for my sister and as a token of my love for her, I carried it to the US. I have kept the exact copy of the Qur'an she gave me for forty years—I still have it!—as it represents sentimental value for my late sister.

The Book of Mormon prompted me to reread the Qur'an and to examine the parallels between the Prophet Muhammed (peace be upon him)[6] and Joseph Smith. I was amazed to discover the striking similarities between Joseph Smith and the Prophet Muhammed (pbuh). As I read *The Book of Mormon*, I couldn't help almost calling Mormonism the American version of Islam, especially as to the core characteristics of the two leaders and the revelations both received from God.

Both the Prophet Muhammed (pbuh) and Joseph Smith were reportedly inspired to start their movements by angelic visits. The Archangel Jibreel (Gabriel) visited the Prophet Muhammed (pbuh). And the Angel Moroni visited Joseph Smith following the visit Smith claimed to have received from God and Jesus Christ three years earlier. In each event, the angel helped the prophet prepare to receive a series of revelations from God.

The significant gap I found was the two men's stances on discrimination. The Prophet Muhammed (pbuh) was more progressive in his views on discrimination. The Mormon Church, in contrast, didn't allow Blacks to be members of their church up until 1979, which was only a few years before I arrived in the US.

From 1849 to 1978, the Church of Jesus Christ of Latter-day Saints (LDS/Mormon Church) prohibited anyone with confirmed or suspected Black ancestry from taking part in ordinances in its temples, serving in any significant church callings, serving missions, attending priesthood meetings, being ordained to any priesthood office, speaking at firesides, or receiving a lineage in their patriarchal blessing. In 1978, the church's First Presidency [the highest governing body of the church—the President of the Church and his counselors] declared in a statement known as "Official Declaration 2" that the Lord lifted the temple and priesthood bans.[7]

As a dark-skinned human, I had been living with a white Mormon family.

What is going on here? I questioned. *How do I fit into their beliefs?*

Nothing made Norma happier than me going to the Mormon church. That was the beginning of the collision course of my belief system.

Because of her generosity and the fact that she treated me as if I were her son, I felt a deep sense of obligation toward her. I wanted to please her as her commitment to me was boundless.

In addition, one Sunday afternoon, when BSU was playing soccer against another college, I scored the winning goal. Norma kept yelling, *"That is my son! That is my son!"*

That was the first time someone had publicly acknowledged me as their son. I still struggle with tears when I think of that moment.

I grew up without a mother or father. No parents showed up at my school to claim me as their child. I have never been acknowledged as anyone's son. When Norma shouted "That is my son!", for the first time I felt I was recognized as a human. I belonged to someone!

My philosophy on religion has always been open and casual. Still, to honor her, I felt I needed to show respect to not only her but her religion as well, thereby making me somewhat of a hypocrite. I wasn't looking to be part of any religion, but for Norma to publicly acknowledge me as her son was one of the most significant moments of validation for me. I thought that if I accepted her religion, I would be paying her back in some small way. I started to consider being baptized in the Mormon Church.

*

While I was living with Norma, Mark Hansen came to Boise to visit me and his former colleagues. During this visit, I mentioned to Mark my involvement with the Mormon Church and my intention to be baptized as a Mormon.

He told me, "You are a disgrace to your race and all Black people if you join the Mormon Church."

Mark wouldn't have minded if I had told him I was converting to Catholicism or joining a Methodist church, but he was looking at the situation philosophically. He pointed out to me that the Mormon Church historically didn't recognize Black people as humans and had, for centuries, prohibited Blacks from joining the church. He thought I was aligning myself with a doctrine that didn't recognize me as a human, even though the ban had been lifted a few years prior. He saw my baptism as an act of betrayal to not only him but especially to myself.

Mark was a moral man. He wanted me to be so as well. I tried to express my reasons for the baptism—that it was my way of honoring Norma and all she was doing for me. I explained to him my stance on religion and that I wasn't necessarily committing myself to the LDS faith but wanted to show my respect for Norma.

He was uncompromising, though. He felt my taking this step was too much of a compromise on my part, especially after all our conversations and the effort he had put into encouraging me to stand up tall and strong, to know and respect myself, and to demand respect from others.

When I spoke to Kathleen about my findings and comparisons between the Prophet Muhammed (pbuh) and Joseph Smith, she said, "Many American Christians regard the Prophet Muhammed [pbuh] not as a fraud but as a great and good man who was instrumental in the establishment of an important world religion belonging to the Judeo-Christian tradition." But she dismissed my interest in religion, entirely. She flat out told me not to "waste [my] time with such crap," meaning Mormonism but also religion in general.

Norma was convinced I was blessed and born with the best qualities of *The Book of Mormon*'s teaching. She believed that it would be most suitable for me to be with a Mormon girl. She also wanted to prove that the Mormons weren't racist by getting the Boise temple to register the first Black member of the church.

I saw deep down she genuinely loved me like one of her sons, and getting me to join the church was the best she could ever do to express her love. From the day she picked me up from the airport, she treated me with dignity and respect and offered her support freely. I figured, *What have I got to lose if I could make this lady happy with a little gesture by dipping myself in the water [baptism]?*

I went through with the baptism, and the celebration afterward affirmed that I had done the right thing. It was a typical baptism, me dressed in a white robe and a man dipping me in a pool of water, but Norma had invited friends to her home afterward to commemorate the event. She put on quite a feast, and all her friends welcomed me. From that day on, her friends and church family saw me as a genuine member of her family.

*

Due to my mixed paternal background and the influence of assorted religions and cultures, I bounced between various religious and cultural practices during my childhood. I didn't think it would be a significant issue here, either. I agreed to travel with Norma's family to Provo, Utah, and attend some religion lessons.

I was introduced to a gorgeous nineteen-year-old girl at one of the church's youth services. As an introverted boy, I had difficulty starting a conversation to break the ice. The girl took the initiative to speak to me, and we started dating. The rules of engagement around dating for Mormon youth were utterly different from the rest of Americans. No one under the age of sixteen could date. Dating was about group study, socializing, and group events. Intimate encounters were forbidden.

I'm not sure if the term *healthy living* had been coined back then, but Mormons were encouraged to eat healthily and take care of their bodies. They were discouraged from drinking alcoholic beverages, coffee, and tea; smoking any substance; and using illegal and illicit drugs. If these are things you enjoy doing, don't consider dating a Mormon.

When talking with non-Mormon American friends, I heard that the biggest issue with the Mormon religion, in addition to the consumption of alcohol, was the Law of

Chastity. The Law of Chasity prohibits sex before marriage and adultery, and it condemns homosexuality, labeling it a serious sin.

I told people that doctrine was the same in Islam and how I was raised in North Yemen. Even Orthodox Christians discouraged such behaviors, but they never strictly enforced them in the manner Muslim societies did.

My friends asked me, "Are you telling us you never kissed a girl, tasted alcohol, or held a girl's hand on a date in Yemen?" My response was always, "Nope." I had never even been on a date before arriving in the US, as dating is not customary in Yemen. They looked at me as if I were abnormal or a complete liar.

"No wonder you go to the Mormon church. You're one of them in many ways," were the typical jokes I received.

After three months of group dating and gathering, the beautiful girl, Martha, started to come to my apartment to drop off church materials or school assignments. We spent several hours visiting, but during our visits, we kept at least six feet apart. Then, she started to pay frequent visits to my apartment after school or church youth services. I really liked Martha, as she was a soft-spoken, intelligent girl with beautiful brown hair, perfect teeth, and blue eyes. She dressed modestly.

Martha was a couple of inches taller than me, but I always made every American girl look taller and bigger than me. When we were on dates, we went to the movies, out to dinner, on a hike, to the beach, to sports events, and anything else the two of us liked. She also came with Norma to watch my soccer games.

One weekend, Martha and I kissed each other. I felt a fever in my lips and spine. I always wanted to touch her body and her hair.

The following Sunday, at a singles' conference, Martha walked to the podium, confessed with some tears in her eyes, and asked for forgiveness from God. She stated that she had conducted an ungodly act the previous weekend. As Martha walked back to her seat, she winked at me. She expected me to confess my sinful act from the weekend, too. I was confused and scared.

I stood up from where I was sitting and said, "I didn't do anything! I just kissed her and only touched her boobs!"

I sat down. The church hall went dead silent!

After the minute-long dead silence, everyone chuckled. Martha was embarrassed and never spoke to me again. That was the end of our relationship. And I never returned to the Mormon church again.

During this time, Mark had been calling since his last visit to check on how I was doing. I wanted to be honest with him so in one of our phone conversations, I told him I had been baptized at the Mormon temple.

It was a deal breaker for him. He was disappointed in me and told me I was a disgrace. He disowned me. He, too, never spoke to me again. Unwittingly, I lost both Martha and Mark at the same time! I felt I was a disappointment to Mark. I felt incompetent in dealing with public or social matters.

Opportunity Lost

In early 2022, I discovered a copy of a letter Mark had sent to Kathleen before I left North Yemen to introduce me to her. I had forgotten about this letter that I had kept for almost forty years:

June 30, 1984

Kathleen,

This letter is a kind of personal introduction of my friend, really like my younger brother, if I had one—Adel Ben-Harhara. Don't let his long Arabic name deceive you; if anything, Adel is less religious than I, and only an accident of birth made him officially a Muslim in an Islamic country.

He describes himself as a son of nature. His father was a Yemeni but from the South under British rule while his mother was—and is, for she is still living in Addis Ababa—an Ethiopian. Adel has apparently inherited far more of the African than the Arab and considers himself neither Arab nor Yemeni but "a good person" with pride and dignity. Adel has been far more than a good friend to me here—but a friend and brother in the real, deeper meaning of those two much-abused words.

Please, Kathleen, do whatever you can to help him should the need arise. He has worked, saved, and dreamed of a chance for a good education at much cost and sacrifice. He had planned on coming in December, but a new law is just now prohibiting all Yemenis from traveling abroad for any reason for an indefinite period. Fortunately, Adel had already gotten an exit visa before the policies were put into effect, so he has to leave now.

I would also appreciate it if you would contact some of my old friends in Boise (if any are left), such as Robertson, Jimmy Schaffer, Ken Sanderson, etc., and ask them to extend a hand to Adel. This will be his first time in a non-third-world country, so to speak. He may need assistance and advice on such matters as finding a small apartment, where public facilities like the library, etc. are located, shopping economically, and other questions.

He will have sufficient funds, but since they must last a long time, he plans on living a very bare, spartan life, except for studying and reading books.

Since his primary interest (passion would be a more accurate word) is in Computer Science, he will invest in a personal computer; he is bringing a lot of software.

When you first meet him, you will probably find him shy and quiet; you may mistake his natural seriousness as a lack of friendliness. Please don't. Adel is a warm, honest young man with deep feelings but also a person who is economical in words and doesn't readily express his feelings superficially.

He is very goal-oriented and fully aware of how hard he will work, especially in the first couple of years. I have never felt so confident that someone would achieve his goals at whatever personal sacrifice as I feel of Adel.

Kathleen, be an older sister to him, do this for me. He is mailing (or delivering) a long, personal letter to you about other matters, so expect it soon. Take care and thanks. I will see you (for sure) in September.

Love,

Mark

I was in tears while reading it; I could not finish it due to my watery eyes! Not because it was emotional or a sad letter, but because it brought back memories from the 1980s.

From this note, after almost four decades, I was correct in believing that Mark treated me as his younger brother, and

I no longer question why he didn't speak to me again the moment he knew I was baptized in the Mormon Church. We only get disappointed in people we care for. He accurately described me as not mainly being a non-religious person; instead, a "son of nature."

Kathleen played a significant role as a sister in my life while I was living in the US. She took the risk to stand witness and put her signature on a fraudulent marriage to assist me in gaining permanent resident status in the US. She was a full-time university professor at BSU when she took the chance to ruin her career and reputation. How many of us will go to that extent to help someone?

She befriended me, listened to my life story, and gave me a record single as a Christmas gift: "God Bless the Child" by Billie Holiday. At first, I was confused as to why she was giving me this song; I didn't know the singer, and I had never heard the song before. She explained the lyrics of the song, talking about perseverance and relaying the connection to the biblical reference the song makes ("For whoever has will be given more, and they will have an abundance. Whoever does not have, even what they have will be taken from them." [Matthew 25:29]). When Kathleen handed me the record, she said, "This is you." Ever since I started writing these three books, I've kept coming back to that song—its meaning and its title. I feel it perfectly encapsulates my life.

In my view, dedicating my first book to her and using *God Bless the Child Who's Got His Own* as the subtitle of my first book doesn't do justice here.

Both Kathleen and Mark have long since passed away and I'm here, left to reflect on those days and write about them.

One regret I have is how my friendship with Mark ended ... that it ended. We say time heals all; perhaps, if he were alive today and I were able to reconnect with him, he may have softened his stance and realized that my decision to be baptized in the Mormon Church was such a small, insignificant piece of my life compared to all else my life has entailed. Perhaps not. Sadly, I will never know.

IX

Voluntary Departure

The path to our destination is not always a straight one. We go down the wrong road, we get lost, we turn back. Maybe it doesn't matter which road we embark on. Maybe what matters is that we embark.

— Barbara Hall, former mayor of Toronto
1994-1997

In the fall of 1992, I was working for the Idaho State Library (ISL) in Boise but in the process of moving to Seattle long-term. I wanted to apply for graduate school at the University of Washington, so I contacted the admissions office for application details. The staff in the office notified me that there were issues with my immigration status in the US, and they were, therefore, unable to proceed with my request. They suggested I approach the local INS office to get further clarification on my visa status.

I was completely confused. I had been under the impression that my lawyer and I were still waiting for a response to the appeal he had filed. I went to the INS office to inquire about the letter that INS had sent to the university's admissions office when I asked about applying. The lady at the front desk took my full name and asked me to wait as she went to the back office.

Within three minutes, she and a man returned, and the man asked me to follow him to an office, which I did. He told me that a decision had been made on my appeal and that I had been given sixty days to voluntarily depart from the country.

"That was about four and a half months ago, and you have not departed."

I was stunned and told him, "I am not aware of the decision. I must check with my lawyer."

"Sure, you can, but if you pay for your flight and leave the country within a couple of days, we can waive the overstay period of sixty days that was given to you. You seem to have zero criminal record, so you should be fine. That way, you can always come to the US without any bad records on your file."

"I still must speak to my lawyer to get proper legal advice," I replied.

He was a bit agitated because he knew nothing could be done at that stage as my departure was to be immediate, and I didn't listen to him.

As I stood up to leave the office, he told me, "I'm afraid you are not allowed to leave."

"Why?"

"You're in violation of the sixty-day voluntary departure, and according to the law, we were supposed to hunt you down and ship you out of the country months ago."

I was even more confused and said, "You know I'm gainfully and legally employed, and I have a resident address. If I were to run away from the INS, why would I come to your office?"

He repeated, "You have violated the sixty-day period, and I must take you to the Seattle immigration detention center."

I asked if I could make a phone call to my lawyer, perhaps a family member. He agreed and let me use his desk phone.

I phoned Dennis, Norma, and my lawyer. The lawyer wasn't available, but I explained my situation to Dennis and Norma.

Dennis Meier at Scientech Inc. had hired me as part of my third-year university computer science and engineering program. The job started as a part-time position and ended up being almost full-time in the latter six months; my work there spanned around eighteen months. We remained good friends after I stopped working for him.

When Dennis and Norma contacted the lawyer, they were told his office had no record of the denial letter of my appeal that INS had sent to the lawyer's office. The matter then became even more confusing and frustrating to me.

The INS refused to accept any request for a bond. Moreover, they mentioned that if I did not pay my own airfare and leave the country within a week, they would pay for my flight and send me back to Yemen, and I would never get the chance to return to the US again. I panicked! Being banned from ever entering the US was the worst situation I could imagine at that moment. I quickly agreed to pay for my airfare so that I didn't jeopardize any future hope to return to the US.

In the meantime, my lawyer tried to find out why his office was not notified about the INS's decision on the appeal. The INS office provided records of my lawyer's office having received the letter four months prior and failing to notify his client (me). Norma and Dennis were furious! They hired a different lawyer and tried to move my file from the current lawyer.

While the new lawyer negotiated the matter with Danilov and explored options to file another appeal, I languished in limbo in Seattle for two months, waiting for my situation to be resolved. I dreaded going back to Yemen, the place I had made every effort to leave forever. Knowing I would likely have to go back was like waiting to hear my prison sentence. I pondered my future and feared that regardless of whether I left the US voluntarily or not, I may never be allowed back. It was an ordeal, and by the time it ended, I was exhausted both emotionally and financially.

The INS said the decision was made. In their eyes, the situation was straightforward: my asylum claim was denied, I had been given sixty days to leave, and I hadn't left. They said I could leave voluntarily but that I had to do so within a week.

The other problem was this all came at me with no warning, and my passport was expired. INS had been holding my passport since 1987 and my passport was expired. I had no opportunity to renew it. Now, I was faced with not only being forced to leave the country on short notice but also without a valid passport.

Norma suggested we fire the lawyer and go with the new one, but I didn't want to get rid of the lawyer in the middle of negotiations. He knew he had screwed up, and he seemed to be trying to redeem himself by making sure I didn't have a record in the US. My employers were trying to get me a new H1-B visa, but INS kept pressuring me to leave the US. If I was going to leave, I wanted it to be on good terms.

Richard Wilson from the Idaho State Library was trying to get the library to issue me a new contract so I could get a visa through them, but INS said the wage the Idaho State Library was offering me was sixty cents per hour lower than the threshold to be granted professional status. Richard couldn't get the additional sixty cents in time as it required statewide pay band adjustments.

When the clock ultimately ran out on me, I chose to pay my own one-way fare, about US$2,800, and return to Yemen. I phoned Norma from the flight to tell her I was on my way.

This flight was a huge contrast to the one I had taken from Yemen to the US years earlier; there was no excitement about reaching my destination. I felt defeated, worthless, hopeless. I spent that flight feeling like I was undoing everything I had done—returning to zero, going backward, returning to a place where I was ridiculed, discriminated against, and had lost my identity as a human. Returning to the place I ran away from was worse than falling into an unknown, unpredictable environment. I was returning to a territory where I knew I had nothing; I didn't want to be there.

On the phone call during the flight, Norma told me she and the new lawyer were prepared to help me sue Danilov.

X

In Limbo

Only those who see themselves as utterly destitute can fully appreciate the grace of God.

— Erwin W. Lutzer, Canadian author

For the first two months after my arrival in Yemen, I was lost. The eight years I spent in the US was not long enough to forget general details, but upon my return to Yemen, I found I completely forgot people's names, street names, and other basic information. This forgetfulness was one sign of the extreme exhaustion and depression I was feeling.

When I wrote to Norma from Yemen, I told her I was surviving, but the only way I could survive was to suppress my emotions, hide my feelings, and deny what had happened in the US with my visa. Coming back to Yemen felt like I was signing a death sentence.

Sharese, my friend and schoolmate from Boise, as well as other friends and colleagues were trying to help me adjust by writing encouraging letters. And Norma had quickly hired a new lawyer to sue the first lawyer; the new lawyer was asking for US$7,500 to file the suit. I had returned to Yemen with pocket money—less than $100—so one of the main hurdles was coming up with the $7,500. Norma liquidated my 401K and sold my car and other belongings I had left behind in the US.

For two months I lived with the Banajah family. Fatuma Banaja was the woman who became my mother figure when I was living in North Yemen in the early 1980s. During those two months, I was in limbo, not knowing whether I would be allowed to go back to the US and if so, when. I couldn't eat; I barely slept and when I did, I talked and walked in my sleep. Even though I was broke, I had no motivation to find a job. One day, she sat me down and we talked about my case.

She fed me and said, "Adel, I see how miserable you are. Listen, I know how painful it is for you to return to the country you had no intention of returning to. I know the ordeal you went through to stay in the US. I know you also want to go back there because you don't fit in here. In your case, I think you're trying to shoot a bird in flight. You have no parachute. You have no means to support yourself or fight this legal matter. To retain your sanity, drop the case. Focus today on how you can sustain yourself in Yemen. Find a job. Start life anew. You started from nothing when you were a child. You can rise above this as well."

She was right. I had sunk so low that I needed to get myself back together and start moving forward. After months of uncertainty, conflicting information, and never-ending expenses, I had no energy to fight any longer.

I wrote a letter to the new lawyer and sent it, telling him, "I'm not pursuing this matter any longer. I'm not interested in returning to the US now. Please drop the case."

The lawyer responded, saying Danilov would settle out of court for US$25,000, even though we were suing for more than $175,000 for lost wages. (Suffering wasn't mentioned as part of the deal.) However, I walked away.

At the time, I didn't consciously think back to what Bansser, my father's close friend and a big supporter of mine in Ethiopia, had done years earlier. He was trying to reclaim the money my father's estate was owed by a man who had borrowed large sums of money from my father over the years to build his hotels throughout Ethiopia. When the man offered him a mere $600 to settle the matter, Bansser had told him, "If that's what you're offering, forget it. I don't need it," and walked away. Bansser was a man of honor, above taking an insultingly low amount of money from an unscrupulous man. Perhaps in my response to this legal case, I was exhibiting a subconscious desire to be an honorable man and emulate him.

"Forget about everything. Send me my file," I told him. This lawyer would have taken 60 percent of the $25,000 I was set to receive. I didn't have it in me to fight for pocket change.

Norma was disappointed. She phoned and asked, "Are you in your right mind?"

"I'm done with the US," I told her. I was frustrated, discouraged, severely depressed, highly anxious, and destitute. Norma persisted, trying to persuade me to continue, but I ended the legal battle. I concerned myself with paying back a few friends who had advanced me legal fees, such as Dennis, and then tried to move on with my life.

And I'm glad I did. After paying the current lawyer, the settlement would have gotten me US$7,000-8,000 after investing more than $10,000 and a seemingly never-ending pile of stress. I asked myself, *What am I getting other than a headache?*

Norma felt the whole situation was very unjust. And it was.

Seventy employees of the Idaho State Library lost the case, not just me. So many people were advocating for me, writing letters, making phone calls, offering advice. The weekly library newsletter published regular updates about my return to Yemen.

What I gained through this experience was recognizing the courage of around a hundred people who were working to get me back: the library staff, Norma, Sharese, Richard (my boss at the library), other friends and colleagues from BSU and soccer organizations, and even the governor of Idaho. What was clear to me was the goodness of the American people fighting against "the system." The evidence of that goodness is permanently recorded in the massive stack of letters (which I still have copies of) pleading to the INS on my behalf and letters written directly to me (which I also still have), encouraging me to come back.

Karma Again?

As with any tragedy, there were heroes and karma prevailed yet again. As a child in Ethiopia, I thought that karma showed its face when my uncle, who took me in when I was five years old only because he wanted the money that came with me after my father's death, squandered the money and then died in poverty. I also felt that karma played a role when the family who borrowed money from my dad and never paid it back eventually lost all of their money; some of them were also jailed for other acts. These events, plus what happened to my lawyer in the US, are proof to me that karma has never lost my address.

My original lawyer, Dan P. Danilov, previously regarded as one of the top lawyers in the US, was disgraced; he was eventually barred from practicing law in the US.

It turned out that other immigrants and refugees had a similar story to mine. In the late 1990s and early 2000s, others came forward and went public, claiming that Danilov had failed to file the proper paperwork or had not filed it in time to meet the required deadlines. They were, therefore, deported. I would have been deported as well had I not left voluntarily; had I been deported, I would not have been allowed to return to the US. I was only one of sixteen people to sue him, all making the same claims against him.

When researching this book, I looked for specific information about his practice and the details of my complaint and others' complaints against him. My status in the US was completely in his hands between 1987 and 1992, and the outcome was not what I had expected or hoped for. Knowing that others filed similar complaints gave me some comfort; my case wasn't the only one that had been mishandled.

I'm not a spiteful person. I don't wish harm on anyone, but to learn that he was suspended and disgraced for his malpractice provided me with some emotional satisfaction and perhaps helped me to finally, mentally, close the door to that chapter of my life.

Part Two

XI

Welcome to Canada

I am a Canadian, free to speak without fear, free to worship in my own way, free to stand for what I think right, free to oppose what I believe wrong, or free to choose those who shall govern my country. This heritage of freedom I pledge to uphold for myself and all mankind.

— John G. Diefenbaker, Prime Minister of Canada 1957-1963

I first heard the word Canada in 1974 in my sixth-grade geography class. I learned that Canada was the second largest land on the planet after the Soviet Union. For sure, I was told that it was a cold country. My elementary school instructor spoke highly about Canada, particularly its educational system and pristine natural beauty (its lakes, mountains, and rivers). Until then, I thought the word "beauty" was only reserved for women.

We learned several facts about Canada: Canada has the longest coastline in the world; it is the largest source of freshwater in the world; more than half of all the lakes in the world are in Canada. Canada has less gravity than anywhere else in the world! Canada is the most educated country in the world. The literacy rate is 99 percent, so almost all Canadians can read and write. Santa Claus's official address is in Canada.

In 1990, when my soccer team from Boise, Idaho, took me to Vancouver, BC, for soccer tournaments, I started to reflect on and think about migrating to Canada. That trip was also when I began to think differently about where my future home would be. Like Boise, Vancouver was beautiful in the summer. It was, however, a much more culturally diverse city than Boise. It had a different vibe and seemed much less of a cowboy town. Vancouver seemed more modern and more vibrant. And Mark had told me, "If you had gone to San Francisco, you wouldn't have been surprised at Vancouver." Had I gone to LA, Chicago, New York—anywhere—I would have had a different experience than I had in Idaho.

During my twenties, my dream to be a US citizen became less desirable and less attainable. Once the honeymoon phase was over and I had adjusted culturally to being in the US, I realized the US incarcerates its citizens more than any other country in the world. In particular, more Black youths were in jail or living in the streets than attending colleges.

Despite the proximity of Canada to the US, in my experience, I found that most Americans, including those who lived closer to the border, knew little about Canada, so finding information about Canada from the people I knew in the US was difficult. In Boise, I was surrounded by people with a small worldview, a narrow scope of life experience beyond their state, and a largely homogeneous culture.

People who were significant and influential in my life at that time—Kathleen, Mark (although he had cut ties with me, his words still echoed in my mind often), and Norma—always supported my intentions, regardless of what they were. Mark was always optimistic about Canada when I spoke to him about it. Although Norma appreciated the natural beauty of Canada, all she knew about Canada were the names of famous hockey players and the existence of the Mormon community in Lethbridge, Alberta. But Kathleen was a well-read individual who seemed to appreciate the Canadian liberal policies and general attitudes of Canadians. She thought highly of the late Canadian Prime Minister Pierre Trudeau. I had a positive outlook on Canada's politics and systems compared to the US because Kathleen and Norma both had positive views of Canada.

I didn't know who Trudeau was, but Kathleen viewed him as an intellectual, charismatic man with a well-rounded political understanding, and she praised his efforts to maintain Canadian unity. She mentioned the Quebec sovereignty movement and talked about Trudeau fostering pan-Canadian identity. She compared him to US President J. F. Kennedy and commented that Trudeau was perhaps even better in her view. She always believed Canada to be a better place to live than the US. From those conversations and impressions, my loyalty began to shift from wanting to be American to being Canadian.

When I was living in Idaho, I spent a good portion of my spare time at the BSU library reading about Canada. Learning about its government system gave me a sense of balance. As a Marxist in my youth, I found the idea of Canada's universal health care system appealing. I learned about Trudeau's alignment with Castro; compared to Idaho, Canada seemed much more left-leaning. I began to understand that most Canadians didn't seem to see communism as a frightening terrorist movement. Instead, Canadian leaders showed great diplomacy by sitting with other leaders in negotiations and talks. And the Canadian public seemed less individualistic than Americans.

I felt empty after the disastrous and sudden end to my time in the US. This notion that there were other options, perhaps better ones, than going back to the US was compounded by the complications of my US immigration status being up in the air. I had been forced to return to Yemen, but I still wanted to live in a Western society. I needed a plan B.

Then, in early 1993, while working for an oil company in Yemen, I met a Canadian fellow named John Rees. He was working in Yemen as a geologist and told me about Calgary, Canada, where he was from.

Like everyone else, I couldn't choose my birthplace, parents, or the religion, language, or culture I was exposed to as a child. I had no control over the socialist revolution in Ethiopia, which led to hundreds of thousands of killings and migrations. My hopeful migration to North Yemen to reconnect with my paternal family was tarnished due to the persecution I endured based on my color and ethnicity, and I was forced to flee to the US. Then, the poor choices I made and the harsh reality of the legal system and crooked lawyer's malpractice forced me back to Yemen to endure further personal suffering and civil war. Finally, in 1993, I made a choice that was a tipping point in my life: to land in Canada— to migrate to a new country as a free man for the first time in my life.

November 27, 1995

Dear Mr. Ben-Harhara:

Your Canadian immigration visa is contained in the enclosed envelope. If you are being accompanied to Canada by your spouse and/ or dependent children, you will also find their visas enclosed. You must arrive on or before the visa expiry indicated in Block 33 of the visa. The visa expiry date cannot be extended. The visa must be carried with you and presented to an immigration officer upon your entry to Canada at which time you will be requested to sign it. As the visa is the only evidence of your status in Canada, it must be carefully preserved and presented each time you re-enter Canada.

May I take this opportunity to wish you every success in your future life in Canada.

The Embassy

*

It took almost three years to complete the paperwork to get my Canadian immigration visa. After securing my immigration papers from the Canadian consulate in 1995, I focused on what city to relocate to. The factors I was looking at were employment opportunities, the cost of living (considering I may have needed to survive for at least six months without a job), and possibly being close to the Rocky Mountains.

The first time I heard of Calgary was in 1988 when I was living in Boise and Calgary was hosting the Winter Olympics. Until that time, I never knew of the existence of the Winter Olympics. And before that, I only knew of three Canadian cities: Toronto, Montreal, and Vancouver.

Even though I wasn't impressed with the winter conditions, I thought Calgary looked like a friendly city. It resembled Denver more than Boise in the winter. There was plenty of snow in Idaho, but Boise received much less snow than the rest of the state, and there was never as much as there is in Calgary. In Idaho, we could see flowers blooming in March because the winters were much shorter and milder than in Calgary. I shuddered when the TV commentator said that Calgary can have snow in June!

Since I'd arrived in Boise during the summer, I had eagerly been waiting to see the snowfall for the first time, which took place on November 4. It was a magical moment for me, and I was mesmerized! But hearing that Calgary was much colder and could have snow any month of the year was frightening.

When John Rees and I worked together in Sana'a, Yemen, in the early 1990s, I often talked to him about Calgary to learn more about the city, mainly job opportunities, educational facilities, weather, etc.

To this day, I am fond of Montreal, perhaps due to my exposure to the 1976 Summer Olympics on TV, but it was easy for me to eliminate Montreal due to my lack of French language skills. Even though the weather conditions were much more favorable in both Toronto and Vancouver, I had to remove them from my destinations due to the cost of living and my fear that I couldn't secure employment immediately.

The fourth possible city was Calgary, as it was the home of significant oil and gas companies. Also, at the time, the unemployment rate in Calgary was low compared to Vancouver or Toronto. I considered that it was not far from beautiful British Columbia and flanked by the Rocky

Mountains to the west. Calgary is within 145 kilometers (90 miles) of beautiful places, such as Banff and Lake Louise. It is one of the cleanest cities I have visited or lived in. Moreover, it is in proximity to the western US, where I lived for many years, so I would be able to travel and meet my former friends from Idaho, Washington, and Oregon.

The downside of Calgary was the harsh winter season and the yo-yo weather patterns (especially chinooks), which trigger debilitating migraines. However, I quickly grew to love Calgary, and it has ended up being where I have spent most of my life. It's true that "home isn't a place; it's a feeling."[8] I feel at home in Calgary. It is the birthplace of my daughters. And Calgary has allowed me to be me.

*

In June 1963, in Berlin, Germany, J.F. Kennedy said, "Freedom has many difficulties, and democracy is not perfect, but we have never had to put a wall up to keep our people in, to prevent them from leaving us."[9] This is how I felt; Canada didn't put a wall up to prevent me from coming, even though I wasn't a citizen of Canada yet.

Reflecting on my life and the opportunities provided to me in Canada, I shall say, as a free man, I take pride in my words, "I'm a proud Calgarian and Canadian!"

XII

Her Rights Versus My Image

I have always thought that if women's hair posed so many problems, God would certainly have made us bald.

— Marjane Satrapi, French-Iranian novelist

When I reflect on my past, specifically my interactions with women, I see how much my social environment, schooling in North Yemen, and my training and working in North America with computers influenced my perspective and actions.

In Yemen, there were strict protocols regarding interactions between men and women. Girls had separate schools. Women wore head coverings, so all that was visible were their eyes. Their eyes were, hence, fascinating and alluring to me. Also, men couldn't speak to women outside their families except for specific business purposes (doing business in the banks, talking to female elementary school teachers, etc.). Even to ask a woman for directions in the street was forbidden.

In our homes, the situation was different. We grew up with mothers and sisters. There was love and laughter. I honored and respected the women in my family and was deeply bothered when they faced misogyny from their husbands, which was rampant in our community. Men misrepresented Islam for their benefit to maintain control of women. Most men wouldn't marry women with a university education; women with a higher level of education were seen as being too difficult to control. Therefore, parents would take their daughters out of school when the girls reached eighth grade so that they wouldn't "emasculate" their future husbands. Islam mandates that all people learn to contribute to humanity in the best way possible. However, men controlled the narrative in North Yemen.

Men's respect for women is manifested differently in Yemen than in Western countries. If someone is harassing a woman on the street in Yemen, a man will protect/stand up for the woman and even go so far as to beat the other person up. Yemen society does not have serial rapists, murderers, and the like. There, women are oppressed but not targeted for violence. They are confined to the home and expected to be submissive. The treatment of women is oppressive but doesn't constitute hate. I've never seen hatred for women in an Arab/Muslim man, but I have in other cultures.

As much as I considered myself different, I believed women should be pretty, good cooks, and good mothers. I was a product of Yemeni society at that time. When I first moved to the US in the mid-'80s and saw that Kathleen drove a pickup truck and spent nights camping alone in the mountains, I freaked out. I felt she should drive a better car, and I asked myself, *Why would a woman sleep alone in the mountains?*

After leaving North Yemen for the first time and settling in the US, I was surprised whenever I would meet a woman of authority. Only men were influential or were leaders in my

Yemeni community. To see women in positions of power was confusing and humbling. I began to realize how much I had to learn and how I needed to expand my thinking. Perhaps most importantly, I needed to know that women had roles beyond simply serving the needs of men.

My work with computers compounded the problem. It's not possible to hurt a computer's feelings. I wasn't looking into someone's eyes when I made a mistake. I would just delete it and move forward. I didn't increase my social IQ quickly because I was immersed in an electronic world.

My weak social IQ and the influence of my upbringing were tested during my marriage. I had entered into this arranged marriage in Yemen with mixed feelings. I was thirty-three years old; it was time to move forward with my life by getting married and starting a family. I had experienced dating according to North American customs when I lived in the US, but in Yemen, my only option was to follow the courtship and marriage customs there. This meant that I wasn't in love with my wife[10] when I married her, but we entered into the marriage the typical way Yemeni couples begin their lives together. But I wasn't solely a Yemeni man in blood or in practice.

In my attempt to modernize myself in the US, I had distanced myself from my faith. I always retained portions of it, but I didn't take the time to tease out the differences between cultural misogyny and Islam. My wife wore a hijab, and after our wedding, I forced her to remove it. The timing and the actions themselves were callous and inhumane. It was on our trip to Canada and her first time stepping foot outside of Yemen. She was expecting our first child, and I performed my initial act as an oppressive husband. I made her remove her hijab even though doing so went against her beliefs and what she wanted for herself.

The Unveiling

The flight from the Sana'a airport to Calgary took us through Frankfurt and was at night. The layover at the Frankfurt airport was about six hours. I took a short nap during the flight, but my wife didn't. She was twenty-one years old and five months pregnant. We didn't know at the time, but she had developed diabetes. She had to take an aisle seat so she could make frequent trips to the washroom.

At the Frankfurt airport, while waiting for our connecting flight to Calgary, I noticed my wife resting her head on the seat and struggling to stay awake. Soon, her head covering started to fall off, revealing her silky dark-brown hair. She seemed too sleepy to realize that her hair covering was practically falling off. I started to reflect on my father's acts when he unveiled his wife Maryam and had her pose for pictures to use for travel documents. What he did that was stranger than anything was distribute her picture to his older brother, whom he had a dispute with, to tell the brother that he had a better-looking wife than his brother. He showed Maryam's picture to his friends, bragging that Maryam was a prettier lady than their wives.

I thought, *My father did that out of an inflated ego, revenge, a rebellious attitude, and without any regard or understanding of her rights. Her rights of privacy or religious requirements. Her culture and value system. I am an educated man. I view women's rights in a better light than he ever did. I want my wife to be free, and by removing her hair cover, I am liberating a woman. I should start with my wife and later with my children if I have daughters.* Moreover, even though I loved and adored my father, I considered him showy and arrogant. Perhaps crazy, too!

I stared at my wife for about ten minutes or so. Then, I leaned toward her to lift the scarf and uncover her hair. She sensed that I had stopped reading my book and turned around to look at me. She opened her eyes and asked me, "Are you okay? Why are you looking at me like that?" I didn't respond for a moment.

Then I stood up and told her, "Your hair scarf was falling off."

As she quickly tried to put it in order, I pretended to help. Instead, I removed the covering and walked away.

She didn't know what was happening. She was half asleep, and I could see her confusion. She tried to hold my hands when I removed her headscarf, but I was too quick.

She put both hands over her head, trying to cover her hair. She was also trying to grab her purse; she was frightened and confused. I walked over to the nearest garbage bin and dumped the scarf. When I returned to my seat, I found my wife holding her hair, as shocked as if I had removed all her clothing. She then started to look for something in her purse she could use to cover her hair. She found nothing.

I sat beside her and said, "You're a free woman."

"What do you mean?" she asked.

"You don't have to wear your veil anymore. You should conduct yourself like all women you see," I said.

"I'm ashamed and embarrassed to go around without a hair cover," she pleaded. She said, "I'm not used to walking in public without a hair cover."

"People would think of you as strange and funny if you wore your head cover in Canada," I added.

"You told me Canada is a safe place to be ourselves and follow our belief system. You said it is a peaceful country," she argued.

"Yes, Canada is a safe and free country to live in, and that is why we are heading there. However, you should look and act like most Canadians. I would like you to look like a Spanish-looking lady, not an Arab with a head cover. Plus, I will be embarrassed to walk around with a wife covering her hair. I feel it looks as if I am oppressing you. That doesn't look good on me."

She didn't respond. She only began to cry.

*

Reflecting today on my actions, I would say asking a woman to uncover her hair is as bad as forcing her to cover her hair. That should be her choice; she should be allowed to follow her religious and cultural values, not mine.

Who am I to "liberate" a woman? As a husband, shouldn't my role be to support her decisions and choices? Was I concerned about my image and, therefore, giving in to social norms, or did I believe in women's rights?

XIII

Finding My Community

The purpose of life is not to be happy, but to matter—to be productive, to be useful, to have it make some difference that you have lived at all.

— Leo Rosten, American author

Calgary

*M*y wife and I arrived in Calgary, AB, Canada, on May 1, 1996. I was thirty-four. I landed as an independent professional, a person who's not expected to be a burden to the taxpayers—an able and productive person from day one.

Except for John Rees, who was traveling between Calgary and Yemen for work in those days, neither my wife nor I knew anybody in Calgary. Within a few weeks of our arrival, we met several Yemeni families who had migrated there. During the mid-1990s, there were no more than ten families we knew who had come from Yemen. The majority of Yemenis in Calgary at that time were from South Yemen. Typically, these families were headed by at least one professional (primarily the father). That is not to say there were no educated women, as a couple of ladies earned university degrees.

Even though most members of the Yemeni community were from South Yemen or were educated in South Yemen, they were also divided by tribe and income status. We met some Indians with Ismaili Muslim backgrounds who were born and raised in South Yemen. Still, most Yemenis had difficulties accepting them as Yemenis because they didn't have an Arab bloodline. Ditto for those with Somali heritage but who were born in Aden, South Yemen.

One elderly Yemeni man kept challenging me about being Yemeni because of my birthplace in Ethiopia and the brown skin I proudly wear. This man asked me if Ben-Harhara was even a Yemeni name. He suggested that perhaps I was mistaken about myself and maybe I was from Harar, a city in Eastern Ethiopia.

I laughed and told him, "I can understand your confusion due to my dark complexion, and perhaps your misperception is compounded by my non-Yemeni attributes. However, how would you classify the tens of thousands of members of the Harhara families living in Yemen, the rest of the Middle East, Europe, and North America?"

Even though he was born and raised in Aden, he knew little about the significant (dynasty) ruling Harhara tribe, which governed the Upper Yafa region in Yemen between 1730 and 1967.

During our first week in Canada, I took my wife to the Calgary Catholic Immigration Society, which was providing English lessons for new Canadians. I registered her for English courses. At the registration and evaluation office, one of the staff stated, "I have never seen an Arab man bringing his wife to sign up for English courses in their first week in Canada. And you keep asking for your wife's opinion. Why?"

Other Yemeni men spoke on their wives' behalf; the other Yemeni women we met never opened their mouths. But without knowing English, my wife wouldn't have been able to learn to drive or do other tasks for herself. I wanted her to live freely and comfortably, not having to rely on me for everything. Learning English was the first tool she needed to be an independent woman.

After the incident in the Frankfurt airport, she didn't cover her hair. Once her English was good enough, she obtained her driver's license. She got a cell phone, and I opened a joint bank account and got her a client card. Within our first two weeks living in downtown Calgary, I showed her where she could walk to go shopping, how she could use the client card for purchases, and how to take local transit. She could go wherever she wanted and do so without my permission. When some Yemenis were handing $50 to their wives, dropping them off at local malls, and picking them up later in the afternoon, I taught my wife to drive a car and walk around with a bank client card.

Her immersion was too fast, however. I threw too much at her all at once: enrolling her in English classes only a week after we arrived; putting her in driving school within the first couple of months before she had a grasp on the language or Canadian systems; and discouraging her from watching Arabic movies so that she would have more exposure to English. My giving her instant and total freedom was about me, not her. I take responsibility for throwing her into the ocean without teaching her to tread water.

And I was embarrassed to walk with a lady who covered her head. I wanted her to be on the same level as a Canadian woman, and I pushed her to be one too quickly. I wanted her to assimilate overnight even though my adjustment to living in the US took years.

Most members of the Yemeni community criticized me as I set a different standard than the other Arab men did, and by doing so, inspired revolt within their households. When other Arabs saw my wife so liberated and immediately straying from the path of typical Yemeni culture and protocols, some members of the Yemeni community became angry with me. I was viewed as not being brave enough to contain her. Some went to the extreme to suggest that if I were a good Yemeni, I wouldn't allow her more liberal behavior. A few expressed that they wanted to tear apart the Yemeni passport I used to come to Canada, as I was a disgrace. I had Yemeni ladies telling me I wasn't a man. I was called a wimp and a faggot; I was told I was weak. I was criticized for failing to maintain my household's Yemeni culture and living standards. I was told I was an embarrassment to my race and ethnicity. Often, others warned me about eventually paying the price, including losing my daughters, by allowing my wife to be liberated.

I can clearly understand their position and respect their viewpoints. If my wife wanted to hold onto and sustain her beautiful Yemeni culture and traditions, I should have given her the choice to do so. But I wanted her to assimilate.

Although my in-laws didn't appreciate my efforts, I would do the same again if I were to marry another village girl from Yemen. However, I drove her to a place she wasn't familiar with, and other Yemenis' reactions, whether based on jealousy or fear, pushed her further away from her own culture.

When we first came to Canada, I tried to attend Yemeni cultural events. However, when other Yemeni families saw my wife's behavior, they got together and agreed not to invite her to their parties and gatherings because they felt she was too liberated. The Islamic community shunned her. They made her feel like she was trying to go after their husbands; some felt she was gossipy, and most thought she was a bad influence. All the men felt she was beyond controllable and was a bad example for their wives; they didn't want to deal with her.

And so, if your people reject you because you are liberated, what choice do you have but to look for companionship elsewhere? She gravitated toward the wrong crowd—individuals who were not focused on their priorities, were lost between cultures, held low self-esteem, or had no purpose in life.

In such a confusing period, I always turned to a longtime friend, Munir Al-Sakaf, and his wife, Huwaidah Basadiq. Munir was born in Jijiga, the capital city of Somali Region, Ethiopia, but left Ethiopia in his late teens in 1967 for South Yemen. This individual was interesting because he had a good understanding of Yemen, Ethiopia, the Middle East, and Europe. Not only were he and his wife helping me navigate through the maze of family life (they were raising four children in Canada), but they had spent a significant number of years in Aden and had a solid grasp on Yemeni social customs. Munir was instrumental in helping me close the cultural gaps between East and West and answering questions I had about Yemen and Ethiopia during the 1950s and 1960s. He earned his higher education in the former USSR and was a professional geologist; he was well-versed in world affairs and politics. I also found him resourceful when understanding how Arab families lived in Ethiopia (during my father's generation). He was full of information and advice, telling me what the Arabic family lifestyle and structure was like and explaining to me, "This is the culture your wife comes from."

He kept reminding me that despite packing their suitcases and coming to North America, most Yemenis continue to operate with a tribal mentality. Despite the academic and technical education they receive outside Yemen, their attitudes and mindsets don't change. Their views regarding women are traditional. Most wanted to come to Canada to obtain citizenship, but their preferred habitat for living is according to Middle Eastern values and norms. The Canadian (or American) passport allows them to roam around Gulf countries for employment but their worldview conflicts with Western values in many ways.

"What did I do to give them such an impression, and why were they reacting the way they did?" I often asked him.

He chuckled and said, "First, you tried to change your wife overnight. Change should come gradually and with a greater understanding of the social norms and economics of the culture you live in [Canada]. You don't force it. Rather, understanding her obligations and freedom should come from within her. You have a good understanding of the Yemeni culture, the role of women, and their place in Yemen. She was only twenty-one when you brought her to Canada. It's easy for her to get confused and rebel against her past and upbringing."

He summarized my situation by stating, "You have to accept that you're different. You were born in Ethiopia and grew up in a different cultural environment. Yes, you're Yemeni and went to North Yemen at a young age, but you had difficulties assimilating there, too. You never did, and you never will. Then, you went on to the US, received a higher education, and were exposed to a different lifestyle. When you returned to Yemen almost a decade later to start a new life, you found it even harder to fit in. Then you picked up a young wife who has nothing in common with you. The two of you have no compatibility at any level. You have been hunting for someone you have not yet become! You will never fit in either as an Ethiopian or a Yemeni. You are different! As long as you stay in touch with your immediate families in the Middle East, I would suggest you forget about the Yemenis living in this part of the world and focus on your wife and your children. As for your marriage, you created a complicated situation for yourself, and you need to deal with it."

I never mingled with Yemenis in Calgary again.

My Other Side

One of the strangest aspects of my life is how much and how far I have been distanced from the Ethiopian community during the past five decades. When I look back and search for the reason, there is none that I can find. For decades, I have missed the food, the music, and the additional cultural aspects of my other half. Every so often, I have wondered what the outcome would be if I were married to an Ethiopian woman or at least someone like me—a lady of mixed race, both Ethiopian and Yemeni.

Repeatedly, I have observed that my work and the social and sports activities I am engaged in seem to determine who my friends are. Over and over, I have found myself gravitating toward radical minds—people who stimulate my mind and soul more than those who share my cultural values. Now and then, I crave friends like those from my youth—Marxist intellectuals. When I was attending junior high school and was imprisoned for political activism, sadly, most of my peers were killed. I lost contact with the remaining few. For reasons unknown to me, many Ethiopians don't use their real names on social media, and the absence of last names in Ethiopian culture has made it hard to find anyone I used to know from my elementary and junior high schools.

The challenge I had in Calgary was how to reach them. I'm not an active member of their community, nor do I attend church services. When one of my half-brothers visited me from Toronto recently, he asked me to take him to his Ethiopian friend's house. The friend asked me how long I had lived in Calgary. When I told him over twenty-five years, he thought I was lying. His suspicion was due to the fact that he had never seen or heard about me.

Another family my half-brother and I visited asked how I came to Canada. I thought they were asking me about my flight. My response was that we came via Frankfurt. My brother chuckled a bit, as I had misinterpreted the question. The other family was asking me by which channel I had entered Canada—had I come illegally? Was I a refugee? There were established routes that refugees and other immigrants used through different countries, and they were wondering which route I had taken. My brother explained that I didn't take the path most Ethiopians did, arriving in Canada as refugees or being sponsored via Kenya or South Africa. None of this was clear to me.

Due to my lack of in-depth understanding of Ethiopian culture and the mechanics of social interaction, which was compounded by my awkward Amharic language expression, I developed an apprehension about jumping in and starting a conversation with any Ethiopian. Unlike Yemenis, Ethiopians are reserved at the beginning and warm up as the conversation continues or as they get to know one another. I tend to be open and childlike, which makes most Ethiopians put up walls, primarily due to not knowing what to expect.

Therefore, the only place I felt safe and was able to be myself was at the home of a University of Calgary professor named Lashitew Gedamu, or Lash. His wife's name is Rani. Rani is a Hadare (Haderes are a mix of Turkish, Indian, Ethiopian, and Arab living in Ethiopia) and is well-versed in Islamic culture. That combination made it easy for me, as Lash was an Amhara from my mother's tribe, and Rani was a Muslim; both of them had exposure to the Arab culture. If I acted or behaved like an Arab, I was forgiven by Lash, and if I joked in Amharic, Rani perfectly understood me. Often, we spoke in English, as it was common ground.

Rani taught me how to cook one Ethiopian dish— ironically, I can cook only the most difficult one! When I was frustrated about how to communicate with my teenage daughters, she taught me how to talk to and, most importantly, how to listen to my girls. When I asked her why my daughter was talking to me disrespectfully and in the same manner as my wife did, she advised me not to take it personally and to respond to my daughter without anger.

"After all," she said, "that is the way she saw her mother communicating with you, and your child understands that that is the way to speak to you."

Both Rani and Lash kept telling me to stay on course and establish a proper structure for the children.

"They may not like it, but eventually, they will appreciate it. Don't change your approach because you fear they may not like you or prefer their mother over you. You must operate in the best interest of the children. Be patient and persistent," they advised me.

As for mingling with the Ethiopian community, like what Munir told me, perhaps I was a misfit in the same way I was in the Yemeni community.

Lash said, "As you know, Ethiopians are good-natured people. However, they have issues at many levels within their communities. Even though you were born in Ethiopia, your appearance looks like theirs, and you speak the language—albeit in a funny way—at the end of the day, you're different. The Ethiopians you knew as a child and those you will run into in Calgary are totally different. They come from different cultural backgrounds and have different expectations in life. With your attitude toward life, and with your experiences and travels, you have become unique. Clearly, you're a mismatch. That is not to say one is better than the other, just different. You can have a superficial friendship, but you won't be able to establish or reclaim the same types of connections you knew when you were a teenager in the 1970s. The years passed by, and the exposure you had in Yemen, the US, and Canada has molded you to be a unique breed. Be polite, respect them, but keep your distance."

That addressed most of my questions.

XIV

Fatherhood

A good father will leave his imprint on his daughter for the rest of her life.

— Dr. James Dobson, *Solid Answers*

Having had no proper parenting due to the absence of biological parents around me as a child, I always second-guessed my parenting abilities. Moreover, growing up in a patriarchal society in a developing country and having mixed ancestral backgrounds compounded with diverse religions left me with insecurities about raising two daughters in Western society. Their mother's approach to parenting further complicated the matter, as we were utterly polarized on how to parent.

What is the right way to raise our daughters?

When my marriage ended, my number one priority was my children. They never saw an excellent example of loving and caring relationships. Neither my wife nor I demonstrated a mutually respectful relationship. Often, she and I argued about what methods to use, and as a result, neither of our approaches was applied. When we divorced, I thought I could better influence my daughters and be a better example if I had joint custody and did half of the parenting under my roof.

When facing something new, I tend to default to reading. That was the case when my wife and I landed in Calgary. She was five months pregnant at the time. During our first week in Calgary, I visited the Calgary Public Library to get some reading material. On that initial visit, I borrowed the book *What to Expect When You're Expecting*, by Heidi Murkoff.

At the time, my wife was twenty-one years old. She didn't read, write, or speak English, so everything that needed to be done fell on me. Besides dishing out my resume and hunting for a job, all my life's energy and attention were dedicated to ensuring my wife and the baby had everything they needed. I found a family doctor, attended her doctor's visits, and listened to and translated the doctor's instructions. In addition, due to her pregnancy, she tested for high blood sugar levels (gestational diabetes), and her diet had to be monitored and adjusted. Reading, preparing questions, explaining, and translating between the doctor and my wife was challenging and overwhelming.

I had an extraordinary sense, which I could not explain, but I felt the new baby would judge me on my ability or inability to provide for the family. The entire commitment— the thought of being a father—significantly boosted me. This was a source of motivation and gave me a sense of urgency to find a job the first week I landed in Calgary.

My wife was out of her natural environment, and she didn't have anyone in Calgary other than me. While not having a support mechanism is a challenge on its own, the shortcoming on my part for lack of understanding of the three trimesters of pregnancy was a significant setback. I had never had any exposure to pregnancy or childbirth. I had to play the stronger person, consoling and comforting my wife to minimize her worries.

Even though my wife was carrying our baby, I felt I was holding both the mother and the child in my mind and my heart! I had to talk to my wife, listen to her, educate myself, give her medication on time, and not be bothered about her wild cravings. When she exhibited pregnancy symptoms such as nausea, weight gain, mood swings, and bloating, I equally felt the pain but mentally and emotionally rather than physically. I was suffering from anxiety, depression, restlessness, and a decreased desire for sex. And I had trouble sleeping. The stress of coming to a new country and settling may have contributed to this as well, but the second half of my wife's pregnancy added a different level of burden and worry.

While visiting the family doctor, who also was monitoring my wife and our unborn child, I opened up and asked for help. The doctor told me I was suffering from couvade. The doctor mentioned that couvade, or sympathetic pregnancy, sometimes occurs in men during pregnancy. Some men exhibit pregnancy-like symptoms such as anxiety, depression, nausea, changes in appetite, trouble sleeping, and changes in libido.

During August 1996, several times during the work week, my wife had to wake me up and drive her to the hospital in the middle of the night only to be told her contractions were a false alarm and be sent home. With the lack of sleep, I went to work with red eyes and the inability to focus. I was under a probationary period, and I was worried I would be let go from work due to poor performance. As a computer network specialist, my work was demanding and required a high degree of attention.

On Wednesday, August 21, 1996, I took my wife to dinner at a local restaurant. After ordering the meal and while waiting for the food to arrive, her water broke, and we had to rush to the hospital. The nurses didn't allow her to eat the meal we ordered; instead, they gave her a bite of bread. In the confusion, commotion, and anticipation, I forgot to eat.

I sat with my wife at her bedside the entire night and translated the information and instructions from the medical staff into Arabic for her. Even though I had read about labor in the book, I had never been in the middle of it.

After five hours of labor, our oldest child was born at 6:37 a.m. on Thursday, August 22. Despite not eating or sleeping for sixteen hours, making sure my wife was okay, and translating all the communication between her and the doctor and the nurses, I was holding myself together. Or so I thought.

The moment I witnessed the baby's head coming out of the birth canal, I collapsed onto the hospital floor not too far from where the nurses and the doctors were working on my wife. They ignored me and kept doing their business. They were clearly unfazed by a passed-out father lying in a heap on the floor. There must have been some radio communication because some other nurses showed up to lift me. They put something to my nose, and the smell brought me back to life. I wasn't dead, but I had fainted.

They kept asking if I would like to cut the umbilical cord. I was disoriented and exhausted. I kept saying, "No! I don't want to be near that area! I don't want to see it again!" I did not.

The baby was cleaned up and put inside a small rolling bed. It was business as usual for them, but I started to cry. I cried like a baby and was unable to stop.

I started to ask myself, *Is this what my mother and sisters went through when having babies?* I felt a tremendous amount of guilt. I was unable to forgive myself for the pain and misery I inflicted on my wife.

Shortly after, they took the baby away for a test of some sort. I panicked, "Don't mix up my baby! She has a birthmark on her belly!"

One of the nurses looked at me and said, "She is all birthmark. We don't have any other light-brown-skinned babies this evening. Don't worry. We won't mix her up!"

She smiled and left.

Despite her assurances, I was dead serious, and I wasn't entirely convinced until they returned the baby to the room and I checked for her birthmark.

Then I noticed a name tag, which read "Baby Ben-Harhara" and listed her birth weight and other measurements. I then protested to the nurse to put the baby's actual name on the tag.

She said, "We do that often as parents may not have chosen a name for the child yet. This tag has no impact and doesn't go on any record."

I insisted the label be changed.

In the weeks leading up to the birth, my wife and I had discussed baby names. I wanted to give our child a name that would work in both cultures—a Western-sounding name as well as one that was meaningful in Arabic. I suggested calling my oldest child Maryam, after my stepmother. However, my wife resisted giving the child a name that her friends' children used. Two of her Yemeni friends in Calgary had daughters,

Maryam and Sarah, so those names were out of the question. We settled on Lina.

I knew that Lina was a nickname for Paulina, Helena, Marlena, or Angelina. In Arabic, Lina means "a young palm tree" as well as "tender" and "delicate." I thought those characteristics matched a baby's sweet, adorable demeanor.

And as a Greek name, Lina can come from "linos," which means "flax." I liked the thought of giving my daughter a name that connects her to the earth.

After a few days, I took my wife and baby to our one-bedroom apartment. I didn't have the money to buy a crib or a swing. I opted to sleep on the floor while mother and baby slept on the queen-sized IKEA bed. Often, in the middle of the night, I woke up to check to make sure my wife didn't roll over and suffocate the child and kill her. For some strange reason, I didn't trust my wife with the new baby. I was the one who was bathing her every day for the first six months.

There were no door-to-door vacuum salespeople in Calgary then, nor could I afford to buy a vacuum cleaner yet. Still, I ended up purchasing a Sony 8 mm camcorder to create a video journal. I started to record everything that was transpiring from the day we arrived home with Lina. It was my way of leaving records of everything in case my daughter wanted to know about her early childhood. Perhaps this was done to overcompensate for the gaps in my childhood.

As for an indoor swing, I put two kitchen chairs back-to-back about 70 centimeters (28 inches) apart, placed heavy phone books on each chair, and then tied a long scarf between the two chairs where the baby could lie down. I set the swing near the couch and started to rock our baby daughter gently to lull her to sleep. Such a humble beginning is one of my fondest memories of my marriage.

Soon after Lina was born, we learned more about Yemenis living in Calgary. Everyone seemed to have advice and strong opinions on how my family should live, and they often presented their views very intrusively. My wife was young and impressionable and was often influenced by those opinions and suggestions. She told me how embarrassed she felt when one of the ladies asked her, "How come you have no baby crib, and how do you have a baby without one?" One other lady was appalled that I didn't have the money to purchase a vacuum cleaner or baby crib; instead, I had purchased a video recorder.

The fact was that I rented vacuum and shampoo machines from a store for several months. As long as I alternated sleeping between the floor and the couch, I didn't think the baby crib was an immediate need. Most of all, I was bothered by the intrusion these families imposed on me. I never commented about their living situation and standards; why should they do so on mine? I appreciated that my wife was making friends, as I did know from when I first went to the US what it felt like to be homesick. Meeting Yemeni people helped ease her homesickness. She also found the opportunity to speak Arabic with the ladies from her country. Moreover, she didn't yet drive or know the way to return home if she decided to walk away from the apartment building. Therefore, meeting the Yemeni ladies was a remedy, but in the long run, the damage they caused to my family outweighed the benefits.

XV

Career Advancement

Live as if you were to die tomorrow. Learn as if you were to live forever.

— Mahatma Gandhi

*L*ater in my career, in the early 2000s, I decided perhaps it was time to learn more and gain an additional understanding of my work from a business perspective. I worked as a computer programmer, data network engineer, and IT architect. I knew how to fix things, but I didn't comprehend why I was doing what I was doing. I didn't see a strong correlation between my work and its impact on the triple bottom line: economy, society, and the environment.

I felt that earning an MBA from a Canadian university would give me a sense of accomplishment and allow me to advance my career. I wanted to write well within the business context, think strategically, and understand the value of my technical expertise in the business world. Most of all, perhaps due to my swollen head, I needed the three-digit acronym added to my name.

When I decided to undertake my MBA, I wrote a business case for my employer justifying the benefits of having a graduate-level degree in business management. I outlined the cost, timeline, and return on investment if I received partial financial support from my employer to help pay for tuition. Naturally, everything had to start at the direct supervisor level, and special requests came up to upper management for approval or rejection.

My direct supervisor, a professionally designated engineer himself, took me out for dinner at a local pub and tried to warn me that it might not be the right time to attend graduate school. Lina was five and a half years old at the time, and my wife was pregnant with our second child. He thought having a young family, working full-time in a highly complex and technical arena, and taking graduate-level courses would be a huge undertaking. His concerns appeared genuine, as he had tried it and was unsuccessful. I always listen to other people's perspectives and entertain their experiences, but I am determined to achieve my objectives. Most importantly, I aim to grow and learn. I applied, and despite his concerns, he supported my application.

My business case was approved, and I started to juggle the three competing priorities: family, work, and MBA courses. As my supervisor had predicted, it wasn't easy. My wife didn't understand the complexity of the courses or the workload I was managing in order to set myself up to better provide for the family. She was extroverted, which was appealing as I felt her outgoing nature was a positive contrast to my introverted tendencies. However, in this case, the personality differences created conflict. Every weekend, she invited friends to our house for parties (most Yemeni women dance during social gatherings). If people didn't come to our house, I was expected to accompany her to others' homes, where she would want to stay and socialize for hours. There were times when I was in the middle of reading a report or doing other coursework, and she would leave for hours at a time, leaving me to look after the children while trying to attend to my schoolwork. Unwittingly, she consistently obstructed my efforts because she didn't comprehend the academic demands on me.

Any IT professional must consistently upgrade their skills every year to keep up. English is my third language, and writing was never my strength. It was always pointed out on my performance assessments that I needed to improve my writing skills. I like to think and solve problems; I don't like to write. Writing requires patience, which has never been in my DNA.

Moreover, the first utility program computer engineers invented was the spell-checker, the primary tool we relied on. If we got the math and the logic right, no one cared about how we wrote anything. Therefore, writing wasn't something most of us engineers invested our time in.

Having lived through business school and having now been out of school longer than I was in school, I can offer a different perspective. I wouldn't say I've accumulated much wisdom since I was a student. I certainly haven't gained from business school as far as becoming a CEO or moving to another geographical location for more excellent opportunities. Still, the passage of time since writing an application to enter graduate school and then graduating with an MBA has given me the courage to write about topics I couldn't express to myself or others then, such as human behavior, economics, and the environment.

Poor Management Skills

Halfway through my courses, my manager moved on to a different role, and I started reporting to a different man— an East Indian man originally from Africa. He was a sound engineer, perhaps book smart, but he was never a good people manager, let alone a leader. He was the most challenging person I have ever had to work with. He was a prime example of the Peter Principle[11] and of someone being promoted despite lacking the proper training and cultural sensitivity. Was he promoted because he was a visible minority—because our employer wanted to show acceptance and diversity by having him in a leadership position? Perhaps, perhaps not. Regardless, he did not have the skills for the job.

His management style appeared to be from 1950 textbooks. When he was assigned to work with our team, he ensured he acquired an office with doors. My previous supervisor had worked out of one of the cubicles amongst the team members, was always accessible, and was a strong leader with supportive attributes. Despite his humble approach, we often mistook his politeness as a weakness. But we did everything he asked for and often went above and beyond.

My new manager, however, created a toxic work environment. He was concerned with exhibiting power, micromanaging everything in his sight, projecting fear, and being secretive. Even though the change of leadership and the new attitude negatively impacted the working environment, including the team dynamics, no one in the team was brave enough to speak up. For the most part, Canadians are polite, and my colleagues complained about him behind closed doors but did nothing formal to improve the situation.

I quickly sensed this man was targeting me as a whipping boy. Anything he didn't like about what my team was doing, he picked on me first and consistently. He wanted to impose his working style on us, which was very individualistic and not collaborative. Instead of fostering teamwork and encouraging us to create synergy, he took ownership of the enormous task and gave individuals certain pieces of the larger project but didn't share with the rest of the team what each person was working on, thereby creating an environment in which everyone was working in silos. No one ever knew exactly how they were supposed to contribute to the whole project. His management style completely contradicted what I had been trained to do and what I had previously experienced.

He monitored who was coming to work and at what time and tracked how many minutes each person was late or departed early. He always watched the clock when we left for our lunch breaks. He told us that the entire team would be punished if anyone were caught surfing the web, checking their cell phone during working hours, or calling in sick without a doctor's note. He preferred to call any of us over the speakerphone to give us work instructions. He treated a group of professionals like elementary school children.

One morning, I notified him that I would be heading to my dental hygienist appointment during my lunch break and would resume work at 1:15 p.m., returning fifteen minutes late. The dentist's office was running behind, and by the time the work on my teeth was done and I made it back to the office, I was forty-five minutes late.

When I sat down at my desk, my phone rang, and it was the boss. He was worked up about those forty-five minutes. He ordered me to report to him over the speakerphone. It always felt like going to the principal's office. He fumed and asked me why I didn't phone him to tell him I would take thirty more minutes. I told him I was in the dentist's chair and came as fast as possible when their work was done. I pointed out to him that I hadn't even eaten my lunch.

He ordered me to get the vacation tracking card (at that time, we tracked our time via hard copy). He made me take forty-five minutes' vacation time, and he approved it. I thought he was being silly, but I didn't care about arguing over stupid stuff and returned my timecard to the administrative assistant.

Even though I wasn't alone in feeling he was a tyrant, no one was saying anything. I suspected they were concerned about being called racist, so they kept quiet, but I knew how they talked about the situation in private. He also knew no one liked or respected him, and he made every effort to make us afraid of him.

One day, he called me to his office to tell me I had an attitude problem. I didn't respond. I stood there waiting to get an order or hear what else he said. He didn't ask me anything related to work; instead, he asked, "Where are you originally from?"

"My ethnicity or place of birth has nothing to do with work."

"I heard you're Ethiopian and Arabian."

"So?"

"Listen, people like you used to wash my feet in Africa. I was born there, you know. The white people were at the top. Then we were next, and the rest were at the bottom."

I asked him, "What are you trying to tell me?"

"Just to let you know that you should be fortunate to be where you are. Adjust your attitude."

I calmly approached his desk, put my right foot on it (yes, I'm extremely flexible!), and told him, "If you think that I'm less of a person than you are, I think you have a problem."

I had never used the f-word in my life, but I said, "If you have a fucking problem with me, let's settle it outside the office building. I may be smaller in stature, but I'm capable of beating the shit out of you!"

I wasn't aware that I was pointing my fingers at him. He asked me not to point at him and to remove my foot from his desk.

Finally, I told him, "Where I came from, in the city of Aden, where the British ruled the country for 139 years, they brought people from your country to clean the sewer system. However, I'm not like you. I don't think about who a superior or inferior human is or isn't. I know you have been treating me harshly on the floor, but I didn't care, as petty acts like yours won't deter me."

He said, "I will report you to HR and dismiss you for insubordination."

I approached the other side of his desk, picked up his phone, and asked him to tell me the HR number. He didn't respond. I handed him the handset and ordered him to call HR. He didn't. He was shocked and rattled.

He had brought the beast out of me. He was a 173-centimeter-tall (5'8") stocky man of approximately 90 kilograms (200 pounds); I was only 167 centimeters (5'5") and 125 pounds. He was scared of me.

I told him, "An elephant might be bigger, but the lion rules the jungle." I left his office.

The next day, he came to my office and asked me to follow him up to his office. He apologized and extended his hand for a handshake. I shook his hand and said, "Water under the bridge." I didn't tell anyone about this situation. Nor did he ever call HR.

*

A year later, as I was writing my final thesis for graduation, he called me to his office. He notified me that my employment status had been reduced from full-time to part-time. Also, as of that day, my employment contract would be renewed monthly. He was within bounds to do this, but as the breadwinner in a single-income family, I worried about how I would feed my children. Once I put my master's degree in my hand, I started to look for more secure job opportunities.

A week after convocation, a global multinational company offered me a job. My manager was away on a month-long vacation. I submitted my resignation to the department's director, giving the required two weeks' notice. Although my manager was away, he was checking his emails, and he immediately instructed the HR department to withhold my wages, unpaid vacation hours, and retirement contributions totaling $180,000. When I asked why this was happening, I was told, "He wants you to pay back the amount the organization spent on your education." I filed a complaint with the employment standards division of the Alberta government, knowing my employer had no right to withhold my wages and benefits. Lawyers got involved when the folks from Employment Standards wrote to the organization about how wrong the department was to withhold the funds. About six months later, after I had started a new job, I was summoned to appear in court.

Four staff members from my former employer's office also appeared in court: my former manager, representatives from the HR and Finance departments, and a corporate lawyer. I was both outnumbered and nervous. The judge asked the lawyer to set the stage regarding the case and state the matter. The lawyer explained that I had used the organization's money to further my education after saying that I intended to serve the organization but hadn't served the corporation. Instead, I had found a better job and moved on. He emphasized that I landed a fantastic job at a global company because of the education my former employee had invested in. The lawyer mentioned because I refused to pay back the money, they had to bring these individuals as witnesses. He claimed I must pay back the entire amount that was paid for my education.

The judge turned to me and asked for my defense. I stated, "I went to graduate school to improve my skills and contribute to the organization I served for the past ten years. I am very thankful to those I previously reported to and the support I received financially and otherwise."

I added, "A couple of months before my graduation, my employment status was reduced from permanent full-time to temporary part-time. My contract was subject to month-to-month renewal. I have two young daughters and am the sole breadwinner of a single-income family. I needed to find a stable job to support my children.

"Furthermore, I don't deny receiving the money. Bringing the HR and Finance departments, as well as my former supervisor, was unnecessary. I didn't leave my employment by choice. Rather, I had to leave under duress due to an unexpected change in my employment around the time of my graduation. I'm not going to ask why a change in my employment status was introduced. I leave it for you, Judge, to ask that question. Moreover, the company policy states that I would serve the organization for one month for every $1,000 received as educational assistance. I have been taking MBA courses for the past three years and have served the organization continually through that period. Payments made during the previous three years have been met."

I handed to the judge the notes my manager gave me on changing my employment status and copies of the corporate policy concerning educational support.

The entire deliberation took almost two hours, and the lawyer handed a massive binder to the judge and me. The binder contained all my grades, invoices, receipts of payments I had made, and the reimbursements I received from the organization.

The judge looked at the corporate policy and notice of employment status change and asked me when the last course was completed or the final thesis was submitted. I had completed my courses in June and presented my thesis in October of the same year. The judge asked when I resigned and accepted the new job, and I told him it was June 1 the following year—eight months after completing my thesis. The judge left the room, and we were instructed to wait.

After approximately fifteen minutes, the judge returned to the courtroom and stated the following:

"The defendant was in a dire situation and needed to find another job to support his family, and he had every right to do so.

"The defendant hasn't denied receiving funds to further his education.

"The defendant left the organization in June and submitted his final thesis paper the following October.

"The defendant shall pay $4,000 only for four months that he didn't serve the organization.

"The defendant may make payment arrangements until the amount is fully paid."

The judgment was fair.

The corporate lawyer argued that the refund should be much higher than $4,000. The judge didn't buy any of the arguments he put forward.

Of course, I was thrilled with the judge's order, as I was only expected to make a small portion of the company's desired payment. I noticed my former manager's face looking like dark kale.

*

What I (and others) experienced working under this manager indicates the clashes that arise when immigrants still operate under the value systems they bring with them. My supervisor's management style directly conflicted with how I had been managed by others.

I have been out for business meals in North America with managers who had immigrated to Canada or the US and, after the meal, refused to use their corporate credit card to pay for the client or business associate's meal if that person ate pork or ordered alcohol. In my business dealings in Calgary, when Yemeni men come to Canada for work, and I entertain them in restaurants, it has not been uncommon for them to ask me to procure their female servers for their entertainment after dining at the restaurant.

The culture clash is understandable, but in both daily life and especially the corporate world, the person's traditional way of thinking needs to be put aside. White people are required to undergo sensitivity training, but it needs to go the other way, as well. Corporate culture must represent the climate of the environment in which people work.

Likewise, people who are not cut out to be managers should not be put into leadership positions just so the company can say they are being inclusive. Foreign-trained employees with little understanding of the North American system should not bring their own cultural practices into the workplace; doing so can be detrimental. That is not to say all individuals from other parts of the world are like that or regularly present themselves in such a way, but in my experience, there seems to be a pattern.

My experience with this manager reminded me of the scene in the movie *Mississippi Masala*, when Denzel Washington's character is in discussion with his girlfriend's father, a Pakistani man, about the father's objection to the relationship:

I'm a Black man born and raised in
Mississippi. Ain't a damn thing you can tell
me about struggle. I know you and your
folks can come down here from God
knows where and be about as Black as the
ace of spades, and as soon as you get here,
you start acting white and treating us like
we your doormats. I know that you and
your daughter ain't but a few shades from
this right here [points to his own face].[12]

How can anyone justify treating another human as lesser
just because of their skin color?

XVI

Harassment at the Workplace

I'm not concerned with your liking or disliking me. All I ask is that you respect me as a human being.

— Jackie Robinson, American professional
baseball player

In spite of my firsthand experience of racism in North Yemen, I like to think that, in general, North American people like or dislike a person primarily based on how they conduct themselves rather than the way they look. For the most part, I think I am correct.

I saw evidence supporting my belief while attending university and working in the US. In particular, the incident when Steve, my Aryan Nation neighbor, defended me and got my calculator back for me reinforced my beliefs that when we get to know people as individuals, we see past skin color, hair (or lack thereof!), style, or language and instead view and value people based on their character. In the US, I had never been on the receiving end of discrimination or bullying based on my color or ethnicity. Maybe I was too naive to notice it, or maybe it didn't occur.

I used to assume racism was a mental sickness, and it only affected white people. Again, I was wrong on many levels. I have always opposed racism, but unconsciously, I was programmed to accept white dominance. Why would I think differently? The first man I saw walking on the moon was a white man. Everything in the textbooks I read concerning science, geography, history, and philosophy was written by white men. I never saw or heard of any modern technological innovations (including medicine) coming out of any other race but Caucasian. With the exceptions of music, athleticism, and a couple of religions, I never expected anyone other than white people to be capable of inventing or breaking ground. If they were, at least I wasn't exposed to it, other than Ethiopian marathon runner Abebe Bikila[13], whose success influenced me when I was a child.

As I furthered my education and assumed professional-level employment in Canada, I started to experience broader discrimination. Perhaps I was perceived as a professional threat to some of the people around me, or maybe there was racism of some sort happening.

The racism and bullying I experienced in my new workplace after receiving my MBA was isolation; the team I was working with left me out of everything. Initially, I thought perhaps it was because I was new and needed to earn their respect by paying my dues. I demonstrated my professionalism by being friendly, working above and beyond the regular working hours, accepting tasks outside the realm of my responsibilities, and being eager to please everyone. However, I was unable to break in and I felt unwelcome.

Team members gathered first thing in the morning between 8 and 8:30. Mostly, the conversations were superficial, focusing on hockey games they had seen the night before or the food and drink they had. Often, they made jokes directed at each other based on who was wearing what on the day. Although I never participated in those socializations, I liked some of the lines they used. Sometimes, I could not help but laugh at some comments and jokes.

Now and then, the topics turned to current affairs like immigration, politics, social issues, and sex. But then I started to hear extreme views on race, ethnicity, religion, sexual orientation, etc. I was alarmed but remained silent. From that point, I became a bit wary of those individuals due to their views.

There were nine of us; one Asian guy and I were the only visible minorities on the team. Of the other seven, the team lead and one other peer kept infusing their anti-immigrant views into the conversations and dominated those early morning gatherings. I vividly recall one of the conversations lasting almost an hour and being heated. The media had reported that a shipload of Chinese illegal immigrants had landed in Vancouver. I had never heard such hateful comments toward other ethnicities and races as I did that day.

I never asked the Asian fellow how he felt about these conversations; I never brought the issue up to him at all, nor did he mention it to me. In my case, I felt out of place and unwelcome. I can only assume he felt uncomfortable, as well.

The team lead encouraged those conversations, and no week passed without him or another member mentioning events such as an African immigrant bringing their parents to Canada for medical treatments and leaving the country without paying the bill. Criticisms were made about Pakistani family members wearing their native outfits and reading religious books on public transit, potentially (in their minds) threatening the Canadian value system and culture; immigrants coming from Hong Kong as investors and only hiring Chinese employees or not paying business taxes; Somali and Bosnian refugees who had just arrived from war-torn areas living in subsidized homes collecting cash, free education, and medical services, potentially bankrupting the health care systems and being a burden on Canadian taxpayers; and the Sikh community insisting on wearing turbans while serving in the Canadian Army and RCMP. The list went on.

At this time, I was mainly a passive observer of these conversations. But this issue started to affect me directly when backlash from the 2001 attack on the World Trade Center entered the conversations.

They all knew that I was part African and part Arab. As a result, they naturally wanted to know my position on the issues they were discussing. Some genuinely wanted to know what drove the 9/11 hijackers to commit such a crime and asked me my thoughts because I was exposed to Arab media. I shared my perspective and condemned the act, emphasizing that it was more of an ideologically based action than a religious act, at least in my view. I assured them that I wouldn't have immigrated to the West if I had that mindset. That was my way of disconnecting myself from the issues and conversation.

Things didn't stop there, though, as the team lead continually taunted me by making provocative comments directed toward me. For example, he would say, "Hey, Adel, you don't look happy today. I hope you don't try to bomb the data center and us. It's my understanding that's what you guys [Arabs] do when you get upset." Or he would call me to his office to show me a game he was playing on his computer:

169

"Kill Osama bin Laden." A couple of times, I told him, "I'm not a religious person or a politician. I left Yemen fearing persecution and seeking freedom. I am here to create a better life for my family. You're passionate about these issues, but my priority is elsewhere. That is not to say I don't care, but I don't want to be the center of hallway discussions day in and day out."

He didn't take my comments to heart. I told him that he should set a different standard for the team and that what he did didn't sit well with me. At the same time, I was so worried he might report me as being an Islamic terrorist sympathizer just because I didn't agree with him on some issues or join the hallway rituals of hate speech. I informed him that I was being targeted for harassment by my peers, as he set the stage for them that it was okay to utter racial and ethnic-based verbal attacks. The situation didn't improve, though; despite my requests, I wasn't getting the help I needed.

Someone began posting racially motivated cartoon drawings in my cubicle. After that happened three or four times, I took the pictures and drawings to my supervisor's office to ask him if he could stop my colleagues' actions. He laughed and suggested that I relax.

"The guys love you here. You are taking the entire thing wrong! You're overreacting. Chill, man!" was his response.

From that point on, I started recording these incidents. I wrote about these events not to gather evidence. Instead, doing so was the default state of the survival skills I had developed since childhood. Journals have always been the safe place where I express my thoughts and fears.

After six months, I took the matter to the department's director, the person my manager was reporting to. I knew they were good friends, and even if the director wouldn't take disciplinary action, I expected he would give my manager a verbal warning to stop what he was doing. The director followed up, calling me to tell me that he had spoken to my manager.

"But he feels that you have been too sensitive and are overreacting," was his response.

He proposed that the three of us go for a drink and smooth the matter out.

I told the director, "I have no personal issues with my manager, but I want this behavior to stop. It is not conducive to a safe and productive workplace. We are professionals. We are not in the high school locker room, and this behavior must be changed."

I also pointed out to him that we were lucky not to have female staff on our team because several off-color jokes and derogatory comments were regularly made toward women.

He did nothing.

*

The following excerpts are taken from some of my journals during that period. I also used some of my journal entries when I put forth my official complaint to HR.

Journal 1 Month 1

As the year began, Brad [my direct supervisor] started to exclude me by giving my duties to others in the group. At about the same time, I started noticing in the hallway the use of excessive derogatory remarks about minorities. Most of the time, these comments were targeted toward other minorities working within our organization and minorities in general. Initially, I thought those were jokes with no intention to harm anyone in particular.

The first time Brad called my name and asked me to join team members in the hallway, he started talking about Black men's penis size. He specifically spoke about a short Black man he had run into in a gym locker room. The man had a larger penis size in proportion to his body size. I have no idea why he wanted me to be part of this conversation, and I have no idea why this topic of discussion was brought into the workplace.

On another occasion, Brad commented, "Adel sets the support group pager in vibrator mode and puts it between his legs" in front of a group of peers and coworkers.

During Islamic religious rituals such as Ramadan or similar holidays, he made comments like, "Why do these stupid people fast all day?"

Because of the example he sets, other team members chime in, adding comments like, "We never heard of people not eating pork till we saw those minorities," and "What kind of people is this government bringing into Canada?"

Journal 4 Month 4

I spoke to Brad about the excessive foul language and derogatory remarks used in the hallway and how I have been treated. I asked if he would consider refraining from making negative remarks about me and also speak to my peers about minimizing such behavior.

He said, "Don't worry about it. The guys like you, which is why they tease you."

One morning, while I was walking back to my office, Brad separated himself from the staff members standing in the hallway and handed me a poster that had been stuck on the wall beside my name on the door of my cubical. It read:

Front Row Seats to Flames vs. Avalanche Game: $265

Replica Hockey Jersey: $225

Beers and Hot Dogs: $22

Picture of you and your friend acting like a couple of FAGS in Sports Illustrated: PRICELESS.

The poster included my picture; the picture was the same as my photo ID.

Where did they get my picture?

I hadn't given security my picture for such purposes. I considered reporting this to security or my manager, but I decided to keep quiet and speak to Brad in private later. Using the usual dismissive language, he told me not to worry.

It was too much to handle and accept.

Why are such things happening to me at my workplace?

Journal 8 Month 8

While I was walking and talking with a white female coworker back from the data center room to my working area,

Brad saw me. After the lady left, he told me, knowing full well that I was married, "Hey, Adel, are you asking her to mix her milk with your coffee?" He made the same comment again after seeing me talking with other white female coworkers.

Whenever I address work-related questions to Brad, he responds, "Of course. It is a free country. You can do whatever you want. No Taliban are living here … are there?"

Journal 10 Month 10

I built a test server that was not configured correctly. It prevented people from logging on to the domain. When I told Jeremy what went wrong and how I could rectify the issues, he started to kick my desk and continued doing so for about a minute. This again happened in front of two other individuals. Staff members and I were surprised as to why he did that. At the time, I said nothing and planned to report this to my supervisor.

The following day, at around 7:15 a.m., before I had the chance to speak to the supervisor and while I was working in the server room, Jeremy approached me and asked me to punch him in the face.

"Go ahead. Punch me in the face if you like."

I knew what he was referring to and told him, "I am not going to punch you or do anything. However, I do not appreciate what you did to me yesterday."

"I know, I know. I just lost it and made a fool of myself."

"As long as such actions won't repeat, I am more than happy to accept your apology."

We shook hands. At the same time, he gave me a National Geographic magazine that was issued in 1962. It had an article on Yemen. I asked him, "Why are you giving this to me?" He said, "I remember you asked me to borrow it. Here you go. It's all yours now!"

"Thank you!"

Such an incident hasn't happened again.

Journal 14 Month 14

Today, Brad told my peers in the hallway, "Adel is playing with his nipples every time he sees me."

This was the most humiliating comment I've heard publicly. He went on to tell a group of people on a different floor of our building that I play with my nipples every time I see him. On two occasions, individuals approached me to ask if that was true.

When I asked Brad to stop humiliating me like this and letting others do the same, he commented, "Stop acting like my wife."

Journal 19 Month 19

I've continued to be stressed out and had to go home sick for a few days. Upon returning to the office, I saw a note on my day timer left open on my desk: "Adel, you are sick, and you never get well." I feel like I am starting to understand how it felt to be a Black man living in Mississippi or Alabama in the 1950s.

Journal 22 Month 22

I saw a new poster on my office door a few weeks ago. George showed me the poster, saying, "This is your recent picture. The new look of you."

The picture was of a cartoon character with a cloud that hung around his head. The character was wearing torn clothing and he had a hole in his shoes. Also, the words "Adel BTFSPLK" were written on the poster. I didn't even know what it meant.

Then I checked on the Internet and found this:

> The world's worst jinx, Joe Btfsplk, had a perpetually dark rain cloud over his head. Instantaneous bad luck befell anyone unfortunate enough to be in his vicinity. Though well-meaning and friendly, his reputation inevitably precedes him—so Joe is a very lonely little man.[14]

During the same week, several people asked me what it meant. I did not comment.

Journal 28 Month 28

Rick [Brad's supervisor] pulled me into his office to tell me he had spoken to Brad the night before. Brad has admitted to Rick that he has misbehaved. I told Rick that I went through a lot of pain to bring such an issue forward and even waited three years to do so after trying to resolve the issue myself. Further, I explained that this was not a personal conflict between us. This is a severe issue that the organization should be concerned with. I asked him to take his time to investigate the matter properly before taking the appropriate action.

Journal 30 Month 30

Rick called me again to meet with him at around 2 p.m. We further discussed this matter, and he instructed me to meet with Brad sometime next week to close the issue quickly. For the second time, I expressed my concerns over how this matter is being handled.

I became alarmed when he asked me how many people knew about this issue and told me they did not mean anything by their behavior. I got the impression Rick only wanted to end this matter as soon as possible without understanding and addressing the seriousness of the problem and its impact on me. I suggested this be passed on to HR as I felt it was not being treated as a serious issue. Rick advised me not to approach or involve HR.

Again and again, I explained to him that this was not a conflict resolution exercise. I do not have a problem speaking to Brad, and I have lived with this pain for years. I asked him if he realized or was aware of the HR violations. He assured me he was. I asked him why he was not taking the proper course of action. I told him that I did not think the two of us meeting and discussing such matters would resolve the existing cultural issues within the department. He kept talking about scheduling a meeting with the three of us; I kept insisting we had an HR person present in the meeting.

I left his office without any hope of a resolution.

Journal 34 Month 34

After reporting the matter to management, I waited six weeks without action. Rick has not spoken to me since our meeting two months ago. I received a renewed request from Rick via someone in HR to accept a verbal apology from Brad.

I finally complained to the HR department and asked them to follow the organization's policies and procedures.

Journal 37 The Resolution

For over three years, I saw drawings on the whiteboard in my cubical depicting my ears, crossed eyes, and similar demeaning images alongside my name. Some were so embarrassing that I had to erase them quickly before anyone saw them.

One of my peers was the ringleader, instigating and encouraging other colleagues to conduct similar acts against me. He was often screaming and verbally abusing me, even when I was working in a different group. And the manager did nothing to stop him. For weeks, sometimes months, I didn't receive any work. I kept asking for projects and received nothing but active demotion. Seeing projects assigned to managers' friends continually demoralized me.

Unsuccessfully, I asked a higher-up to prevent and stop these aggressions. I kindly requested management to localize the issue, gather facts, and take the appropriate action. I also expressed an interest in being part of the solution. When I exhausted every avenue to earn respect and equal treatment, I felt my only option was to leave the group and seek a new role in the company. My departure from the group minimized the direct threats. However, the harassment and discrimination continued as I was still employed in the same organization and saw the same people even though I no longer worked directly with them.

Initially, I was told by my manager an investigation would be conducted, and disciplinary action would be taken accordingly. On numerous occasions, I highlighted that my case was not a personal conflict between two individuals but a workplace violation that concerned the organization.

I knew the situation had nothing to do with my performance, as I was getting superior reviews from my previous boss and the other department managers I supported.

Several times, I was asked, "What would satisfy you to bring this case to closure?" They asked if I would accept a verbal apology, and I insisted it was to be a written one, as they may make me pay a price for standing up to them. I needed a written record. I said I would expect a letter of apology from those two individuals indicating their acknowledgment of all of the allegations; I also asked management for assurances that no other person would be subjected to similar bullying and discrimination in the workplace. Above and beyond this, I asked, "What is the organization's policy in dealing with individuals who conduct themselves in such behavior over the years?"

In the end, the whole leadership team was sent for bullying training. The department had to take courses on discrimination, cultural awareness, and sensitivity. And the written letter of apology I had repeatedly requested was finally granted, so to speak:

Adel:

Please accept my apology for allowing the environment in the work area under my responsibility to evolve and escalate into a culture that was caustic for you and hurt you.

If you want, I am open to meeting with you to discuss these issues if you think it will help.

Regards,

Brad Smith

How many times had I met with him, pleading for him to work to ensure the workplace culture would improve? How often had I requested that certain colleagues be asked to refrain from their unprofessional behavior? How much more discussion would have to take place before something changed? I had had enough.

I left for another organization.

I wasn't the only person in our organization to be on the receiving end of this treatment. But what bothered me the most was that they all tried to cover it up and dismiss it because they were friends. I didn't want anyone to make me "happy." I wanted to do my job without harassment or intimidation. All humans have the right to a safe and productive work environment.

*

Bullying. Gaslighting. Racism. Black Lives Matter. #MeToo. We hear these words in the media and use them in our daily conversations. We designate certain days to raise awareness for mental health, we acknowledge Orange Shirt

Day, and we express outrage on Facebook when a Black American is shot and killed by a white person for no apparent reason. But what are we *really* doing to improve our treatment of one another?

XVII

International Assignment

Why do you go away? So that you can come back. So that you can see the place you came from with new eyes and extra colors. And the people there see you differently, too. Coming back to where you started is not the same as never leaving.

— Terry Pratchett, British author

As part of my graduate studies, I learned that job outsourcing helps North American companies be more competitive in the global marketplace. It allows them to sell to foreign markets through overseas branches. Hiring in emerging markets with lower living standards lowers prices for goods they ship back to the US or Canada.

While working for a multinational corporation, my responsibility was outsourcing. I was typically assigned to a deal's opportunity/engagement phase and worked with the client and the engagement team to build and validate the scope, complexity, timeline, and delivery cost of outsourced deals.

As we closed domestic firms' operations or downsized in the US and Canada, I started to see the impact of offshore outsourcing as a reduction in US and Canadian employment.

Although the executives told us that outsourcing increases labor productivity, employment, wages, and costs and improves the standard of living, none of that was visible to me.

For seven consecutive years at my job in Calgary, I kept sending Canadian and American employees home with pink slips and actively outsourcing their jobs to India, Malaysia, the Czech Republic, Mexico, Argentina, etc. I continued to interact less and less with North American technical staff. Despite what the executives said, outsourcing has caused high unemployment, loss of income, and loss of competitive advantage, leaving Canadians and Americans without financial support and employment. Soon, management positions were also sent overseas. I started to wonder what would happen to me. Yes, as the North American opportunities began to disappear, I, too, needed to be relocated to operate from overseas offices.

The first opportunity that came my way was to work in Dubai in the United Arab Emirates (UAE). It appealed to me as I speak Arabic, and many of my relatives live in Abu Dhabi, the capital of the UAE, which is roughly a one-and-a-half-hour drive from Dubai. In consulting with a few of my peers assigned overseas, I learned that working in Dubai could be lucrative for many, with high wages and low taxes; it is a desirable place for anyone wanting to earn big bucks.

I arranged to move to Dubai to support the company's Middle East, Africa, and Eastern European initiatives. Even though my wage didn't increase substantially, the agreement was that I would receive a tax-free salary and an accommodation allowance. The term of the agreement was two years. I agreed to an annual salary of US$149,864; an annual housing allowance of $55,000; an annual car allowance of $12,000; and a one-time moving allowance of $18,000. In addition, I would receive a hardship allowance based on the number of nights I spent working in Saudi Arabia. (A hardship allowance is a bonus given to those working in Saudi Arabia to entice people to work there.) Moreover, my employer was responsible for securing all the proper work permits, residence visas, and other documentation required to legally allow me to work in the UAE and Saudi Arabia.

I spent eight months in Dubai and traveled to and from Saudi Arabia every week during that period, working seventeen hours a day, seven days a week. Staff in India, Canada, and England worked the typical Monday to Friday work week, taking Saturdays and Sundays off. In the Middle East, because the Islamic holy day is Friday, the weekends at that time were Thursday and Friday, and all offices were operational on Saturday and Sunday. Therefore, I had no option but to work seven days a week.

Saudi Arabia and the UAE are vigilant and aggressive in ensuring that all foreign employees have the proper authorization to work in their respective countries. Due to logistical roadblocks, my employer couldn't provide me with the appropriate documentation for either country, as had been agreed upon. In Saudi Arabia, on many occasions, while conducting a business meeting, I had to be swiftly escorted out from office buildings every time the immigration authorities arrived.

Realizing the magnitude of the risk and fearing for my safety, I brought these issues to the attention of my North American and European superiors. I was stressed, as being in Saudi Arabia's prison system is more frightening than anything one can imagine. I started to think of a book I read and a movie I watched: *Midnight Express*.

Midnight Express is a 1977 nonfiction book by Billy Hayes and William Hoffer about Hayes's experience as a young American who was sent to a Turkish prison for trying to smuggle hashish out of Turkey. I could not unsee the things I saw in the movie. My vivid imagination went wild about what would happen to me if I got caught and put in a Saudi jail. I had flashbacks of the horrors I witnessed when I was imprisoned in Ethiopia in 1977 and imagined that being incarcerated in Saudi could be even worse. Nightmares night after night!

One Night in Dubai

While I was in Dubai, it became clear to me that the sex trade in Dubai had been prevalent for years. Whether it was the hotel I stayed in or other hotels my staff and colleagues stayed in, I always saw prostitutes frequent the hotel bars and nightclubs.

The way the women dressed surprised me. They looked like professional women—well-dressed and wearing clothes that were not too revealing. They weren't dressed like CEOs, but they looked like they were young women dressed to go out for a fun evening with their female friends. Most of them wore nice pants and tops that showed a bit of cleavage. Some of them wore a business jacket or other type of cover that they removed when they entered the clubs. They had nice hairdos and their overall appearance had some modesty; their appearance wasn't overly sexual.

Some women, predominantly from Eastern Europe, Central Asia, South and Southeast Asia, East Africa, Iraq, Iran, and Morocco, were sent to work as prostitutes in the

UAE. In the conversations I had with expats who had lived in Dubai for many years, I was told there were many Iranian prostitutes in Dubai, and some of them stayed in the city for several years. The UAE attracts a lot of foreign business people, and it is gaining a reputation as the Middle East's top sex tourism destination. Are they coming because of the sex trade, or is the sex trade flourishing because of their presence? It's a vicious cycle at this point.

One day, while I was sitting at the bar with my peers, a girl approached and started to talk to me. Due to the high volume of the songs played, the dancing not too far from where I sat, and perhaps her accent, I could not understand what she was saying. I asked if she could text me so that I could read what she was trying to say. I requested her phone number; she wrote it down on a napkin and handed it to me. I texted her and asked what she was looking for.

Her prompt reply was 5,000. I was confused. I asked her what she was referring to with 5,000. She responded, saying, "For you and I." Again, I didn't get it. I asked what 5,000 meant. She used her index finger and thumb to make a circle and pushed her other index finger through it. From that, I suspected what she meant. Just to be sure, I texted her back, "Sex." She smiled and nodded. I was happy we had communicated, but I was also confused, perhaps because I was in an unfamiliar situation where I was faced with negotiating for sexual services for the first time in my life.

I texted back, asking what currency she used; was this for a year or a month? She burst out laughing. And she didn't stop. I thought she had lost her mind. At the same time, I was worried that my questions were a dead giveaway of my naivety and being too green for the game. Once she collected herself, she texted me back, stating "for tonight" and "AED." (The

Emirati Dirham is the official currency of the UAE, abbreviated officially as AED and unofficially Dh and Dhs.)

I quickly turned and did the calculation on my cell phone. The 5,000 AED she asked me to pay her for two hours that evening was equivalent to CAD$1,700 or US$1,400. I thought, *Holy cow. That is almost my weekly wage.* Even if it were $50, I wouldn't have gone through with spending the night with her, so I politely declined. She left me alone with a disappointed look.

Not long after that, another lady approached me. Unlike the first one, this woman looked like more of a businesswoman. The way she introduced herself was like a real estate agent or a furniture salesperson would. She looked professional and dressed as such. She engaged me in casual conversation. Primarily, she wanted to know who I worked for and what I did for a living. She spoke English eloquently.

When I mentioned my profession and background, a look of disbelief crossed her face. In North America, when exchanging greetings, I never encounter anyone dubious of another person's profession or role. She asked for my business card, and I pulled one out and gave it to her. She acknowledged it and showed a satisfied look. I asked her why she suspected I wasn't telling the truth.

"I thought those jobs were only for Europeans or Americans. I didn't even think you would be a Black American, as you don't look like them," she replied.

After fifteen minutes, she pointed to a girl sitting across from us having drinks.

"What about her?" I asked.

"Do you like her?" she responded.

Again, I was confused.

"I didn't even know she was sitting there until you pointed her out." I added, "I don't know her, so I can't form any opinion about her."

She said, "You will like her. She works for me. She is from Kyrgyzstan."

I almost stopped breathing. I gathered she was a madam.

She continued, "I have many girls from Azerbaijan, Kazakhstan, Kyrgyzstan, Tajikistan, Uzbekistan, and Russia."

I wasn't listening to the rest of what she was saying.

I told her, "Where I come from, I buy chicken, beef, and fish, but I don't buy women, and I never will. I'm a father of two daughters and a brother of many sisters."

She did try to persuade me. I appreciated her effort and persuasiveness, but I had none of it. I approached the bar and asked the bartender to ring up my bill. All I had was a couple of ginger root sodas. She then demanded that I pay for her drinks as I had wasted her time with useless conversation. I left some cash for her drinks and left.

My colleagues, a Black American from North Carolina and another man from Denmark, asked me why I was rushing to return to my room. I debriefed them about my two encounters during the previous hour or so and how distasteful I thought it all was. They laughed at me.

One of them said, "What do you expect, man? Of all the girls you see here, nearly 125 of them are hookers." I thought they were professionals and having a good time after work. I was dead wrong.

Breaking Point

Before my work assignment, I last visited Saudi Arabia in the early 1980s while living in North Yemen. After thirty years, returning to the country required special preparation. For one, I had changed how I was interacting with other humans. I had lost the Arabian manners I was previously accustomed to using. I had become more direct and less tolerant of the usual small talk before getting into the core of a business conversation. I had also forgotten the mechanics of etiquette around prayer hours and greetings. I was acting like a Western person without having the physical appearance of one.

I stayed in a hotel the entire time I worked in Riyadh, the capital of Saudi Arabia. Almost all of the staff members were men. When most of my peers flew to Dubai as an outlet to break the confinement, I often stayed in Riyadh to finish work. I didn't feel the need to fly to Dubai to consume alcohol or procure sexual services. That is not who I am, and flying to Dubai just to stay in another hotel room wasn't worth the hassle or expense of flying back and forth.

On weekends, I often got lonely. The only females around were the Lufthansa flight attendants. They arrived once a week, and I quickly learned their schedule. I could only view the women's hair and legs as they entered the hotel because once they got into their respective rooms, they emerged for meals dressed like locals—covered. Those moments reminded me of my youth years in North Yemen when I hardly saw a woman's face other than my sisters'. I started to reflect on and wonder about the impact on men who barely know a woman, let alone interact with them. Liking, respecting, and appreciating is knowing. How can we understand half of society without studying and working with them?

I went for long walks when I got tired of working in my hotel room. In the middle of my walks, I got stuck in prayer hours. When that happened, the *muttawa*, the enforcers of the Islam rules in Saudi, would catch me walking. The *muttaween* monitors observance of the dress code, gender segregation in public spaces, and whether shops are closed during prayer times. They enforce conservative Islamic norms of general behavior, as defined by Saudi authorities. When I happened upon them, I immediately pulled out my passport and informed them that I had just arrived from overseas and was looking for the nearest mosque. They often drove me to the nearest mosque for me to pray.

Now and then, I went for a short run with my friends at 4 a.m., when the weather conditions were a bit cooler. A couple of times, the local police officers told us not to run in shorts and T-shirts, as our legs and arms were showing.

We told them, "We are men. What is the issue?"

"Women can see your legs, and you must be appropriately covered."

With the temperature around 25°C (77°F), wearing long sweatpants and jackets was impossible. I started running indoors but could not run more than ten minutes on a treadmill.

If I got caught with a non-Arabian, such as a white European or North American person, I was the one who got hassled and pushed around because I'm an Arab and I spoke Arabic. The locals felt there was no excuse for my slackness.

The things that should have worked as an advantage turned out to be drawbacks to my survival in the Kingdom.

At the same time, even though I flew to Canada every four weeks, I missed my two daughters terribly; they were both under twelve, and I was missing out on their childhood. The potential of earning tax-free wages rapidly became less and less desirable to me.

Eight months passed, and neither Dubai nor Riyadh appealed to me. The possibility of being caught working in Saudi Arabia without the proper documentation was real. My immigration visa to enter Saudi Arabia was only to teach my North American staff at my company's office. Ditto for Dubai—I was supposed to enter Dubai as a tourist and limit my activities at my company office on a short-term visa. My company was trying to get me a work/resident permit in Saudi Arabia, but the process would take up to six months. Moreover, the authorities had to keep my Canadian passport with them, and I could only leave the country when the authorities granted permission.

In some ways, I felt like I was back in Yemen; everything I had wanted to run away from was coming back to me. The government had complete control over me. They may not have kept my passport too long, but the fact that they could keep it and that I couldn't leave the country without the government signing paperwork giving me permission to do so triggered me. I was reminded of all the times I had to resort to bribing, fighting bureaucracy, etc., in order to try and live a normal life in Yemen.

I wrote a long email to my superiors to identify my concerns, shortcomings, and nervousness about continuing to work in the area without proper documentation. After eight months with no end in sight, I had no stomach to take the risk any longer. I packed up, flew to London, and waited for a response, expecting a contract and a work permit.

While I was in London, I sat in my hotel and waited. I was not prepared to return to Dubai or Saudi Arabia until my paperwork was sorted. During this time, the VP of the European and Middle Eastern division called the North American VP and told him I had left multimillion-dollar projects in disarray. After about ten days, the North American VP summoned me to Ontario to meet with him immediately.

Upon arrival, I was taken by the receptionist to the boardroom and asked to wait. I was expecting the VP to come and meet with me. Instead, an HR manager came. He took my badge and laptop and told me my job was redundant. The company offered me a severance package and I was dismissed.

Professionally, I had always felt I was a high performer and a hard worker. I was consistently ranked as an A+ employee, always getting bonuses and rewards for my work. At this stage, to be told I was redundant left a large dent in my professional ego. My worth was largely attached to my professional title, so I felt I had nothing. Alpha men are competitive; we need to make sure we fit in. I realized I was at the bottom of the food chain because I was unemployed. I had to separate my ego from my professional identity.

Personally, I felt discarded ... useless, as if none of my education or experience counted for anything. I had a family to support and a mortgage to pay and I was suddenly left without means to do so. I thought there was no humanity to the situation and I felt I was disposable. For several years I had given everything for this company, and during my time in the Middle East, I gave seven days a week, seventeen hours a day. I even took my laptop camping so I wouldn't miss anything. I felt like I had given the company the highest priority and they just tossed me away. I was humiliated.

XVIII

Yemeni in Western Society

Divorce isn't such a tragedy. A tragedy's staying in an unhappy marriage, teaching your children the wrong things about love. Nobody ever died of divorce.

— Jennifer Weiner, American author

The topic of how Muslims fit into Western societies is a much more comfortable one for me than it would be for most Western people to talk about. After all, I'm from the Middle East, and I feel that I have a good understanding of both cultures. Many people in the West base their assumptions of Middle Eastern society on what they see in the media or movies, which is, of course, slanted and almost always depicts only poverty or terrorism. The Western suspicion of Islam and the chaos in the Middle East are understandable, but they blur any level-headed conversation.

It's impossible to cast members of Middle Eastern society in the same mold, as people from Morocco, Iraq, or Yemen may have limited similarities to one another besides the religion itself. But the one commonality is that the more the person is attached to Islam and the cultural values of their country of origin, the harder it will be to reconcile life in Western society.

On the other hand, for a person who drifts away from Islamic cultural values, the adjustment is also tricky when trying to maintain the balance or stay on course within Western society. If someone has family in the Middle East but doesn't follow Islamic norms, they are caught in the middle. I don't attach myself to Islam, or any other religion, but I want to remain connected to the society I come from; that is, after all, my heritage. It's a balancing act—keeping ahold of food, music, and basic values while developing and maintaining my own unique identity. I don't want to offend others but I also need to be true to myself. And the values and ideologies I hold have been influential in my work and my family life in Canada.

Many individuals who don't know the mechanics of my irreconcilable marital differences ask me why the breakup occurred. Those who knew us a bit said, "She is a beautiful woman and cooks delicious meals. What else do you want?" This is a typical Yemeni perspective. My standard answer was that the major issues of my marriage at the foundation were because it was an arranged marriage rather than a union based on love and compatibility. She didn't fit my criteria; we were a complete mismatch due to cultural and traditional barriers, intellectual incompatibility, and the clash of Arabic culture—her foundational culture—with Western society, which I had long since adapted to. I take responsibility for the breakup; I knew from the start this union was a mismatch, yet I entered into it much to the detriment of my ex-wife and me.

If one chooses to hold on to the tradition of arranged marriage as it is practiced in most Middle Eastern countries, one should stay in the communities where that practice is most suitable. If the couple in an arranged marriage ends up in a Western society, perhaps it's best to renew the commitment or terminate the union. I've seen a lot of arranged marriages end in divorce after the couple moves to a Western country due to the change in environment. Once the woman has more choices, her and her husband's commitment doesn't hold up. It's similar to what happened to the husband and wife in the movie *Not Without My Daughter*; their relationship changed drastically once they landed in Iran, and the husband's culture dominated the rules of his behavior. Essentially, once the couple arrives in Western society, they are prone to break apart because the values and the environment that held them together in their homeland don't exist in their new culture.

Even though the root cause of my failed marriage wasn't our relocation to the West, the move significantly contributed to it. My wife emphasized Islamic Eid (holidays), and she expected me to attend a mosque for prayer services as a demonstration of my love and respect for her. Doing so had never been part of my routine.

Yemenis send remittances to their family members back home. My former spouse greatly valued how much money I could send to her family and how often. I feel I have no obligation to send any money to anyone, as I got nothing nor expected anything from anyone. Until I was eleven, I raised myself and depended on three people for survival: me, myself, and I. I send money to my extended family because I love and want to support them, but they neither demand nor expect it. And I would rather put a couple of hundred dollars into education for my children than send money to folks who continue to expect it for the rest of their lives. In most cases, families from back home assume that those who came to the West freely collect money, and we must share. I say no.

My wife and I had completely different views about money even before we were married. After we had booked and paid for a reception hall for our wedding, she heard about another one she felt would be better and pressured me to cancel the first reservation and book the second one. I told her the deposit on the first reservation was non-refundable and that canceling it and booking another would be a waste of money. We never agreed at that time. I was headed toward a collision course because of this issue alone: money.

XIX

Cultural Incompetence

[I'm] not a police officer, but [I] responded with [the] PD once to a twenty-nine-year-old man who called 911 because his mother didn't respect him. He "couldn't even" talk to her anymore because she would insult him, and he wanted the police to talk to her for him and get her to stop disrespecting him. He was living in her fairly nice home rent-free while unemployed since high school.

— It's Cool I Got This, anonymous
Internet poster[15]

In addition to my short stint working in the Middle East, I also visited several times to spend time with my family members in the Gulf countries.

During one visit to Abu Dhabi, when my wife, children, and I were staying with my sister Sheikha and her family, my wife met a lady claiming to be from Aden, South Yemen. My wife kept asking to meet this lady and her boyfriend, who was from France. My understanding was that my wife was so taken by the lifestyle in the UAE that she wanted me to find a job so that we could move there. She was thinking and hoping this lady and her man would be able to assist us.

But this lady and man had a different plan. They were making multiple phone calls to my niece's house during the night and coming to the house to pick up my wife. While the lady and man were parked and waiting outside the house to pick up my wife during one of these visits, my nephew saw the car and recognized one of the men sitting on the passenger side. This man was known to the UAE authorities for pimping and was suspected of human trafficking. This man also happened to be from Yemen.

My nephew didn't want to create a scene but went on to speak to Wejdan, my niece, about it. He thought the parties waiting outside were perhaps known to me. My niece, who was close to me and knew me well, assured my nephew that she didn't think I had any connection to these individuals. She came to me and asked if I knew anything about them. She also asked me if I would be interested in approaching them to inquire why they were there and perhaps suggest they leave. I agreed.

I walked up to the Mercedes SUV and asked the man on the passenger side why they were there. At the same time, I glanced into the back seat and noticed my oldest daughter, Lina, and the Yemeni lady seated in the back. Before the man could respond to me, the lady started to talk.

"I am here to pick up your wife and children. Your family has been unkind to your wife, so I am taking her to stay with me."

"How have you reached that conclusion without even knowing my family?" I asked her. "My family should not be of concern to you. My wife, children, and I are in the UAE for two weeks, and we will return to Canada in a few days."

I then turned to Lina.

"Lina, get out of the car."

"No, no, she is fine. She can stay in the car," the lady said.

"She is my daughter. Lina, come here."

Lina did as I instructed. Once she was out of the vehicle and standing with me, I then spoke to the driver, the French man.

"Drive away from here. My wife and children will not be joining you for whatever you have planned."

The lady continued to protest. "We will not leave here without your wife."

That was a surprising and frightening demand. Alarm bells were going off loudly in my mind. I gathered myself assertively and insisted they leave, emphasizing again that my family had nothing to do with them. I grabbed my daughter, walked away, closed the main gate door behind me, and went inside to speak to my wife.

When I approached my wife in the guest room, I found her packing and getting ready to leave with the crew waiting outside.

"I asked the people in the car to go, as they seemed to be questionable characters," I told her.

"Where did you get such false information? You are being controlled."

"At least one of the people you have been associating with for the past week or so is wanted by authorities."

"I don't want to hear this."

She elbowed her way out the door and rushed outside to meet them. By that time, the vehicle had already left. She ranted and screamed at me until she exhausted herself and then locked herself in another room.

My sister asked me to join her and the family for breakfast the following morning. Everyone asked where my wife was. We went to check the room where she had spent the night, but she was nowhere to be found. The house had eight bedrooms, and we checked them plus all the bathrooms. Nobody had any clue what had happened to her. We asked the guard if he had seen her depart the house. He told us she had left around 3 a.m. with the people who drove the black Mercedes SUV. She had asked the guard to inform us that the Canadian Embassy had collected her.

My niece started to look through the call display on the phone for all missed calls, particularly any calls received past midnight while we were sleeping. She also wrote down all the phone numbers from the calls that had come to her house for the past week or so.

I googled the Canadian Embassy and consulate to find their phone numbers.

"Good day. My name is Adel Ben-Harhara. My wife, children, and I are visiting my family in Abu Dhabi from Canada. I am looking for my wife, as she left my family's home last night and told the guard that someone from the Canadian Embassy had collected her around 3 a.m. I'm not sure who I should speak to about this."

The lady on the other end paused briefly and said, "Why do you think the Embassy picks up citizens?"

"I don't know. The guard told us that so I thought I should ask."

She said, "Sir, that doesn't make any sense."

"There was a small argument between my wife and me last night. My wife left the house at around 3 a.m. and told the house guard that people from the Canadian Embassy picked her up," I repeated.

The receptionist assured me, "The Embassy doesn't operate that way. We don't keep individuals at our site. And we haven't heard from your wife."

I asked her, "Where could she have gone, and why did she leave a message stating she went to the Canadian Embassy?"

"Sir, I will repeat: we don't collect parties from residences just because of a minor family dispute." She said, "If I were you, I wouldn't report this to the local authorities."

The warning to locate my wife using other venues and not to notify the authorities further confused and alarmed me.

"Why shouldn't I contact the authorities? I have to in case something has happened to my wife. Plus, my wife has a seven-month-old infant with her."

The receptionist again insisted, "Do not notify the local authorities. If you do, your wife will be deported and never be allowed to return to the UAE."

I was getting nowhere, so I handed the phone to Wejdan. They talked briefly, and Wejdan returned the phone to me. The Embassy staff member wished me luck and ended the call.

Our only option was to start calling all the numbers we found on the call display in hopes that the lady my wife had been contacting had reached out. We discovered that two-thirds of the calls that came in on the call display were from married Arab men in the UAE calling for escort services. The lady had called my wife using two men's mobile phones. The men were both surprised to receive calls from us. It was clear to us that the lady played with many clients.

At about 3:30 p.m., roughly twelve hours after my wife had left the house, we located her and the baby at one of her girlfriends' residences. My niece went to collect her. It was a most shameful, embarrassing, and scary incident for me. We had only two days left before departing to Canada, and those were the most prolonged forty-eight hours for me, waiting to see if another embarrassing and scary situation would occur in front of my family. As per Arabian culture and the Islamic religion, what my wife had done was cross the line at all levels, violating all customs and traditions and showing great disrespect to my family.

Plus, these people she trusted were not worthy of her trust. They put her in a position where she only interacted with another man for a moment, but they took pictures of her and then sent them out to blackmail her, saying they would show the images publicly to make it look like she was misbehaving.

On our last day in Abu Dhabi, my sister's children brought me many gifts, and as I was busy packing to fly back to Canada, my sister came to my room and made sure no one was nearby.

"My brother, I'm concerned. I don't think your wife is aware of the potential danger of this situation. She doesn't seem to understand the protocols of the family's cultural values that she stayed with. I suggest you pay close attention to your daughters' well-being and priorities. I don't believe she has their affairs in her mind and *Allah Ma'ak*."

Allah Ma'ak means "God be with you. May Allah bless us all with success, health, happiness, patience, and strength. May all your dreams come true and live the life you have always dreamed of. May Allah bless you with victory in this life and eternal life, too. Amen!" She meant, "May Allah bless you with tremendous courage to stand for humanity throughout your life."

I was astonished at how my sister could read my wife and arrive at such a conclusion, and I was embarrassed. My nieces and nephews are close to my age, so my sister, their mother, is older. The whole time we had been visiting, I was mindful of wanting to show my respect to her, but the way my wife had behaved on the trip was a great shame.

*

Ten years after visiting my sister Sheikha on this trip, I received a call in Canada from the UAE to inform me my sister had passed away. I cried like a child—I cried because I was unable to be present when either of my oldest sisters passed away—Hind and Sheikha.

I started to recall what Sheikha had told me—that I should earn my doctorate because she knew I had stopped my education at a master's degree. In the Hadhrami tradition, boys must be successful businessmen or scholars in religious matters or achieve the highest education level, a Ph.D. I wasn't a wealthy businessman, nor was I religious, as I don't even pray or fast; therefore, she wanted me to earn a Ph.D. to achieve a higher social status.

I reflected on her advice to pay attention to my daughters as I was divorced by this time and was learning how to co-parent.

Despite the loss of my sisters and as a result of their deaths, I ended up having a closer relationship with my niece. Wejdan filled the gaps created by my sisters' deaths, and she was kind enough to give me my sister's earrings to keep for sentimental value. Although I enrolled in a Ph.D. program, my divorce and the custody arrangements took priority. I ended up not pursuing a doctorate as my sister had hoped, but I kept my word concerning her advice on how I treated my daughters and did my best to look after them.

Summer

On that trip to Abu Dhabi, we were a family of four. My second daughter, Summer, was a baby during that trip.

Even though I knew my marriage wasn't going anywhere, I felt that Lina needed a brother or sister, and so Summer was born in 2003.

I wanted my second child to also have a name that was easy and meaningful for both Western and Eastern cultures. The word "summer" has a lot of meanings: an early morning fragrance, wind, air, Creator. In Arabic, "Sama" means holy, jovial, loyal, or charming. The connotation is closer to exquisite, superb, or perfect. In Yemen, we often associate this name with a sunset-time conversation.

And of course, summer is a beautiful season in Alberta!

Not a Crime

One Sunday, my wife arrived at our Calgary home at around 11:40 p.m. with our children, who were eleven and five. This wasn't the first time she had come home so late with the children, and we had already had numerous discussions about the issue. I asked that the children be fed, cleaned, and put to bed at a reasonable time.

She had a habit that she was unable to break, which was roaming amongst Arabs' homes to visit. During these visits, the women would mostly eat, dance, and chat on the main floor while the children were often left unattended in the basement or other rooms. My oldest daughter kept telling me about beatings and the kicks she was enduring from older, unruly children during these visits. I also tried to raise awareness of this with my wife and suggested she cut down on the number of visits and leave the children with me when she went on these outings. It was important for Arab families and children to mingle so the children could learn Arabic, and families could keep the culture intact. We didn't see the issue in the same way, and we had a different understanding of these visits' impact on our children.

When they walked into the house that Sunday night, I hugged the children and told them to brush their teeth and go to bed. For Lina, Monday was a school day, but she hadn't finished her homework, and I knew that after such a late night, she would have trouble getting up early for school. That was typical after these outings, and I wasn't happy about it. While I was getting the children ready for bed, my wife was on the phone finishing the conversation she hadn't managed to finish during her visit.

Once I put the kids to bed, I approached my wife to try and understand why it had been persistently difficult for her to stick to our agreement about the children. I mentioned that the oldest hadn't done her homework, which had been the pattern for several years.

"I'm unable to help her with her homework and put some structure around their routine, as you're taking the children everywhere. The priority seems to be your social gathering at the expense of our children and family."

She said, "I'm done with you, and I'm leaving the house with the children. I want to do what I have to do. I'm free, and I'm Canadian."

"The matter is not about your freedom or being Canadian, but rather about our children's well-being. You have been telling me you're free and Canadian for several years. I don't think you understand what it means to be a Canadian. Also, there is an obligation to your freedom. The two are not mutually exclusive." I added, "You have been physical with me, hitting me in the face, yelling at me with offensive and obscene language, and threatening to kick me out of the house. I have stayed calm and patient with you because you might be going through phases, and I had the hope you would outgrow your childish behavior."

She said, "Fuck you!" and picked up the phone and called 911.

I went to the bedroom. Within eleven minutes, two police officers showed up at the door. I heard them talking to my wife. Shortly after, they asked to speak to me. As I left my bedroom and headed toward the entrance, our children followed me, as they hadn't yet fallen asleep. I ordered them to get back to their rooms. They pretended to go but returned and stuck around, hiding between my legs and listening to what had transpired.

The two officers were a Black man and a white female.

The female officer asked me, "What is going on here?"

Before responding to her question, I asked the officer if she had children.

Instead of replying to my question, she said, "Sir, I'm here to deal with the domestic matter, not to answer your question. Your question has nothing to do with the call."

I asked, "Please?"

She said, "I have two."

"How old?"

"Seven and five," she replied.

"Are they in bed by now?" I asked.

"They'd better be, at least by 7 p.m."

"I now can address your question, Officer," I said. "My wife came home about twenty minutes ago with our children. My wife and I have had several discussions and agreed the children are to be fed, bathed, and put to bed early. It's now past midnight. The girls are still awake and not bathed. Nor was their homework done. I only asked her why this kept happening week after week for years. She wanted to take the kids and leave the house, but she didn't tell me where and what would happen to the children. Then I said, 'You can leave, but the children aren't going anywhere tonight.' So then she phoned 911."

The female officer approached Lina, went into one of the bedrooms, spent about five minutes, and then came out.

She looked at my wife and told her, "Madam, he hasn't attacked you, prevented you from leaving the house, or abused you in any way. Do you have a ride to where you plan to go?"

My wife responded, "I have a car."

"Then you can leave, but the children should stay home."

My wife yelled back, "I want to divorce from him! I thought you guys would kick him out of the house!"

The officer said, "Madam, 911 is used only in emergency and life-threatening situations. If you choose to divorce your husband, I recommend you call a lawyer, not 911."

The officers left the house.

*

Later, I found out that one of my wife's girlfriends, who was from Yemen too, provoked her husband to hit her and then called the police. The man was kicked out of the house and arrested for domestic abuse. Then I realized why my wife had been physical with me a couple of times. She was hoping I would retaliate, and if that were the case, I would be kicked out of the house. Most likely, a restraining order would have been put in place. I would continue to pay the mortgage, child support, and more while living in someone's basement. However, I had dealt with many challenging situations, which helped me to control myself in heated situations, so I always kept myself in check. Moreover, I am not the type of a man who hits women.

Some male refugees who come from countries where women don't talk back have a hard time seeing their spouses change drastically in Western society. For example, for an Arab man, to be slapped by a woman is shameful; he would prefer death.

The Canadian government invests a lot of money in language training and providing other assistance to immigrants, but there are gaps. Some immigrants don't understand the legal system; specifically, they don't necessarily understand that 911 is for life-threatening situations only.

Some immigrant women want to be as independent as Western women but fail to understand their obligations. Western women fought and earned voting rights, equal salaries to men for the same work, and equal treatment at home and on the work front. Western women are also aware of their obligations in society. I shared domestic chores and worked in an office. I helped look after the children, drove them to sports activities, and worked hard to maintain a good standard for my family. Many Middle Eastern women know only their rights but not their responsibilities. And they see child support as a revenue stream rather than what it is intended for.

In Islam, whatever a woman earns is hers, and whatever the husband makes is shared. For the most part, women don't work outside the home. Their roles are limited to being in their homes and ensuring the children are appropriately fed and cleaned and completing their school assignments. A father is a provider, but the upbringing of a successful child is left to mothers, and mothers both in Yemen and Ethiopia take the role seriously. When children complete university, only mothers get the credit.

My wife and her girlfriends wanted to draw what was best for them from Western and Eastern cultures. They stayed home rather than working but spent their time in malls, eating, visiting, and shopping. They left the kids running wild and didn't read for them or put the proper structure in place for them to develop and learn.

That is not to say all Islamic or Arab families are like that, but a good majority of Arab immigrants are. There are also those parents who are both working multiple jobs to provide for their children but cannot find time to spend with their children. They try but are unable to. Their children, born in Western society, sound like native English speakers but lack a well-developed English vocabulary. When my daughters' teachers commented on that issue early on, I used to automatically assume the teacher was a racist. But from my experience over time, I see that such comments are accurate. Those children who were unable to assimilate or be academically successful ended up in the drug business. That was my worst fear for my children.

Over time, I sensed that instead of accepting our differences and trying to work through them, my wife wanted the house and the children but wanted me out of her and our daughters' lives. We became water and oil. That is not to say she was terrible. We were just too different. Moreover, I enabled much of her behavior, as I thought I was doing the right thing by allowing her to adapt to Canadian culture in her way. She was a sheltered nineteen-year-old when I married her and a twenty-one-year-old with no world experience when we moved across the globe. She was thrust too quickly into a significant life change. And over a dozen years, we grew worlds apart.

I wanted to end the marriage peacefully and told my wife, "I am done, and I am filing for divorce."

She said, "Sure," as she had been looking for a way out of the marriage.

XX

Raising Teenagers

*I have three daughters, so I can't be as tough as I want to be. When you
have kids—especially daughters—they know how to work you. They're a
lot smarter than we are, that's for sure. But I'll be more tough on their
boyfriends.*

— Tim McGraw, country music singer

Teenagers can be challenging even when they have two
parents who are always on the same page about how
to raise them. The situation gets further complicated
when the two parents play tug of war, especially when one
parent feels the other should have no rights in parenting.
Teens are brilliant when it comes to exploiting gaps and
inconsistencies between parents.

In my case, I ended up being the primary caregiver for
my children. Raising my daughters without losing my mind
when I didn't have the support of my former partner was a
huge challenge.

When I was in Yemen, I once heard a wise person say,
"Your children are a version of you." I always worry about
this comment because I was a difficult child. Just in the way I
did, I know my daughters will each branch off and become

her own person over the long run. Their adolescent personalities, in particular, were created from their genes and the time they spent with me and my ex-wife. And my ex-wife and I have set completely different examples for our daughters.

In 2010, when we decided to end our marriage, Lina was thirteen and a half and Summer was seven. I didn't trust or respect their mother's ability or judgment for raising two daughters. Modeling and reinforcement had an enormous impact on my relationship with my ex-partner. I felt, with due respect to my former spouse, the word "we" had changed to "me." I sensed, throughout the divorce proceedings, that the details of the agreement were all about a way to get her own needs met rather than find a place where we mostly set ourselves aside for the good of the children. This calamity had a terrible hidden effect on our adolescent daughter.

You Have No Rights

Between the ages of sixteen and eighteen, Lina chose not to visit me or spend any time at my house, while my wife and I were moving toward our divorce. Lina didn't dislike me, but she didn't like my rules. She felt that I was a control freak who said no to everything. I made many mistakes; I was more about rules than why my rules were put in place. I was unable to communicate with or listen to her. As an engineer by profession, I'm all about fixing the problem pragmatically.

As our relationship got increasingly tense, confrontational, and challenging, and the more she resisted me, the more my imagination started to get out of control. The more disconnected and disengaged I was from her life, the more I began to wonder and worry about what was happening. My primary concern was that she wouldn't do well in school and couldn't complete high school, let alone go to university. I didn't believe she would have any future as a female minority without a good education. My perspective was more a reflection of my fear and my state of mind than the space my daughter was in, but I didn't know that then.

Despite knowing the moral compass and other situations in my marriage were going south, I didn't think about getting professional help. I thought I could fix everything just because I felt I was on the right side.

But what does it mean to be on the right side, anyway? I reflected on how I was dealt with as a child. I didn't like the way I was treated and never wanted to apply any of the severe punishments I experienced: beating, screaming, name-calling, or demonizing a child. At the same time, I had no experience with proper discipline.

My ex-wife changed Lina's address on her student record without my knowledge, so I wasn't getting school reports. When direct communication failed between me and my ex-wife, I chose to approach Lina directly. I begged and convinced her to meet me for coffee. At the coffee meeting, I came up with a list of violations and disrespect she had exhibited during the previous eighteen months. I lost sight of the fact that my only concern at that time was my inability to view and review her school report card. When we circled back to the report card, she said, "Since I don't reside at your place, you have no right to view my report card." How could I argue with this logic?

Social Media

Having two daughters made me a better human than my own life experience and the schooling I received ever could. I'm unsure, but my view of women could have been shaped differently than if I were a father of sons. Therefore, having girls was the biggest blessing and most enduring contributing factor in my adult life.

The learning and personal enhancement didn't come without a price, though. The world preys on women, as exemplified by the situation in the UAE with my wife and the human traffickers.

In 2010, as a natural protector, I started to read everything I could find on child abuse, pedophiles, kidnapping, and molestation. I was always overly alarmed and often unnecessarily worried. Sometimes, I could not sleep based on what I saw, heard, or assumed. When Lina signed up for a Facebook account, I started reading up on all the possible risks of being on social media. I knew I wouldn't be able to stop her from being on it, as she could easily use her friend's account or create an account with a fake name. I chose to join Facebook and monitor her online activities.

Summer thought that Facebook was for older adults, including her sibling, who is only six and a half years older. Therefore, she opted to join Instagram and Snapchat instead. I did, too. Beyond reviewing their social media posts, I used my computer engineering background to track all network traffic to identify sites the children were visiting. I found nothing, but I didn't stop there. Often, I took away their cell phones at 10 p.m. and kept them overnight.

After I started monitoring the Internet traffic, the principal of Lina's junior high school called me and wanted to speak with me about my daughter. The call came in the middle of the day while I was at work. The first thought that came to my mind was that she was in danger or injured. I excused myself from work and rushed to the school.

The principal informed me that my daughter had been engaged in an inappropriate text exchange from 11:37 the previous night, lasting past midnight. He went on to say that it would be shocking for me to read the chat, though. He was holding my daughter's phone in his hand while talking to me.

After he finished, I asked him a couple of questions: how he found out about it and, as a principal of a school and possibly a parent, what kind of advice he would give me to deal with the matter.

The principal indicated that the boy she was chatting with had similar chats with a different girl at school. The girl's parents had reported the issue to the school. The principal then approached the boy to confiscate his phone and address the matter. While browsing the boy's phone chats, he discovered a similar conversation with Lina. The principal read all the chat threads. I was thinking, *Why would he want to read the entire transaction of these teens' conversations?* I decided to keep that thought to myself.

We then further discussed the impact of the cyber world on today's children's lives, including cyberbullying, sexuality, parenting, and the roles of parents and schools in dealing with such issues. What I took away from that conversation was that today's youth have two kinds of personalities: an online personality and a genuine and physical personality known to us parents. Students treat their peers less humanely and respectfully when dealing with each other online versus in person. (The same can be said of adults, I guess!) Online, students tend to be vulgar, harsh, and less concerned about the feelings on the other end of the keyboard. Moreover, schools and parents are unprepared to deal with the harassment.

Even though the principal asked me to read the thread of my daughter's chat with the boy, I chose not to. It was Friday afternoon, almost the end of the school day, and I drove Lina home. In the process, I spoke to her about it—primarily, how embarrassing it was for me.

She asked me, "Is it all about you?"

I paused and thought, *She's right.*

I apologized. Then, I started to ask her why she had engaged in this type of interaction and what lessons she could learn from it.

First, she was upset that the principal had read all the chats on her phone from all the students and implicated her in the mischief. Second, she argued that the incident occurred outside the school facility and should not have been the principal's concern. Third, she was unhappy that the principal involved the parents, as this was between friends and classmates. She thought he was weird to have discussed the details of their online conversation with me. Not only had she thought about it, but she'd also discussed with her peers that they thought the principal was strange and that it was not his business to investigate messages on their cell phones that had been exchanged outside school hours.

Her comments somehow diluted the focus of my questions to her. She also deflated my concern about my image—the self-image I wanted to project of being a good father raising a well-behaved child. I wanted to be proud of her, but her behavior had embarrassed me. Her comment made me realize that this situation was not about me. I set aside my ego and focused on her—or rather, her actions. However, I was stumped by the three points she introduced. I decided to navigate the matter by agreeing with her that the principal shouldn't read everything and ask those embarrassing questions. Then I went back to insisting on her telling me the lessons she had learned or should have learned. I also informed her she would be grounded for a week without access to her phone.

As a typical teen, she brushed me off and didn't entertain my questions. She told me she couldn't wait to return to her mom's home two days later (the children were rotating between my house and their mom's). I was irritated by her dismissive attitude toward the entire drama. I couldn't help returning to making it about me, and I kept telling myself, *I left my work worrying about her. Then there was the bad news at the principal's office and now look at her attitude.*

I kept the phone with me. But I didn't want to read the chat. I didn't think it was appropriate for me to do so. I was also scared of what I would discover in the chat and that it would upset me more or, even worse, provoke me to say something to her. Knowing my personality, I would never forget it. It would haunt me for the rest of my life. I convinced myself to forget about the chat. *After all, how bad could it be?* I thought. *It's only words.*

At the same time, I started to wonder whether I should read it to prevent further damage. I kept asking myself, *Were they talking about suicidal actions? Or are they planning to commit a crime? What could it possibly be?*

I could not forget the principal's warning: "You will be shocked when you read it."

What could there be for me to be so shocked about? Did they talk about sex and sexuality? Did they exchange nude pictures?

I was fuming and bothered. But I chose not to know anything about it.

The following day, I received a call from my ex-wife asking me to drop the children off at her place. It was Saturday, a day before the agreed schedule, as we usually exchanged the children on Sundays. We had been apart for about two years at that point, and in that time, my ex-wife had never asked me to drop off the children. Most of the time, when I dropped our daughters at their mom's, their mother was never home. This request didn't make sense to me, but I didn't think much about it and decided to take the kids to her.

As I was standing by my ex's door, I told her it would be best if she booked a time with the school principal to hear the details of an incident at school and read the thread of the chats (if she chose to). I suggested she discuss the situation with Lina and impose the grounding I intended to apply as a measure of discipline (no access to the phone for a week). Lina had already phoned my ex-wife via landline, explained her predicament about being grounded, and asked for help to get her phone back.

I wasn't aware of the communication that had taken place between the mother and child between Friday afternoon and Saturday morning. The immediate response I received from my ex-wife was, "Go fuck yourself." She turned around, called Lina, and handed her the cell phone. The demarcation pointing to our different parenting styles had never been more apparent than at that moment.

I left without uttering another word.

Menstruation

Muslim women who are menstruating are exempt from fasting during Ramadan, according to the Qur'an. Both Islam and Judaism prohibit sexual intercourse with a woman on her period. In Ethiopia, conversation about menstruation is still considered highly taboo; the topic is rarely discussed or taught in schools. This leads to stigma and shame for many girls, which is exacerbated by the difficulty of obtaining sanitary products such as pads and tampons. I grew up learning that women are dangerous to be around while they're on their period and hearing people use derogatory names to refer to a woman's monthly cycle.

I'm a product of my formative years and the teachings I received in Ethiopia and North Yemen. I had never discussed or learned anything to prepare me for this issue. Having to deal with it with my daughters was new territory for me.

One weekend, while my daughters and I were grocery shopping, my ex-wife phoned me to inform me that Lina had started getting her period a couple of months prior. She said, "She didn't want me to tell you that, but you should buy her pads while shopping."

I said, "Okay," and continued to shop.

No more than fifteen minutes later, my ex phoned again to remind me about the pads.

I told her, "I'm aware that I'm absentminded, but you don't have to remind me every ten minutes."

I continued to shop. My daughters had two other girls with them who were the same age, too.

I finished shopping and lined up to pay at the checkout. My phone rang again. It was my ex for the third time.

Oops!

Half of the groceries were on the conveyor belt then, and many customers were lined up behind us. I quickly turned around to the girls, who were also behind me, and told Lina, "Go and get the ladies' diapers."

"What diaper?" she asked.

Everything froze! The cashier, who happened to be a lady, stopped everything. The ladies who were lined up behind us were looking at me.

"What size of pad do you need?" the cashier asked Lina.

Lina mumbled her reply.

The cashier pushed a button.

"Can I get a 36-pack of Always ultra-thin maxi pads with wings on checkout three please?" she called out over the intercom. Now everyone in the store knew my daughter needed these!

I not only embarrassed myself, but I humiliated my daughter and exposed my lack of understanding of or respect for the most straightforward natural event.

I grew up with sisters and stepmothers. But most men don't want to talk about periods. They blush when someone says "period" or "menstruation" and avoid talking about it at all costs. My sisters and my stepmothers acted the same way. This is due to various factors ranging from not wanting to say the wrong thing to being embarrassed by a lack of knowledge and the cultural shame surrounding periods. All these things need to end. This can end with education and a willingness to talk and make mistakes.

It took a period (no pun intended!), but I had to learn and grow. Even though Lina has never been open with me in this regard—possibly because I had humiliated her beyond repair!—Summer openly reminds me of her mood swings and often gives me a heads-up when she knows it's coming. I grew to be a better man and a more informed human.

Donuts

I tend to buy brand-new vehicles and pass the previous one on to my children when I do. When Lina turned eighteen and enrolled in university, I purchased a new car and gave her my old one. Once she graduated from university, was employed, and bought herself a new car, we passed on the older vehicle to Summer. Summer started driving the car with her learner's license while her mother, older sister, or I was in the vehicle.

In November 2018, I received a phone call from the Calgary Police Service while giving a presentation at work. The officer asked me if I knew where my car was.

I said, "Downstairs in the parking lot."

He asked me, "Are you sure?"

"Yes. I drove it this morning to work."

The officer sensed that I may have had multiple vehicles and asked if I owned more than one car.

I said, "Yes."

"Do you know where your 1998 Jeep Cherokee is?"

"Parked in front of my house."

He quickly said, "Sir, we found your car inside a church door and are looking for your daughter to speak to her."

I froze. Unlike the call from the school principal about Lina, this time, I had my phone set on speaker phone, and my colleagues were hearing the conversation. I was a bit embarrassed and had no option but to run home.

I knew the church's location, as it is within our community. Once I arrived at the site, I started to talk to the officer to get more information. Eight teenage boys between the ages of fourteen and sixteen had taken the car for a joy ride and started to do donuts in the church parking lot. The driver lost control on the ice and drove into the church's main door, resulting in a significant amount of damage to both the building and the vehicle. When the car crashed into the church, the teenagers fled. Neighbors who saw the accident called 911.

I noticed the police had apprehended the driver of the car, and the boy was already sitting in the back seat of the patrol vehicle.

While I was still talking to the officer, he asked where Summer was. She hadn't been in the vehicle when the incident occurred. Thank God nothing had happened to the boys. I was relieved to learn the only damage was to property not person. The police wanted to know if my daughter had given the car keys to the boys willingly or if the vehicle was stolen.

At that moment, the father of the driver was trying to open the police car and beat his son for what he had done. When the man realized the doors were locked, he started to scream at his son, "I will kill you! I will break your head! You're useless. I told you to stay out of trouble!"

His tirade went on and on!

The police officer and I calmed the father down. Then a second officer visited my home to check on my daughter. Summer told the officer she had been home the whole time and willingly gave the boy the key.

The officer told me, "The car is written off. You cannot enforce any recovery since your daughter gave him the keys, and it wasn't stolen. You may take the family to small claims court."

I said, "I will see what I can do about that."

Then, the boy's father approached me, wanting to speak. He was delighted my daughter hadn't lied despite her friends asking her to tell the police that the boy had stolen the vehicle as the charge would have been much more severe on his son.

I told him, "I would rather lose money and the vehicle than have my daughter lying to the authorities."

He promised to pay me the car's value, which he did in total.

I Am Twenty-One

Father's Day, June 21, 2017. I had been thinking about what I should do with my daughters on Father's Day the entire week. The three of us had lunch and supper in the Banff area and went for a hike in the mountains in the afternoon.

Before we left for the mountains that morning, I went into the basement for a photo album. I wanted to put together a collage for my daughters. I rarely went into the basement. It was where my daughters had their bedrooms, a recreation area, and other facilities; it was their space. As I was standing in the middle of the entertainment area, I thought I heard a male voice. Initially, I thought the TV must have been on, and I tried to locate the remote control to turn it off. I turned the TV on instead, as it was already off. I was perplexed and quietly went to check the washroom and the yoga room, not wanting to wake up my daughters.

My mind started to wander, and my heart began to beat fast. I didn't want to believe what I was thinking to be true. I slowly walked toward the door of Lina's bedroom. The male voice was coming from her room. I felt my throat quickly dry up. I was also clueless about what to say or do. I gathered myself and rushed to the upper floor to get my mobile phone.

I texted Lina, asking if a man was in the house. When I didn't get a reply, I started phoning her. No response. Then, I wondered whether I should grab a knife and head to the basement again. As I headed to the kitchen to grab a sizable butcher knife, I noticed a reply to my text.

She simply said, "Yes."

"Who is this person, and how did he end up in the house?"

She mentioned the name. I knew the boy, but it had never crossed my mind that he would take the liberty to spend the night without my permission.

Once I knew she was safe and set aside my fear of battling the intruder, I turned my attention to my parental role.

I rarely get angry. The problematic childhood I had taught me to stay calm despite the situation and to focus on navigating through the circumstances. In this case, I was unable to contain myself. The situation brought the beast out of me.

I texted her stating, "I want him out of the house in two minutes. If not, I am coming down with the butcher knife."

She said, "He was drinking last night, and I brought him home and allowed him to spend the night in my bed. I spent the night in the other room with my sister."

I didn't care what kind of excuse or justification was provided to me.

The boy left the house within five minutes.

After he left, Lina and I sat at the kitchen table to discuss the situation. She said, "I'm twenty-one and old enough to know what I'm doing."

My response was that one sentence every parent says to their children at some point. "You could be seventy-one. As long as you live in my house, my rules for this house must be respected."

She replied, "Mom allows it."

I was boiling inside, but I calmly spoke with her about boundaries, respect, and personal safety.

Where I came from, a Yemeni man could quickly kill his daughter, sister, or cousin, or at least beat her if she was found to be talking to a boy, let alone allowing a boy to spend a night at the parent's house. I started to blame my ex, as I felt she had lowered the standard family rules and lost moral authority since when my children were living with her.

Then, I started to question myself: *Why did I accuse my former spouse rather than work on the relationship between my daughter and me?*

XXI

The Bosnian Connection

Invisible threads are the strongest ties.

— Friedrich Nietzsche, philosopher

In 1972, when I was in elementary school, I read a magazine covering Emperor Haile Selassie's visit to Yugoslavia. This was when I learned about the country and their late leader, Josip Broz Tito. The Ethiopian king was the first African head of state to visit Yugoslavia in 1954.

The magazine was full of black-and-white pictures, and the story covered political and economic relationships between the countries. The news coverage also talked about the Non-Aligned Movement (NAM), an international organization dedicated to representing the interests and aspirations of developing countries such as India, Ethiopia, and Yugoslavia. Moreover, it was an organization of countries that did not formally align with the US or the communist block like the USSR and sought to remain independent.

The political situation didn't make any sense to me at the time. However, Tito's biography piqued my interest. He was born to a Croatian father and a Slovenian mother. I started to normalize mixed parenting as being no different from my situation.

A couple of years later, I developed an interest in the Yugoslavian national soccer team (it was only second to the other national team I liked—Brazil). I had no connection to the country, nor did I know anyone from there. However, I thought that the Yugoslavian soccer team played soccer similarly to South American players. I used to call them the South American team in the middle of Europe.

From 1997 to 1998, while living in Calgary, my wife attended an English language course to upgrade her high school diploma. She befriended a girl named Uranela. Uranela was a young lady from Bosnia and Herzegovina who was without her parents at the beginning of 1997. She made the trip across the ocean on her own. Shortly after she met my wife, Uranela came to our house for a visit, and I started to pose questions about her background and the war that took place during the early 1990s. She was an intelligent lady with a good insight into what had transpired where she grew up.

During the war, she was an interpreter for the International Committee of the Red Cross (ICRC), a Swiss humanitarian organization. She used to work on family reunifications, missing person files, and prisoner exchanges. Whenever she shared her stories with us, she told them intensely and courageously. During one of our visits, she mentioned that her parents were moving to Canada, and she was eagerly expecting their arrival.

Her parents arrived in the fall of 1997. I asked to meet them as I wanted to welcome them into this country. Her parents, Ismet and Rasema, and her younger brother, Adis, used to come to our home on weekends. During their visits, we began to unravel and share our stories of the past decade. We talked about our everyday struggles of being new to Canada, and we discussed cultural differences in hopes of creating some shared understanding about what it meant to be Canadian and live in a new country. We also had many conversations about war, loss, trauma, and grief experienced as a family.

Their family had experienced unimaginable loss. Adis and Alis were identical twins, born in 1981. In 1995, a tragic accident enfolded, and Alis passed away. He was only fourteen years old. The parents lost their son; the siblings lost their brother. After moving to Canada, Uranela was excited to see her younger brother again. They enjoy each other's company and have spent a lot of time together since reuniting in Canada. Adis is now in his early 40s and is living with loss, pain, and grief; he often thinks about his twin brother.

Ismet was full of energy. He was a man who wanted to start a new life in Canada. Rasema, on the other hand, was a calm, focused, and generous woman. Adis was fifteen years old and in junior high school when they arrived in Calgary. We quickly grew from casual acquaintances to family-like units with frequent visits between us. Ismet noticed I wasn't a handyman and always offered to fix any broken items around our house. Rasema always cooked excellent meals, and I spent considerable time fixing the family computer and installing software.

He and his wife had attempted to smooth the feathers between my wife and me, advising us to try and work on the marriage, telling us, "Marriage is a work in progress." Once they knew it was a dead issue, they turned their attention to helping me maintain my psychological well-being. Rasema taught me how to cook. They invited my kids to activities and visited my house, ensuring they were looked after.

When my marriage ended, this Bosnian family and I continued our friendship. Similar to the way Munir Al-Sakfa, my geologist friend, and Lash, my friend the university professor did, this family encouraged me that life would be all right. Ismet encouraged me to do hiking and running to manage my stress. He started taking me for walks, and he took me running and biking for the first several months after my separation, helping me maintain balance.

"We lose a lot of things in our lives, and we still survive," he told me.

Adis grew to be a solid professional with a master's degree. He morphed from the boy I used to show how to use a computer to a man I converse with about international and intercultural competency. He now works as a counselor for immigrants and their children. He sees their challenges as going beyond a lack of food or struggles to meet basic needs. Instead, he focuses on helping them build cultural competency.

"A lot of the children of immigrants don't know how to survive in this culture," he says. He affirmed to me that my family is not unique.

XXII

Mountain Therapy

It's not the mountain we conquer, but ourselves.

— Sir Edmund Hillary, mountaineer

*I*n March 2016, Summer's school reported that she was suffering an academic setback, creating a lack of confidence and behavioral concerns. The school administrators asked me to move Summer out of French immersion. I pleaded with Summer's core teachers and the principal for a chance to work with her to improve her grades. They agreed.

During spring and summer, due to the living environment at my ex-wife's residence, Summer continued to reside at my home most of the time. At the time, five additional people were living at my ex-wife's residence: her mother and father, her partner's father, and two exchange students. Summer didn't have a room or bed and spent nights sleeping on the floor at her mother's house.

While I spent evening hours with my daughter at the dinner table, assisting and encouraging her to finish her school assignments, I told her I would pack my bags and challenge myself to climb Mount Kilimanjaro if she improved her grades.

In spring 2017, I received a letter from Summer's school stating that she had been selected for the most-improved student award. I was thrilled and shared the news with Summer, telling her I would take time off work to attend the ceremony at school when she received the award.

She told me, "I would rather receive the award in private," and requested that I not come to the school.

"Why, my love?"

"I don't want any of my friends to know that I was struggling academically."

I agreed to her request and hugged her.

After a moment of silence, she looked me in my eyes and said, "If I recall, you told me you would climb Kilimanjaro if I happened to improve my grades."

At that, she walked away to her room.

Kilimanjaro

I knew Kilimanjaro, or Kili, as its climbers call it, was in Africa, but I had forgotten my elementary school geography entirely and could not recall if this mountain was in Kenya or Tanzania.

Mount Kilimanjaro is one of the Seven Summits—the tallest mountain on each of the seven continents. Its summit is the highest point on the continent of Africa. It is also the tallest freestanding mountain in the world.

In April 2017, Lina and I went to Boston, Massachusetts, for my participation in the 121st Boston Marathon, which made my financial situation even less favorable for me to make the trip to Africa to climb Kilimanjaro.

When you tell your friends and family that you plan to climb Mount Kilimanjaro, most people become concerned for your safety.

"Don't people die there?" they ask.

Those who have reached the summit say that a determined person with above-average fitness could probably summit Kilimanjaro, especially if the pace is *polepole*, pronounced po-lay-po-lay. It's Swahili for slow, but it's spoken fast. Like so many Swahili words and phrases, rolling it off the tongue is fun. Catchy, even. Take a moment and say it out loud: *polepole*!

Some 30,000 people climb Kilimanjaro yearly, and the reported number of tourist deaths is about ten annually. That means there is only a 0.0003 percent chance of death; it's practically zero. Put another way, there is only one death per 3,333 climbers.

Summer wasn't old enough to comprehend the risks involved, and I started to think about how horrible she would feel if something happened to me on the trip. I had promised her; how could I break that promise? But I was conflicted.

Will I be that one out of the 3,333?

*

It was almost 2 a.m. when the designated person picked me up from Kilimanjaro International Airport in Tanzania. A tall, dark man was holding a sign with my name. When I approached him, I greeted him and asked him if he could assist me with carrying a duffel bag. I took plenty of hiking gear and clothing for two weeks as I also planned to travel between Tanzania, Kenya, and Ethiopia for an African safari.

The man wasn't friendly at all. He had perhaps waited for me for over four hours while I stood in line with 300 other people to get my entry visa, and it was clearly past his bedtime. The only sentence he said was that he expected me to be a woman. That was because a few Europeans had a similar name with different spellings (Adele, Adelle, etc.).

As we departed the airport parking lot in the pitch dark, I was in the back seat. We didn't talk at all. I was exhausted from the long flight, and he too was exhausted after the long wait. From the information the tourist guide company gave me, I remembered that it would take around fifty minutes to get from the airport to the designated hotel. This trip seemed further, even though we had been on the road for only seventeen minutes. I kept checking the time, but my watch was still set to Calgary time, and with a ten-hour difference, I was further disoriented.

Halfway into the drive, I started to worry and question myself.

I don't know these people. What if I signed up with a fake tourism company? All my communication was online, and I never verified whether this was an honest or fake tourist company.

What about this man? What if he takes me to a remote site to kill and rob me? No one in the world would know I was with him alone. After all, this is Africa, and my US$2,000 cash, clothing, and hiking gear could easily change someone's life here.

I was concerned, and I began to believe the scene I had created was true. I started thinking of escape plans. I planned to run.

I'm a marathoner. I can outrun him.

I also thought, *Wait. Africans are born runners. I may* not *be able to outrun him!*

I thought about hiding my cash in my socks and perhaps negotiating everything I had in exchange for him sparing my life.

I started to ask myself, *Why am I here? Why didn't I wait for other passengers or tourists and share taxi fare to the city?*

Wild imagination!

A speed bump brought me back to reality.

We approached a checkpoint where soldiers were standing on the side of the road and inspecting cars. Initially, I thought the men must be his buddies, and we had arrived at the destination where they were going to rob and possibly murder me. At the same time, I was happy that there were signs of human life besides the driver and me.

One of the officers checked the car, and after he briefly spoke to the driver, we were allowed to proceed.

I asked the driver what they were checking and why they were at that spot.

"The airport is within a different jurisdiction, and we are now entering the next one, where the hotel is. When vehicles cross between jurisdictions, they are always searched. We are now in Moshi[16] and the hotel is about ten minutes away."

I breathed a sigh of relief.

237

I'm not going to get murdered after all!

I started to wonder about my imagination. I said to myself, *I began to act and feel like a white person who is afraid of Black people! Why did I think Africans are bad?*

Once I checked in to the hotel, the driver told me the guide would be in the lobby to meet me at 6 a.m. to start the trek.

The hotel room was okay. It had showers, a small soap bar, and a faded towel.

I thought, *I have seen better hostels. Calling it a hotel is a bit of a stretch.*

But it was a clean and safe resting place before the demanding trek.

Perhaps because it was daytime in Canada, or maybe due to the caffeine I consumed during my thirty-six-hour-long trip from Calgary, I could not sleep. I did manage to text my daughters to let them know I had arrived in Africa safely.

Babu

On June 25, 2017, at around 5:30 a.m., I visited the hotel lobby to meet Rama, the guide. I knew I was early, but it didn't matter because I had been unable to sleep anyway, so perhaps it was best to be away from my room and to study the surroundings.

More foreigners were arriving. Most of them spoke English, but not as their first language. After chatting a few sentences at the front desk, they all defaulted back to their respective native languages: French, Dutch, Portuguese, German, Croatian, Bulgarian, and Polish.

Rama showed up at 6:10 a.m. and greeted two Danish boys. I heard their conversation as they sat on the other side of the couch I was sitting on. He had met them the day before. Rama didn't know what I looked like and told them, "I'm waiting for this girl to ask if she could join you guys."

The boys asked what her name was and where she was from.

"She is Canadian, and her name is Adel."

Like the driver the night before, they all mistook me for a female. The tour office administrator assumed I was a woman and sent everyone a note to tell them I was a woman. I stood up to correct that.

I was teamed up with two intelligent men from Denmark: Vincent and Sebastian. They were cousins, and both were twenty years old. My first thought was how I would keep up with them. The guiding company had decided to keep the three of us together for cost-saving and logistical purposes. Otherwise, I would have had a set of porters, and they would have, too. By combining the support team, we could share the tips and have a sizable caravan.

After an orientation meeting, we decided to have fun regardless of the outcome. The lead guide, Rama, the assistant guide, Hamid, and the cook, Steve, plus twelve porters, were dedicated to the three of us. I made sure I remembered those three names, as they were the key players amongst our fifteen helpers. When I looked at the entire crew, none exceeded the age of twenty-six. When I told them I was fifty-five, not only did they make me feel old, but I felt like a senior citizen. The porters immediately called me Babu. I asked what Babu meant; apparently, it means grandfather. Rama clarified by saying, "It means 'respectable name given to an old man, a figure like a patriarch as in progenitor.'"

From my childhood Judaism teachings, I remembered the patriarchs were Abraham, his son Isaac, and Isaac's son, Jacob, the ancestor of the Israelites.

I asked, "Are you guys telling me I'm as ancient as Abraham?"

Rama was worried I would take it negatively and started to apologize. I told him not to worry; I would use it as an incentive to kick some young peeps' butts during the hike. He laughed.

The entire trek, my name was Babu.

"Have you seen Babu's poles?"

"Put up Babu's tent first."

"Make sure to get Babu's hot wet towels ready for him to clean himself first thing in the morning."

I finally told them, "It is always best to have fun with the younger generation and to listen to the elders, like me."

They liked that!

Conquering Kili

We took the Machame route, also known as the Whiskey route, which is the most popular approach to Kilimanjaro's summit. Machame's draw is its scenic beauty. However, due to its shorter itinerary, the trail was considered complex, steep, and challenging. Rama told me this route was better suited for more adventurous folks or those with high altitude, hiking, or backpacking experience. I said, "Why not? I live every day, but I die once." I chose this route. The Danish boys agreed.

The route approaches Mount Kilimanjaro from the south, beginning with a forty-minute drive from Moshi to Machame Gate. The path leads hikers through the rainforest to the Shira Plateau. Here, many of Kilimanjaro's routes converge. Then, the Machame route turns east and traverses underneath Kilimanjaro's Southern Ice Field on a path known as the Southern Circuit before summiting from Barafu Camp. The descent is made via the Mweka route; this route is now only used for descent.

Day 1 Moshi to Machame Camp

Elevation: 1640 to 2850 m/5,380 to 9,350 ft

Distance: 11 km/7 miles

Hiking Time: 4 hours

We drove from the hotel in Moshi to the Gate, which took about fifty minutes. The drive passed through the village of Machame, located on the mountain's lower slopes. Once dropped off at the park gate, we walked through the dense rainforest on a winding trail up a ridge until we reached Machame Camp.

As soon as we arrived at the camp, I vomited. The trip had been purely exhausting already; starting in Calgary, I had flown for twenty-one hours and had three- to six-hour layovers in Toronto and Addis Ababa before arriving at Kilimanjaro International Airport.

Day 2 Machame Camp to Shira 2 Camp

Elevation: 9,350 to 12,500 ft

Distance: 5 km/3 miles

Hiking Time: 5 hours

We left the rainforest glades and continued ascending to a steep, rocky ridge. We passed through heather and open moorlands on the Shira Plateau, then crossed a large river gorge before getting to Shira 2 Camp.

I felt much better on this day. I was able to take pictures and even spent time conversing with Sebastian and Vincent. Both were about six feet tall. Vincent was the first to speak to me, but Sebastian was always there to hear our conversation. While Vincent had a contagious smile and often burst out laughing, Sebastian was reserved but very engaged.

As the hike progressed over the next several days, I was sandwiched between these young men, engaging in conversations about politics, current world affairs, Canada, the US, genetically modified food, Europe, and Islam. I wondered how educated and advanced these young fellows were compared to those I met when I first migrated to the US. They were intelligent, well-rounded, and well-spoken young adults.

They, too, found me interesting for having a mixed ethnic background, attending universities in the US and Canada, and being able to maintain physical fitness as a fifty-five-year-old! They also thought that I had a better perspective on life than most African and Middle Eastern people they had met. Not surprisingly, I was even older than their fathers, and they found me to be a motivational figure.

On this day, we started to play songs on portable music devices. Vincent and Sebastian joined the African porters in a dancing circle. They didn't understand the Swahili, but they were enjoying themselves. While taking pictures and recording short video clips, it occurred to me that despite the differences in skin color, income, and educational levels between the African porters and the Europeans from well-to-do families, they could enjoy life together. One thing was in common: their body movement according to the beat.

Day 3 Shira 2 Camp to Lava Tower

Elevation: 3810 to 4630 m/12,500 to 15,190 ft

Distance: 7 km/4 miles

Hiking Time: 4 hours

We continued to the east, up a ridge, and then headed southeast toward the Lava Tower, a three-hundred-foot-tall volcanic rock formation. We descended to Barranco Camp through the strange but beautiful Senecio forest to an altitude of 4267 meters (14,000 feet). The forest was like a jungle with thick lush green plants and flowers everywhere. Looking up from the forest, all we could see was the bare mountain, volcanic rock. The contrast between the dense forest and the dry mountain was astounding. Although we began and ended the day at the same elevation, the time spent at a higher altitude benefited acclimatization.

Vincent got sick from the altitude and could not keep anything in his stomach. Even though the cook made fresh meals with lots of variety daily, Vincent was vomiting and started to get dehydrated. Both Sebastian and Vincent came unprepared for such a situation. They hadn't brought painkillers like Advil, first aid supplies, or electrolytes. We still had a two- or possibly three-day hike before reaching the summit. I started to be concerned about him.

I thought the third day would be more leisurely as we adjusted to the altitude, but I struggled somewhat on this day too. As we moved to higher elevations, the night hours got cooler. I began to sleep with multiple layers of sweaters and socks. The septic washroom smell started to irritate my sinuses. It gave me a severe headache, so instead of using the designated washrooms, I held my bowel movements until the middle of the hike and opted to squat in the bushes. There were hardly any bushes for the most part, so I had to look for big rocks or anything I could hide behind.

My daughters gave me three rocks when I decided to go on this trek. Each rock had one word painted on it: Live, Laugh, and Love. They told me, "When you go to the mountain, throw these out there." Some rocks fell out of my pocket while I was getting out of my tent on Day 3, reminding me of my commitment to my children and inspiring me not to stop. When they fell out, I noticed, stopped, and picked them up.

Despite our struggles, there was no shortage of laughs or topics of conversation. Often, we passed many trekkers who were also on their way up.

Day 4 Barranco Camp to Karanga Camp

Elevation: 3976 to 3995 m/13,044 to 13,106 ft

Distance: 5 km/3 miles

Hiking Time: 4-5 hours

We began the day by descending into a ravine to the base of the Barranco Wall. Then we climbed the non-technical but steep, nearly 274-meter (900-foot) cliff. We crossed a series of hills and valleys from the top of the Barranco Wall until we descended sharply into Karanga Valley. One steeper climb up led us to Karanga Camp. This was a shorter day, again meant for acclimatization.

On Day 4, we reached the peak of our difficulties, both mentally and physically. Vincent hadn't eaten for twenty-four hours. I kept giving him electrolytes I had brought with me from Canada. That helped, but it wasn't enough. Sebastian morphed from being his cousin to acting like an older brother. He showed compassion and care I had never seen between two individuals since my imprisonment in Addis Ababa.

Although we didn't discuss it in front of Vincent, I talked with Sebastian and Rama about possibly sending Vincent back to the base, as we were sure he wouldn't be able to make it to the summit. We didn't want to risk his life or take the chance of any other issues coming up as we proceeded on the trek. I asked if the porters could bring a portable stretcher to quickly evacuate Vincent, who was, by then, unable to walk on his own. Rama and I were inclined to send him back with several porters and Hamid, the assistant guide. But Sebastian wanted to include Vincent in the conversation before making any decision. We agreed.

We asked Vincent for his opinion about returning to base camp as he hadn't eaten for two days and looked too weak to carry on with the hike.

He looked at the three of us and said, "I didn't come this far to quit halfway. I must finish even if I die."

The four of us went silent.

I told Vincent, "You've got the spirit of John Stephen Akhwari from Tanzania."

He asked, "Who and why?"

I told him, "In 1968, during the Summer Olympics, while competing in the marathon in Mexico City, at the 19-kilometer (12-mile) mark, he fell badly, wounding his knee and dislocating his shoulder as he landed hard against the pavement. However, he continued running and finished the race as the last person to cross the line. When the reporters asked him why he hadn't given up, he said, 'My country did not send me 5,000 miles to start the race. They sent me 5,000 miles to finish the race.' That is you!"

He was so happy!

We dropped the notion of sending him back. Instead, I gave him the remainder of the electrolytes I had brought from Canada, and an American family we ran into at the Barranco Camp gave us plenty of painkillers and other first aid supplies. Rama continued to monitor Vincent's situation three times a day using an oximeter and stethoscope to measure pulse, temperature, blood pressure, and oxygen saturation. Sebastian continued helping his cousin by carrying or supporting him.

Day 5 Karanga Camp to Barafu Hut

Elevation: 3995 to 4673 m/13,106 to 15,331 ft

Distance: 4 km/2 miles

Hiking Time: 4-5 hours

We agreed to continue.

During our lunch break, Rama asked us if we wanted to spend the night at Karanga Camp or head directly to Barafu Camp to save a day. Vincent, Sebastian, Rama, and I discussed whether we should continue hiking or spend the night. Knowing how frail and tired Vincent was from altitude sickness, we didn't think spending two more nights before heading to the summit was worth it, even though we needed an additional rest day. We decided to continue to Barafu Camp.

We left Karanga and hit the junction, which connects with the Mweka Trail. We continued up the rocky section to Barafu Hut. At this point, we had completed the Southern Circuit, which offered views of the summit from many angles. The two peaks of Mawenzi and Kibo were viewable from this position.

Here, we made camp, rested, and enjoyed an early dinner to prepare for pushing on to the summit.

Rama told us he would wake us up at around midnight. Leaving then meant we would reach the summit in time for sunrise. He checked on Vincent, and we all went to bed early.

During the trek, every time we reached a new campground, the porters arrived ahead of us to set up the tents, cook fresh meals, and boil water with clean towels so we could clean ourselves. The porters also greeted us with dance and song. On this day, neither Vincent nor Sebastian danced with the crew. We barely finished our meals before heading to our tents to sleep.

Day 6 Barafu Hut to Summit

Elevation: 4673 to 5895 m/15,331 to 19,341 ft

Distance: 5 km/3 miles

Hiking Time: 7 hours

Around midnight, we arose and began our push to the summit. This was the most mentally and physically challenging portion of the trek. The wind and cold at the elevation and time of day were extreme. The temperature was around -5°C (23°F) but felt more like -20°C (-4°F). We ascended in the dark for several hours, taking frequent but short breaks.

Near Stella Point (5761 meters/18,900 feet), we were rewarded with the most magnificent sunrise I have ever seen, coming over Mawenzi Peak. Imagine there is a huge flashlight pointed at your closed bedroom door. As soon as you open the door, the light blasts your face. It's a special kind of sunrise—it looks like the sun is approaching you. At lower altitude, the sunrise differs from that at 5791 meters (19,000 feet). It's blinding; it covers the whole sky. The sun looks like a pancake, and there is nothing but orange above the clouds.

After we hiked for several hours toward the crater rim, the rising sun lifted my spirits. From that point, it was only a short trek to Uhuru Peak, the highest point on Mount Kilimanjaro and in Africa. The warmth drove us to finish what we planned—summit Kilimanjaro!

Vincent, who had barely been walking the previous two days, regained his strength.

He screamed, "We made it!" and started crying.

He wasn't sure if we were at the true summit, and he kept asking Rama, "Is this it?"

Rama kept telling him, "Yes, you made it! You made it!"

It was a jubilation! I jumped up and down, and we all laughed like children.

I stopped taking pictures. I was speechless and felt like a zombie. I've never been drunk, but I was walking like a robot—due to the lack of oxygen, I felt as if I were floating in no gravity. Sebastian, Vincent, and I continued laughing and hugging.

I gave my camera to Rama and asked him to take a summit picture of me. I pulled the Canadian flag from my backpack and stood by the sign showing the peak's elevation.

Rama kept saying, "Adel, you have the flag upside down."

I saw his lips moving and heard the voice, but I could not comprehend what he was saying. Later, I realized that was due to a lack of oxygen, putting my brain into a fog.

Rama was frustrated and requested the assistant guide, Hamid, to assist me in flipping the Canadian flag so he could take a decent summit picture.

Later, he asked me why I wasn't carrying the Ethiopian or Yemen flags.

I told him, "First, I could not find them before coming to Kilimanjaro. Second, even though I was born in Ethiopia and I'm partially Yemeni, Canada is the country that has provided me the opportunity to be here."

I gave him the Canadian flag and the three rocks my daughters had given me to carry with me to pass on to his newborn son.

I turned around and raised my hands in the air, facing the sunrise. I asked Rama to take a few shots. These photos, for me, capture the most unforgettable sunrise of my life. After a six-hour climb on the summit night of a five-day trek, I stood on the highest point in Africa, the land of my birth.

The summit of Kilimanjaro stands at 5,895 meters (19340 feet). Here, we saw the sun rising over Mawenzi, one of the three volcanic cones of Kilimanjaro.

Day 6 Continued, Summit to Mweka Hut

Elevation: 5895 to 3068 m/19,341 to 10,065 ft

Distance: 12 km/7 miles

Hiking Time: 4 hours

From the summit, we descended, continuing straight down to the Mweka Hut camp site, stopping at Barafu Camp for lunch. The trail was rocky and quite hard on the knees; trekking poles were helpful. Mweka Camp is situated in the upper forest, and we experienced mist but no rain in the late afternoon. Later in the evening, we enjoyed our last dinner on the mountain and a well-earned sleep.

Day 7 Mweka Hut to Moshi

Elevation: 3068 to 1640 m/10,065 to 5,380 ft

Distance: 10 km/6 miles

Hiking Time: 4 hours

On our last day, we continued the descent to Mweka Gate and collected our summit certificates. At lower elevations, it was a bit wet and muddy. From the gate, we continued another hour to Mweka Village. A vehicle met us at Mweka Village to drive us back to the hotel in Moshi.

Final Thoughts

To me, climbing Kilimanjaro can be compared to completing a Ph.D. or master's degree or paying off an expensive house. I was filled with a tremendous sense of relief; reaching the summit felt like a massive accomplishment.

The ascent to Mount Kilimanjaro's summit was a mix of misery and a vast sense of achievement—a wonderful, once-in-a-lifetime experience. Climbing through the five ecosystems of Mount Kilimanjaro rewarded our tour group with a visual display of brilliant and unique plant life. We saw flowers, plants, and trees we were told could be found in no other part of the world.

Did I do this?

My feelings after summiting were mixed: I felt complete and yet empty. I was spent, physically and emotionally. But I also felt a massive sense of satisfaction. And I realized at that moment that if I set my mind to doing something, I could achieve it.

If I can do this, I can do anything. Any age, any time.

Rama, our main guide, and his twelve crew members led the way on the entire trek. Roughly four porters were assigned per climber on this journey. The porters carried our stuff, cooked hot meals three times a day, and treated us like royals from one campsite to another. Their working conditions were deplorable, though. They were underpaid, overworked, and underfed. I made sure I tipped them all well, and I noticed the Danish boys were generous, too.

We climbed 50 kilometers (31 miles) one-way (up) to reach an elevation of 5,895 meters (19,431 feet) above sea level. One-third of people didn't make it. I was climber number 860,722 since organizers started keeping records of the climbers, and only those who summited received certificates.

My initial plan had been to reach the summit in six days and come down in two. I carried the Canadian flag so I could wave it and pose for a picture at the summit peak on Canada Day, July 1. However, we reached the summit after five days instead of six, on June 30 at 6:23 a.m., just in time to watch the sunrise. There is … simply nothing like it.

XXIII

Darken the Mountains

Nothing is more destined to create deep-seated anxieties in people than the false assumption that life should be free from anxieties.

— Fulton J. Sheen, American Catholic
bishop

One day in spring 2021, a couple of people sent me a link to a news story with the message, "How often do you experience discrimination in the mountains?"

I read the article. The gist of it was that a woman founded a movement called "Darken the Mountains." Her aim was to break common stereotypes and increase inclusivity for outdoor sports. She was prompted to do this after someone said to her on a hiking trip that they didn't usually see someone darker than themselves out on the hiking trails.

The article and the movement bothered me. I don't like seeing the media focusing on the negative aspects of the human experience. Most people are good people; good people don't get as much attention, especially in the press, as those who stir up problems. Because of my love for the mountains and the amount of time I spend in them, I felt the need to respond to the article, so I wrote an email to the reporter.

In my email, I described my hiking and running decorations and my mixed paternal background of Ethiopian and Arab descent and explained that I proudly wear my dark skin. I had to mention this to her so she would have some context and understanding of the person pounding the keyboard to send her the email.

I further stated that I support and encourage any effort to get every person to engage in a healthy lifestyle, including hiking. However, I take exception when all matters are racialized. I have faced zero opposition or discrimination in my quest to become a better cross-country skier, hiker, and runner. The fact is that countless people, regardless of race, religion, or minority status, have supported and guided me to be successful in my outdoor endeavors.

Even though I rarely write or engage in politics or religious topics, I am compelled to write to you. If I remained silent, I would be doing a disservice to those good men and women I have interacted with over the years.

The vast majority of people I have encountered over the years are good, particularly those who are running and hiking. There is something special about active people bonding together. Sometimes, we call it the runners' high! Brain chemicals associated with feeling happy, confident, and less stressed when we exercise are triggered by increased endorphins and dopamine. We are less likely to see the color, race, ethnicity, gender, and any other differences we may have.

There are several reasons preventing people of all *stripes, including those in minority groups, from taking part in many outdoor activities: financial means, know-how, family history, etc.*

Most members of minority groups tend to hold multiple jobs to provide for the family or send financial support back home to relatives, which leaves zero disposable income for extracurricular activities. Unfortunately, skiing and hiking equipment is costly, and these sports are very time-intensive. But there is no lack of cost-effective or even free opportunities for everyone to enjoy the mountains.

Unlike office towers and just like the sky, these mountains are open and accessible to everyone. No application or screening process is needed to start a hike. The trees, the rocks, and wild animals have no opinion about ethnicity: whether we are Black, yellow, brown, pink, or white. No license or permit is required to hike other than the pass you need to take a vehicle into the provincial or national parks. I never saw or heard of a white person preventing me from going to any destination. The conclusion is simple: get your brown butts out there, with whomever and wherever, and get busy. Participate.

The things people do not like are when we leave items behind (such as littering nature with plastics, cigarette butts, etc.), when we put other hikers' safety at risk by taking unruly children, and when we let our dogs off-leash. These are just a few of the fundamental problems we should be addressing.

To suggest there is racial discrimination on a hiking trail or any other sport is simply a flimsy excuse to bring the topic of racism to the table.

To encourage inclusiveness and accessibility, I don't create minority-based hiking groups. Why? I try to be part of some of the existing hiking circles that prompt a healthy lifestyle. Inclusiveness is done organically by working together, not creating a separate group. Every week, I post several pictures and video clips on social media, not because I seek attention or affirmation, but to promote, encourage, inspire, and motivate people from all walks of life.

I am appreciative of your report and the importance of highlighting the concerns members of the minority group are facing (hate-related). I just worry that we are reporting a situation that could be a fleeting personal perception and an isolated incident that is not representative of the general experience. Hiking the Rocky Mountains is a beautiful and joyous experience that unites us all.

That said, I would like to propose a story for you to cover. It's a very Canadian, multicultural story of a Lebanese immigrant hiking expert who regularly hosts hiking trips to share his wealth of knowledge about hiking the Canadian Rockies. His hiking groups are often a mixture of enthusiastic people of diverse backgrounds from the Philippines, China, Central Asia, Africa, and the Middle East (including Canadians whose ancestors came to this country generations ago). He has more than 1,000 followers on his social media presence. They all share the same interest in acquiring that firsthand experience one can only achieve by reaching the spectacular mountain vistas and summits.

Combined with his and my experiences, you can present a different story focusing on some positive aspects of hiking our mountain trails while highlighting the inclusion of our immigrant (minority) communities. We have a story that will unite us more. What do you think?

We have over 500 jaw-dropping pictures too!

The reporter didn't take me up on my offer. It seems to me that news agencies are attracted to negativity. Why?

Alibaba

The friend from Lebanon whom I mentioned at the end of that letter inspires and scares me. Alibaba regularly participates in extreme hiking and climbing adventures, including ice climbing. I enjoy challenging myself on outdoor excursions, but Alibaba goes a little too far for my comfort level, jumping from cliff to cliff and asking me to take pictures of him in precarious positions and locations.

I went ice climbing with him, trying it for the first time in winter of 2022. I was frightened. Unlike rock climbing, if you fall while ice climbing, there is nothing to grab onto. Any miscalculation could result in disaster. You're carrying an axe. You also need to wear ice crampons, which have much more prolonged and sharper spikes than regular crampons, so if you fall, you could impale yourself on the axe or crampons. My apprehension was high. However, I was encouraged when I saw a couple of people ahead of me. When I reached 10 meters (32 feet) above the ground, I told myself I should stop but I continued anyway. I got to the top of the waterfall and then descended.

When I came down, I felt happy after doing it, but I thought I didn't need to do this again. I have daughters, and I have a life to live. I tried it once, and doing that kind of activity is not worth the risk.

Alibaba was amazed that I went 100 meters (328 feet) above the ground in my first (and only) attempt. Most people go only 3 or 4 meters (10 or 13 feet) their first time!

"Oh man, you did it! You did it! I'm proud of you! I didn't think you'd go that far!" He slapped me on the back, congratulating me as I reached solid ground.

Alibaba's first trip to the Rockies was in May 2017. He says that from the moment he immersed himself in all of that natural beauty, he was addicted. Like me, he heads to the Rockies almost every weekend.

"While other people are partying, going to clubs, I am in the mountains. Hiking, climbing. My party is in the mountains," he says.

He also prefers going solo.

"It's like the first time, every time. If I go with a group, I can take care of them, but if I go by myself, I can take my drone with me, take pictures, and do my own thing. I don't eat when I'm hiking. I'm wired; I can't relax."

XXIV

Becoming a Stereotype

Only after a marathon can I say I have given everything. Because of the enormity of the attempt, the cleansing of the pain, I can sit, even stiff and blistered, and know a kind of peace.

— Kenny Moore, American Olympic
athlete

*A*seasoned runner once told me, "Anyone can run, but it requires a special type of stupidity to run a marathon." Crossing the finish line after 42.2 kilometers (26 miles) delivers a feeling of gratification and accomplishment, but a similar sense accompanies the finish of a well-run 5k (3.1 miles), 10k (6.2 miles), or a fast mile.

I didn't start running marathons like we all learned how to ride a bike: just start and after many rounds of trial and error, cuts and scrapes ... success! No! That's not how it works. The process was complicated and staged.

After my marriage ended, I was in the midst of a custody battle and multiple court cases. And I lost my employment. I needed to do some soul-searching to deal with the pressure of all those significant life changes. I was undergoing therapy to help me find ways to manage everything I was dealing with.

I gleaned many strategies and tools from my therapy as I discussed managing my swollen engineer head, the denting of the inflated ego of an MBA holder who found himself suddenly unemployed, a failed marriage, and lifelong struggles including suppressed childhood trauma. One of the tools my therapist suggested to me to manage my stress was physical exercise.

When I told one of my Yemeni friends that I planned to run, he told me, "You cannot."

I told him, "I can because I have Ethiopian blood in me."

He responded that the other half of me was a rotten, lazy race (referring to my Yemeni blood. I guess he can say that as he is Yemeni himself!).

Humility 101

Not all Canadians are good hockey players; not all Brazilians can juggle a soccer ball like Pele. And not all Ethiopians are marathon runners. But I enjoy running and exercising, so I formally became a runner. I registered at a running club near my home in my later forties. The club manager put me in a group called Learn to Run. I felt a bit offended and degraded. Most people in the group were much older than I was. I almost left the group and went home but decided to stay at least for one clinic as I had paid for the course.

My group and I walked from the building to the designated starting point. The clinic leader told us to run for two minutes and walk for one. The total distance was about 3 kilometers or 1.5 miles. I took off first and ran as fast as possible to prove I was better than the other group members. About 100 yards (91 meters) or so in, I ran out of gas and started gasping for air. The rest of my group passed me. In a few minutes, a seventy-four-year-old man from my group paused to ask if I was okay.

I said, "I'm good."

But I wasn't. Despite my sincere effort, I could not keep up with the other group members and was glad when the session was over.

When we reached the building again and while stretching, the clinic leader approached and talked to me about pacing and appropriate running wear. I had shown up wearing soccer shorts from the 1980s and Walmart sneakers. Over the next three months, I learned the fundamentals of hydration, nutrition, proper clothing, and especially about selecting running shoes.

Little did I know that eventually I would be able to run a full marathon, but first things first. The day I completed a 3.7-kilometer (2.3 miles) run nonstop, about twelve weeks after that embarrassing intro to running, I texted every person I knew to let them know about my accomplishment. I kept posting my running routes and distance on my social media platforms. After another twelve weeks, on October 6, 2012, I registered for a 5-kilometer (3.1-mile) race and ran it. I dedicated my run to a cousin who had passed away from breast cancer.

Gradually, my running community and circle of friends expanded, and I was encouraged to run more 5k (3.1 miles) races. I moved on to 10k (6.2-mile) runs and then the half-marathon. And more and more people started encouraging me to run a full marathon. Apparently, within the running communities, you're not a runner unless you run a marathon. I knew that the first person who ran the 42.2 kilometers or 26 miles from the city of Marathon (Greece) to Athens had died while running. He was a Greek soldier who was asked to deliver the news of winning a battle against the Persians, and he collapsed and died upon delivering the news. Of course, I would die someday, but I didn't want my life to end during or even at the finish line of a marathon!

After many months of training, at fifty-two, I ran my first marathon on June 1, 2014, in Calgary. I recorded a time of four hours and twenty-seven minutes. It was the most grueling and painful experience I had physically endured. I was happy it was over and vowed never to repeat it. I was unable to walk for several days.

I continued to meet more people through running, and one day, I encountered a group of runners outside the running club. They organized their schedule and gathered like-minded people for marathon training year-round. Two-thirds of them were older than me. The oldest was an eighty-four-year-old man named Gerry, and the youngest was my age or maybe a year younger. They called themselves the Beaners because, after long runs on Sunday mornings, they clustered at a coffee shop called Extreme Bean, where I was also spending a lot of time. I started to see them sporadically at the running club, too, but they used the club's location only as a meeting point.

Shelagh was the organizer and the head of the group, along with her husband, Al. She had started the group some twenty years prior. They agreed to include me on the email distribution list so that I would be informed about different locations they met to run three times a week. I didn't think the rest of the group liked me, but I felt comfortable with Al and Shelagh. The two of them had run a combined sixty marathons at that point. They knew about runners' injuries and the appropriate remedies. I stopped reading books on marathons and started to listen to them because most running books and schedules were made for elite runners and didn't necessarily address the type of gear and clothing essential in the unique climate I was dealing with in Calgary. In particular, Al and Shelagh were more knowledgeable about how to best gear up for running in Calgary's harsh winters and the altitude here.

Al asked me if I had ever considered running at Boston. I was shocked by that question because I wasn't even considering myself a runner yet, let alone thinking I could run the Boston Marathon.

I responded, "I don't know."

Lina had just graduated from high school, and I wanted to take her to Maui as a graduation present. I also had a couple of ulterior motives for the trip. My relationship with her had suffered after the divorce, and I saw the trip as an opportunity to spend time together, reconnecting and enjoying a beautiful island. Also, she wanted to have a break for a year before attending university. I was concerned that if she took a year off to work, she might not ever go to university. I needed to be with my daughter alone and discuss her future. In particular, I wanted to impress upon her that a girl like her, who is a visible minority, will have limited opportunities in Canada, and education would be a key to her success. Perhaps Maui was an excellent location for deep one-on-one conversation with her. When she heard about my plan to take Lina to Maui, Summer argued that she should come along too, so I took both of my daughters on this trip.

When I mentioned the trip to Shelagh, she asked if I had considered running the Maui Marathon.

"While you're there," she said, "just do it."

Both Al and Shelagh guided me in preparing for the Maui Marathon. Since it was held in late January, my training had to be done during the winter season. Often, during the cold days, when I showed up to run, I was underdressed. Al allowed me to borrow his heavy-duty gloves, wool hat, and buff.[17] Shelagh had run the Maui Marathon in the past and prepared me to hydrate and run a marathon in hot conditions.

I completed the marathon in Maui and placed fourth in my age group. I shaved nearly thirty minutes off the time of my first marathon in Calgary. My daughters drove along the course line and waited for me at different water stations to cheer me on.

The funny part was that my daughters suggested that I remove my running shirt when crossing the finish line. They would take pictures while I was waving my shirt. I agreed. However, I didn't like my white chest hair, and we decided to color it. We didn't know how to apply the chemicals or do it right, and my chest ended up all blotchy, looking more like a world map. Then they told me not to take off my shirt! I could have shaved it instead, but it was too late to do anything about it by then.

Later the same year, with the guidance of Al and Shelagh, I ran my third marathon with them in Hamilton, Ontario. I finished in three hours and thirty minutes, nearly an hour less than my time for my first marathon! Shelagh congratulated me and told me that I had qualified for Boston! I didn't know the qualifying time, and I had to check with the Boston Athletic Association to confirm; she was right!

The Boston Marathon 2017

The Boston Marathon is special to many people—runners and non-runners alike. Marathoners across the globe aspire to earn their place in Boston, and completing Boston is considered a highlight of a runner's career. Boston has earned its status at the top of the marathon running heap for several reasons.

First, the Boston Marathon is a qualified race. Runners who wish to run Boston must have already run a marathon at a specified, relatively fast pace. The qualifying times change each year and differ for each age group. Unlike any other elite event, Boston is achievable for non-elite runners despite the qualification requirements. Everyone who sees someone in a Boston Marathon T-shirt or jacket knows that runner met a high standard to get that jacket or shirt.

Also, Boston is one of the world's oldest marathons. The first in 1897 was inspired by the success of the first modern-day Olympic marathon in 1896. The Boston Marathon is steeped in tradition and history and has some of the best spectators in the world. As the marathon occurs on Patriot's Day, a regional holiday, locals have the day off, and many come out to the race and cheer. The course passes by several colleges, including Wellesley College. Students of Wellesley College cheer on the runners in the Scream Tunnel—a 0.4-kilometer (0.25-mile) segment of the race. The female students wait along this segment, screaming, and offering kisses to race participants. The screaming is so loud that runners say they can hear it from a mile away.

Finally, and sadly, the bombing at the 2013 Boston Marathon prompted the event to become an even more unifying and patriotic event for both runners and the city of

Boston. The city declared the day "One Boston Day" in 2014 as a way to remember the tragedy and honor those who were impacted by the bombings.

I didn't realize the enormity of qualifying for Boston until I started receiving congratulations. Most importantly, I had promised Lina that I would run Boston if she decided to enroll in university, which she reminded me of later on when she enrolled in her undergraduate program in 2015.

I took Lina to Boston when I ran the marathon in 2017 so that she could visit Harvard University. I hoped doing so would motivate her to do her master's degree. We visited the John F. Kennedy Presidential Library and Museum, as JFK was one of my childhood heroes. We roamed around to explore the city and try all types of cuisines.

As for the race, I took qualifying more seriously than the marathon. Instead of resting and rehearsing my approach for the race, I was roaming around the city on foot and by car. By the time the race came around, I was exhausted and felt like I was coming down with a cold. I didn't care. I just wanted to run to finish anyway. This was the most significant event I had participated in to date, and the experience was overwhelming.

The race started on schedule. As per corral,[18] the runners were driven to the starting point in Hopkinton, a town 48 kilometers (30 miles) outside of Boston. Due to the number of runners (37,000), we needed to be separated into different groups with staggered starting times to make the race manageable.

As I got off the school bus, I rushed to the nearest wooded area to pee. Halfway through the process, I turned around and saw a lady sitting next to me doing the same business. I guess nothing mattered at that point … we all are human and were answering Mother Nature's call.

The atmosphere felt surreal as I walked toward the starting line. I was surrounded by people from so many cultures, all there for the same reason. The mood was wonderful; I imagined it was like an Olympic village, with athletes worldwide. Everyone was happy, and the air was filled with excitement. Families came to cheer on their loved ones. Only four years since the bombing, the energy and the spirit were so fresh.

When in my life did I ever think I could run the Boston Marathon? I thought. *This is such an achievement!*

I'm sure every runner feels that way when doing Boston for the first time. It was like walking down the aisle in a wedding—or like I was a lamb being led to slaughter.

Boston is a special race. It's so prestigious!

I pumped myself up, and I kept walking. But I had to walk 2 kilometers (1.25 miles) to even get to the starting line. I was exhausted before I even started the race!

The elite runners were finishing their race when I reached the starting line. Their success motivated me even more. I was ready!

During the race, I stopped to kiss about five Wellesley College girls and high-fived many children cheering us on.

Around the 32-kilometer (20-mile) mark, even though my group had started about thirty minutes ahead of him, Al, my running mate from Calgary, came up from behind to finish ahead of me. I finished in four hours and nine minutes, much slower than my qualifying time, but I was thrilled to have completed the race. If Al hadn't encouraged me to run with him for most of the last 10 kilometers (6.2 miles), it would have taken me more time to finish.

I didn't do well in Boston, but I knew I could return to redeem myself. In the following years, I qualified three more times but I decided not to run it again. I know several runners who have run Boston multiple times because they wanted to best their personal record, but I don't care about that. At first, I wanted to go back and finish with a better time, but over time, personal records lost their appeal. Most runners care about their time, but my daughters only care about whether I finish or not and I began to focus on that as well. Completing it was enough for me.

The Chicago Marathon 2018

With the Boston Marathon out of the way, I started diversifying my physical activities, including hiking, biking, and cross-country skiing. Between 2014 and 2018, I ran ten marathons in Dubai, Toronto, Honolulu, Edmonton, Banff, and Vancouver, and I ran the Calgary Marathon four times. I even qualified to return to Boston three different times. However, my family doctor gave me something to consider: participating in the six Majors and seven continents (one marathon per continent) rather than repeating Boston.

The Abbott World Marathon Majors is a series of six of the largest and most renowned marathons in the world: the Tokyo Marathon, the Boston Marathon, the London Marathon, the Berlin Marathon, the Chicago Marathon, and the New York City Marathon. Competing in a Majors race is a significant accomplishment for athletes across the globe.

For organizers and sponsors of the marathons, the Majors are financial events. Any runner can get sponsorship, but winners are also paid well. A Kenyan runner, for example, who wins $100,000 in a race can be paid more than the annual GDP of the city he or she comes from. For elite athletes, such as those from Africa, running marathons is like a job—a way to rise above poverty. For the rest of us, for everyday people like me, it's a sport. Completion is a personal accomplishment! As of the completion of the Tokyo Marathon in 2023, fewer than 12,000 runners had completed all six Majors.[19] I wanted to be part of that number!

After completing Boston, I let go of my thought of returning to Boston to improve my time. I turned my attention from running just any marathon in any city to completing the six Majors first, followed by the seven continents. Some major marathons, such as New York City and Berlin, are not easy to get into as the qualifying times are nearly impossible.

After Boston, I ran three different races that secured me a qualifying time for Chicago and Berlin.

In October 2018, it was time to fly to Chicago for the marathon and to visit the city. I spent several hours on a river cruise learning about the architecture, food, and street life. The hotel I stayed in had a spectacular view of the lake.

And I made some great new friends. When I was at the starting line waiting to begin my race, I was shivering and covering myself with plastic to try and keep warm. A lady with minimum clothing was nearby.

"Aren't you cold?" I asked her.

"Where I come from, this is a comfortable temperature." She smiled at me.

"Where are you from?"

"Canada."

"Where in Canada?"

"The western part," she replied.

"Where in the west?" I persisted. "Alberta? BC?"

"Alberta."

"Calgary? Edmonton?" I continued to drill down.

"In the middle," she laughed.

"Ah, Red Deer!"

Red Deer is less than a two-hour drive from where I live. We became friends and still keep in touch.

I also made a new friend, Mark Gershman, who lives in Phoenix. When I released Volume One of my memoir, Mark wrote the following on his Facebook page:

> As mentioned many times, running offers
> me endless opportunities to meet
> wonderful people throughout the journey.
> Short-term and long-lasting relationships
> are priceless. A few years ago, in a shared
> van going to the Chicago Marathon, I met
> a wonderful new friend, Adel Ben-Harhara.
> In that short ride, we became instant
> friends and have stayed in touch since. I'm
> looking forward to seeing him again at the
> NY Marathon this fall (the slowest finisher

buys dinner—I've already surrendered). I was incredibly humbled and honored to be allowed to read an advanced reading copy (ARC) of his new book *To Have Nothing: God Bless the Child Who's Got His Own*. It's just been released on Amazon. The book is his first of a three-volume memoir. It is raw and heart-stopping. You'll be captivated from the get-go. It's a story of resilience, courage, drive, perseverance, and a mindset well beyond his years. Adel, thanks for sharing this with me from the onset. I'll see you in a couple of months.

Mark and I have remained great friends. Although we live in different countries, we've had the chance to spend a lot of time together over the years when in the same city to run marathons.

The London Marathon 2019

While in London, I wanted to achieve a few things besides the marathon. The first and most important was to visit the National Army Museum, where military records are kept, with the hope I could view pictures of the war my father participated in.

My second objective was related to artifacts stolen by Britain. I vividly recall reading, as a child, books that mentioned Britain sending 64,000 people (including 12,000 fighting men) under Sir Robert Napier to invade Ethiopia to release European hostages whom the Ethiopian King Tewodros had captured.

Napier not only destroyed Tewodros's fortress but also allowed his troops to pillage Magdala.[20] An enormous auction of loot was then held. It took fifteen elephants and nearly 200 mules to carry the bounty back to the coastal area. The stolen goods were then shipped to the UK. The British also took the king's son Alemayehu with them. His son's name was the same as my mother gave me when I was a child. I wanted to see the artifacts and recapture and reconcile the images I had in mind with the tangible items left at the museum. I still ponder this question: Why did Europeans steal African treasure (not just in this case but throughout history)?

The London Marathon is the most prestigious of the six Majors and famous for drawing most of the world's best runners. Some runners call it the major race of the world's major marathons due to the level of competition.

The route went along narrow streets with lots of turns. London is the only marathon I know of with two different starting points; the route forms a Y, with the two starting points merging at roughly the halfway point.

In 2021, as I was working on my memoir, my friend Gerry Miller, an octogenarian from Calgary, ran the London Marathon, becoming a world champion and six-star finisher.

Gerry and I met many years ago when we were both engaged in marathon training. Neither of us has ever been in a runner training program, but we always join up with marathon friends, sharing our thoughts, fumbles, and most importantly our friendship through rough but generally happy times.

At the time I am writing this, Gerry is in his late 80s. He is fifteen years older than my mother! Despite the age difference, we have become great friends because of our common love for running but we have also bonded for a much stronger reason. We both had a difficult childhood and grew up without our mothers.

Gerry's grandfather, Willham Mueller, arrived in Canada in 1903 from East Germany. In Winnipeg, where he immigrated, his surname was changed from Mueller to Miller. Gerry's dad, William Miller, was born in a farming community in Saskatchewan and later moved to northeastern Alberta for work.

On Gerry's mother's side, his grandfather was sent from France to investigate French colonies in Northern Alberta. While there, he dated a young French lady from the St. Paul area. The lady friend gave birth to Gerry's mother, Dorthy Revardie, and shortly after that, Gerry's grandmother passed away. His grandfather did not like the isolation of northern Alberta and asked to be returned to France. The young girl, Gerry's mother, was adopted by a caring and loving Scottish couple, the Firths. She grew up as an only child, rather spoiled, and lacking for nothing. While in college, she began dating Gerry's dad, William Miller. They married and began a family.

William and Dorothy had several children: Ken, Marie, and in 1937, after a horse wagon ride across the North Saskatchewan River, Gerry and his twin brother, Donald, arrived at Elk Point hospital.

When Gerry was three and a half years old, the family split in a bitter dispute. In a court case, Ken received an excellent arrangement, living with the Firth grandparents across the alley from their mother's newer house in Vermilion, Alberta.

Marie was able to stay with their mother; soon Gerry was put on a train with our Father, to Edmonton, then on another train, east to a very isolated end of the line town, Alliance, Alberta. A young farming couple needed help with their expanding farming operation, and so Gerry and Donald became foster children and were placed with the couple, the Jacksons.

About twice a year, his real mother would drive with Ken and Marie from Vermilion to visit Gerry and Donald on the farm, but those were frustrating times due to some estranged feelings between the families.

For the first two years of school, Don and Gerry rode an old mean horse three miles to a one-room school. Gerry was the driver, with Don riding behind and hanging on to Gerry. Most mornings, the horse would buck them off in a ditch, and they had a terrible time getting back on that horse.

Before Gerry started Grade 3, the family moved to a larger farm near Galahad, where they began a dairy operation as well as farming six quarter sections of land. He and Don had to help milk the cows and separate the milk. In retrospect, he said their chores resembled slave labor.

However, he also told me, "We must always remember to count our blessings. We enjoyed the best farm food, and we were allowed to participate in sporting activities. As well, we socialized with many church-related young people groups. I remember the hayrides and bonfires, and always some snuggling with pretty young girls. My brother and I enjoyed going to school. We excelled in sports, especially hockey. During the winters, we would eat noon sandwiches quickly, then run over to the skating rink to play scrimmage hockey."

Gerry was anxious to leave the farm. Upon graduation from that rural high school, he received a bursary to attend the University of Alberta. He became a teacher and then soon a school administrator; he was a school principal for three years. Then, he received a research scholarship to complete a master's degree and became a Doctor of Philosophy.

Yes, we have a similar story, coming from humble roots and growing up without our mothers' guidance, but we both worked hard to become well-educated men with a positive attitude and a love for life.

Gerry, at 87, having completed the 6 World Major Marathons at least 20 times.

When I told Gerry I would like to include a bit of his life story in my memoir, he told me the above information. He also said this to me:

"Adel, I have always appreciated your positive and very thoughtful interactions and helpful ideas relating to many life issues. These aspects of our friendship are far more important than marathoning. As an accomplished author, this being your third book, you are providing the world with a progression of such an intriguing life history, coming from nothing and getting to where you are now in life. You are a lifelong friend and running buddy to me, often quizzing me about my childhood, later life situations, and running experiences. Yes, we share a few life similarities. I'm very humbled, nervous, and mostly honored to accept the invitation to be part of your memoir."

I guess I have inspired him, just as he inspires me!

The Berlin Marathon 2019

In 1990, the Berlin Marathon hosted more than 25,000 runners who, for the first time, ran through Brandenburg Gate and into East Berlin. Runners were crying while they stopped to kiss the ground. Since then, runners have continued to flock to Berlin each year to experience one of the best-organized marathons in the world.[21]

I, too, cried when I was in Berlin to run the marathon but not because of the race itself. I visited several historical sites: Jewish cemeteries and other WWII memorials. The bunker where Hitler committed suicide. The Parliament building. And, of course, with my knowledge of and involvement in Marxism as a youth, I wanted to see the statue of Karl Marx. I knew more about the history of Germany than I did about the UK or France from my childhood studies. During my time in Berlin, I tried to marry images I had from my childhood with reality.

When touring through the memorial museum, I saw letters written by boys and girls explaining how they were being treated in the concentration camps. I started imagining my daughters, who were the same age as these children would have been. I couldn't finish the tour; I had to leave and I cried.

And, of course, I, too, was deeply moved when I visited the Brandenburg Gate, where JFK had spoken and where Reagan pleaded with Gorbachev to "tear this wall down."

The marathon was a minor event and I endured small suffering compared to those depicted in the historical sites of this city.

Without knowing COVID-19 would be on the horizon, I planned to complete the six major marathons by November

2020, before I turned sixty. I qualified for and was supposed to run the New York City Marathon in November 2020. However, my plans to run the New York City and Tokyo Marathons had to be put on hold due to the pandemic. As of January 2022, I had secured entry for New York City in November 2022, and I planned to run the Tokyo Marathon in March 2024.

I was looking forward to running the same route as Ethiopian Olympic marathon champion Abebe Bikila ran … but I would be running with shoes!

The New York City Marathon 2022

When I first heard the name New York City, as a twelve-year-old boy, I believed that I was thinking of the capital of America. I remember seeing the city's streets and buildings in movies when I was a boy. As I grew older, my understanding of the city and history evolved. Yes, it is the largest and most influential American metropolis and the country's most populous and international city, but it is not the capital.

I learned that there are probably hundreds of languages spoken daily, and the habits, food, and dress reflect the vibrant diversity of cultures in the city. I always felt it was the most diverse city in the country. Some say that no matter what you do, you will always "fit" in. However, I always felt I didn't belong there, and I am unsure why.

The New York City Marathon presented me with an opportunity to re-examine my impression of the city. I had never been, but I had read and heard a lot about it. In addition to assembling race gear, I listed sightseeing destinations I wanted to visit: the Statue of Liberty, the Empire State

Building, 9/11 Memorial & Museum, 9/11 Ground Zero Tour, One World Observatory, the Metropolitan Museum of Art, the city's cathedrals, Broadway shows, the New York Public Library, a walk over the Brooklyn Bridge. I also wanted to see some of the famous sites that are important to Black American history: the temple in Harlem where Malcolm X used to preach as well as the Apollo Theater, where some of my musical heroes, such as Sammy Davis Jr. and Billie Holiday, performed. It all had to be done in five days, and I also had the race to run.

For a boy from a humble background who only read about those sites, being able to see, touch, and process the significant historical value these places carry was overwhelming. I captured many pictures and video clips and added them to my vlog on YouTube and other social media accounts for the world to see.

The race itself wasn't that different from other races I have run. I arrived in New York exhausted as I had run a marathon in Victoria, BC, only three weeks earlier. I also completed two major hikes in the Rocky Mountains in the previous two weekends. Nothing was left in my tank, but I didn't want to miss this opportunity.

As usual, the running community was excellent. I picked up the race bib and spent time visiting with Mark Gershman and Fuada Velic, two marathoners I'd met in Chicago in 2018.

I completed the race in perhaps the slowest recorded time in my running career—more than four hours—and was glad it was over. It was a hot and humid day for a run; the temperature was 27°C (81°F). While I was running, I encountered a Ukrainian lady, Svetlana, who was struggling. I encouraged her to keep going, to run faster and to cross the finish line. The race organizers recorded the lowest number of finishes in the race's history because of the weather conditions. Brazil's Daniel Do Nascimento suffered a frightening collapse after jumping out to a decent lead after a fast start in the unseasonably warm conditions in New York that day.

When I crossed the finish line, I found myself feeling the same way I did when I reached the summit of Mount Kilimanjaro: exhausted, exhilarated, relieved. Many runners had collapsed but I wasn't one of them. During the race, I needed to adapt by running more slowly and hydrating more. I realized I had the maturity of knowing that running is not about getting out of the gate but about finishing and feeling accomplished. I felt I was a wiser runner after this race than I had been previously.

Tokyo Marathon 2024

I'm amazed at how our adult lives are intricately linked to our childhood. Everything we heard or read as a young person tends to turn into a reality of touching, hearing, smelling, feeling, and seeing during adult life.

During the 1970s, when I was learning how to read and write, the sports magazines in Ethiopia were full of articles about Abebe Bikila, the Ethiopian marathoner who won the Olympic marathons in 1960 and 1964, making him the first athlete to have won the race back-to-back.

Even though Ethiopians won many more medals in long-distance running over the years, understandably, Bikila was hugely celebrated both for being the first African and also Ethiopian to achieve this feat.

The 1960 Olympics in Rome were held long before I was born. And in 1964, Japan was the first Asian country to host the Summer Olympics. However, the news of Bikila's victories was fresh and current to me a decade later. I tried to vividly imagine the streets of Rome where Bikila ran barefoot and the Tokyo city streets where he ran while the Japanese spectators watched him on a hot and humid day.

Sixty years after his win in Tokyo, I was in Tokyo to run my sixth Major. The Six Stars of World Major Marathons had been my journey since 2017, and it came to an end at the Tokyo Marathon in March 2024.

Completing a total of thirty marathons prior to Tokyo was a great accomplishment, one that my family and I are proud of. Tokyo was going to be my final one. It was at a time when I decided not to take part in any more marathon races in order to preserve my knees for old age. Since my passion for running will never die, I chose to run distances up to half-marathon only after completing Tokyo.

With the intent to climb Mount Fuji after the race, I packed winter hiking gear I normally use in Canada like my ice-axe, heated gloves, helmet, GoPro, crampons (ice cleats), headlamp, winter clothing, etc., and left for Japan.

On arrival at the hotel in Tokyo, I discovered I had lost my wallet with my driver's license and three of my credit cards either on the flight or on the shuttle from the airport to the hotel. Luckily, my two running mates from Calgary, Gerry and Jody Raby, stepped in and bailed me out. They covered my meals and other expenses until my oldest daughter, Lina, arrived from Canada.

Over 38,000 athletes from all over the world took part in the 2024 Tokyo Marathon. Even though Boston is the hardest to qualify for, Tokyo seems the hardest to get into, perhaps because of the number of applicants.

I have never approached a marathon race with as much fear and apprehension as I did this one. There were a couple of reasons: After COVID-19, I hardly ran, trained, or took part in any race; therefore, my physical condition was not at the level it used to be. I'm not sure if it has to do with the coronavirus, which I contracted in 2023, or due to my body's reactions to the vaccine, but my breathing rhythm is not the same as it used to be.

The Tokyo Marathon is held during the first week of March. Training for a marathon must start at least twelve weeks in advance, and in this case, that meant training in the middle of Calgary's harsh winter. Training outside in the ice and snow is difficult. To be able to finish the race without injuries, I needed to travel to Vancouver a couple of times to do long runs (32 to 34 kilometers/19-21 miles) and fly to the Bahamas to take part in a half-marathon.

And lastly, the possibility of being disqualified was looming in my head. Compared to other marathons, Tokyo has so many rules, I was worried I might accidentally do something to get disqualified.

One of the rules of the Tokyo Marathon was that a runner must cross the 5k, 10k, 15k, and 20k checkpoints within a specified time. That added an extra pressure; I feared that they would stop me from continuing the race if I did not cross the checkpoints under the specified time.

Another rule was not to litter the course with sports gels or clothing, etc. We had to line up for about ninety minutes before the start of the race. It was near 0°C (32°F) that morning at 7:30 a.m. so I was wearing extra layers to keep warm. There were designated places where we could drop clothing. I was worried whether I would be able to see or find them; dropping clothing elsewhere on the course would result in automatic disqualification.

My normal placing has been corral C for those with a target finishing time between 3:30 and 3:45. However, perhaps because of my poor result in the New York Marathon in 2022, I was put in the back of the pack for Tokyo (corral G).

In any big-city marathon races, in particular in the six Majors, thousands of marathoners are lined up to hit the road. Tokyo was no exception; it was hectic. Being put in corral G and feeling like a human penguin—feeling like I was waddling instead of running—was not a problem; my challenge was how to navigate through the number of runners, which required additional energy. The number of runners in corral G was much higher than I was used to, so I felt crowded.

Because of the congestion, I tripped and fell into a railing. My right arm was injured and I felt the pain through my shoulder and neck. I had to gulp down my pain and show no sign of injury so that I wouldn't get pulled out of the race.

Overall, I didn't enjoy this race as much as I have most others. I was happy to be quickly escorted away from the finish line and back to my hotel. Unlike many races I have run, this was the most worrisome and least motivating. I just wanted to get it done. And I did. I received a special medal for completing all six Majors. A wonderful accomplishment!

Even though I'm not really into keeping track of stats or records, I was surprised and proud to learn that only 716 Canadians have completed the six Majors. I checked the Hall of Fame, and I was ranked 41st out of 716 Canadian finishers and 14th out of 392 Canadian male finishers, and as of March 2024, no Yemeni and only three Ethiopians have completed the six Majors. Therefore, I'm the first Yemeni and fourth Ethiopian to have my name listed in the Hall of Fame. Life is good!

Completion of the Tokyo Marathon was also a moment for me to sit back and take the opportunity to express my gratitude to my running mates, friends, and relatives for their continued support over the years, and to Canada, which provided me with the opportunity to achieve this milestone!

*

Often what we learn from Hollywood and media and what we experience in person are totally different. The first detail about Japan that amazed me was the number of Japanese people who didn't speak English. Given the level of advancement in technology and science Japan has achieved, I had assumed that to a large extent, people might be versed in various international languages. I have traveled in remote sections of Africa; many locals were able to carry on simple conversations and market their merchandise in English. That was not the case in Japan.

Japan is clean and Tokyo is perhaps the cleanest city I have seen. I didn't see a garbage bin on the street. It speaks to the fact that cleanliness is simply a lifestyle for Japanese people. Even the water is so clean that koi fish are able to live in the street drainage canals. Koi can only survive in extremely pure water, which proves the quality of the water in the country.

Japan is the home of the busiest crosswalk with 2.5 million people crossing Tokyo's Shibuya Crossing every day.

And there are more than 6,000 manhole covers throughout the main island (Honshu), decorated with art. Each one is unique, reflecting the local culture.

Yes, the requirement to go silent in restaurants and on train rides was the hardest thing for me to adjust to. Even though I'm an introvert, I'm a chatty man and can talk someone's ear off for hours.

While on the train ride to Mount Fuji, my daughter Lina asked if she could eat one of the bananas I was carrying in my backpack. I told her we could not eat on the train.

We were amazed at how the public transportation system manages to keep to a precise schedule accommodating millions of people on a daily basis. But if you miss it, you need to purchase a new ticket as each ticket is for a specific time, car, and seat.

Overall, I enjoyed the culture and my experience. I was impressed with how clean and orderly Japanese society is. The systems are well-structured and the people are polite and disciplined. The only disadvantage for me in this regard was that because of their adherence to discipline and following rules, I was not allowed to climb Mount Fuji, as it is closed in March.

XXV

Danakil Depression 2020

It's been called one of the most alien places on Earth — a "gateway to hell" and, in the words of British explorer Wilfred Thesiger, a veritable "land of death."

— Monica Pitrelli, editor for CNBC Travel

*L*ife has ups and downs, as does our beautiful planet. I saw the rooftop of Africa by climbing Mount Kilimanjaro, the highest mountain in Africa. I found it irresistible to be at one of the lowest and arguably hottest places on the earth, also in Africa (Ethiopia).

Temperatures at the Danakil Depression average 34.5°C (94°Fahrenheit) but have been recorded above 50°C (122°F).

Two mountains at the southern end of the Danakil Depression, Mount Ayelu and Erta Ale, are also active volcanoes. Mount Ayelu is the westernmost and the older of the two. Erta Ale is one of several crater lakes in the area with lava constantly bubbling in it. The area also contains the hot springs at Dallol.

Volcanic activity heats spring water, bringing sulfur and iron to the surface leaving behind yellow, green, and orange deposits. For centuries, locals have been trekking in with camel caravans to mine the salt by hand, and in recent years, a few have been guiding tourists into the alien-looking landscape.

I asked a few of my friends from Calgary if they would consider accompanying me on a new adventure. As with most international trips, it was hard to coordinate multiple parties with diverse work commitments and other vacation plans, so I had to tackle this trip solo. I booked my flight and tour with a local company and headed to Ethiopia during the cooler, more comfortable season—January and February 2020.

From Addis Ababa to Mek'ele is only 500 kilometers (310 miles), and the flight takes only an hour. But the cost, US$350, is way too expensive for locals, given the average income of the people living there is about $75 per month. During my trip, security was on high alert due to tensions in Ethiopia between the central government and the local authorities. Even though several foreign visitors were on the flight and at the airport, I noticed security personnel kept an eye on me. Primarily, I looked like a typical local but with a few odd body movements. After living in Canada and the US for almost forty years, I have lost the mannerisms that Ethiopian people use; I use different hand gestures and other types of body language. Locals seemed to know I was new to the environment. The funny part was my introduction to the tour guide, who was waiting for me at the airport terminal holding a sign with my name. I approached him to introduce myself, and he was perplexed due to my name, as my name isn't Ethiopian but my face is; my last name confused everyone.

I was part of a group of twelve, and we were put into a couple of minivans and driven to the tour office. We were assigned to smaller groups, and each small group was designated a Toyota 4WD Land Cruiser at the office. I was impressed with the condition of the cars. Knowing the country's situation and considering our destination, I had been worried about the type of vehicles that we would be in.

The twelve individuals were from Brazil, Germany, Canada, China, and France. I was grouped with a French family—a mother with her son and daughter. They took the back seat, and I sat in the passenger seat. The children were twenty-four and twenty-two years old. They spoke English, but the mother didn't. We quickly got along. The guide, who was also our driver, spoke limited English, and he was pleased about this combination, as I could talk to him in Amharic and relay information to the French family in English.

He admitted to me that he had thought that I was from Sri Lanka.

"Why?" I asked.

He said, "You look Ethiopian but don't act or talk like us. Moreover, I have never seen Ethiopians coming to this place to visit the Danakil Depression. Most Ethiopians don't know about the existence of Dallol or where it is located." (Dallol is the local name for the Danakil Depression.)

Day 1 Berhale to Hamed Ela

We began at Berhale, a small village at the edge of the Danakil Depression; the Danakil Depression can be said to start here.

We trekked through the small town of Berhale, where camel caravans stop before they proceed to the northern highlands. En route to Hamed Ela, we saw many long caravans going to the salt mines and others coming out of the Danakil with their salt-loaded camels.

We ran into a camel caravan carrying salt to the nearest major cities. I asked the guide to pull over for pictures. The man who was leading the caravan stopped to greet us. I spoke to him in Amharic and asked if he would let me walk with the camels. He agreed.

Leading the camel caravan was like an out-of-body experience. These very tall animals were so calm. Pulling them made me feel that if I had stayed in Ethiopia, this would have been my profession—my daily routine. I automatically defaulted to putting the stick on my shoulders and leading these huge animals. Fifteen of them followed me without question, without resistance. I felt connected to them in a way I had never experienced before. There was a deep sense of mutual trust that these animals would remain calm and just plod along behind me, and I sensed that they trusted me as well. Knowing that these fifteen animals were behind me took me back to Yemen; I felt immersed in this unique experience.

I told him, "If I hadn't left Ethiopia over forty years ago, I would have competed for your job."

He was unable to stop laughing for a while. Finally he said, "I'm glad you left. I would be unable to compete with you."

Day 2 Hamed Ela to Dodom

We started early, shortly after a 6:30 breakfast, and drove to Dodom at the base of the volcano Erta Ale. The 80-kilometer (50-mile) drive took about six hours, passing through a changing landscape of solidified lava, rock, sand, and the occasional palm-lined oasis. We passed several small hamlets scattered about in this desert before reaching Dodom. We then trekked the rest of the way; the trek from Dodom to Erta Ale took about three hours.

Camels transported all the camping and sleeping materials, food, and water to the volcano's rim, where we spent the night watching the dramatic action of the boiling lava.

Seeing the lava boiling and bubbling was similar to watching a pot boiling on the stove, but the difference is, the pot is self-contained and much smaller. Watching bubbling lava over the size of a football field was scary. I started to wonder if the ground I was standing on would give in. I feared becoming part of that boiling mixture. The air was smoky and I had to wear a mask. I felt puny in comparison to the natural phenomenon in front of me. I was split between excitement and fascination and fear; I kept wondering, *Has anyone checked to make sure this place is safe? Am I standing on stable ground? If I get swallowed by the boiling earth, is that worth this trip?*

The world's only permanent lava lake is in Erta Ale. Erta Ale is a shield volcano (one that is created by constant flowing lava) and is one of Ethiopia's most beautiful natural attractions. The diameter of the base is 30 kilometers (18.6 miles). We spent an unforgettable night on the top of the mountain. The quiet, the stillness, watching the sky, sleeping under the moon on a foam pad without a tent or any other shelter ... I felt free and liberated.

Day 3 Dodom to Erta Ale and Back to Hamed Ela

Early in the morning, we rose with the sun and had time to walk around the pits and craters. The main crater, 200 meters (219 yards) deep and 350 meters (383 yards) across, is sub-circular and three-storied. The smaller southern pit is 65 meters (71 yards) wide and about 100 meters (109 yards) deep. The walk started around 7 a.m., and we returned to our camp by 10:30 for breakfast. After some time to relax, we drove on to Hamed Ela, a village with a total population of about 500. We spent the night camping at Hamed Ela.

I noticed the checkpoint security officials were focusing on me on this day, too. They pulled the cruiser aside for regular checks, but they asked about me, "Who's this person? Why is he here? Where is his ID?"

I was asked to step outside the car at almost every stop during the entire trip, and the security officers carefully examined my passport. The French family that I was traveling with noticed the same pattern. The mother asked me if I was on a wanted list or if someone who looked like me had perhaps escaped from prison. We laughed. My only explanation was that I wasn't European-looking, and hardly anyone of my color traveled with Europeans. Therefore, I caught the attention of the checkpoint officers.

There were two other funny incidents as a result of my skin color.

Every time we got organized and needed to move on to the next stop, the tour leaders would count to ensure they weren't missing anyone. They kept looking for fifteen people but assumed they were looking for European- or Asian-looking tourists.

"Where is the other foreigner?" they always called out.

They counted fourteen people, but they ignored me when counting because they thought I was a local.

The other incident was a bit of a financial plus for me! When we went to the natural hot springs, each person had to pay around $50 for the admission fee, but they didn't charge me because they thought I was a local!

Day 4 Hamed Ela to Dallol and Lake Assal

We drove to Asebo in the morning, where the colorful salt is mined. We observed workers breaking the salt from the ground, cutting it into rectangular pieces, and loading it onto camels.

After that, we drove to Dallol—116 meters (380 feet) below sea level, one of the lowest places in the world—and visited the different landscapes formed by volcanic activity. We then saw Lake Assal, a crater lake in the Danakil Desert, and followed up with a walk with the camel caravans and the local Afar people.

Finally, we drove back to Hamed Ela and proceeded to Mek'ele, the capital city of the Tigray region.

One of the most amazing aspects of this trip is that when I went to Addis Ababa, four out of five Ethiopians I talked to had never even heard of this place; they didn't know it was in their country. Some asked me why I went there. It was like talking to a Canadian who had no idea that Niagara Falls or Banff was in Canada.

XXVI

Blue Nile Falls with My Daughters

The Nile, forever new and old,

Among the living and the dead,

Its mighty, mystic stream has rolled.

— Henry Wadsworth Longfellow, poet

*I*n 2010, I took my two daughters to Ethiopia to visit Lake Tana and show them the Blue Nile Falls.

We took an hour-long flight from Addis Ababa to Bahir Dar, where we spent one night. From there, we took a boat trip to Lake Tana to explore the ancient island's monasteries before visiting the falls in the afternoon. We saw about five monasteries and were told we wouldn't be able to go to at least four other monasteries as women and girls weren't allowed on the islands.

While visiting those five monasteries, the tour guide shared with us the rich history of Christianity in Ethiopia and the history of the Queen of Sheba. He explained that the Queen's son, Menelik, was Ethiopian. While showing us the images painted on the walls of the monasteries depicting the

Queen's visit to King Solomon and then back to Ethiopia, he explained her visit.

From my Ethiopian Christian, Jewish, and Qur'anic studies, I knew the exact geographical origin of the Queen of Sheba has been extensively debated for centuries. Lina quickly reminded me that I had told her the Queen of Sheba was Yemeni.

In Arabic, I politely responded to her, "Let's have this discussion away from the site," as I didn't want to upset or embarrass the tour guide, who passionately explained the links between Ethiopia and the land of Solomon (Israel). The guide was adamant and proud of the Queen of Sheba being Ethiopian, and I didn't want to question him.

My children kept looking at the paintings on the wall and asked why the figures were lighter-colored than typical Ethiopians. Lina stated, "If this is Ethiopian heritage and history, the images should also represent the identity of locals." I had no words to explain the contradiction, nor did the guide!

The Blue Nile Falls are located about 300 kilometers (186 miles) north of Addis Ababa. While the river is flooding, the water is so high that it looks almost black. In the local Sudanese language, the same word is used for both "black" and "blue" so it is called the Blue Nile. Before arriving at the falls, my children saw a wooden shack by the side of the road with an Ethiopian flag waving near the entrance. Lina requested we stop the vehicle.

She asked the guide, "What's that building?"

"It's a school," he replied.

"Can we visit?"

"Sure," he said.

As we approached the gate of the shack, we found around fifteen students—boys and girls in a single room. There was one female instructor.

The lesson paused when the teacher and students saw us by the door. The teacher came to inquire why we were there. I told the teacher in Amharic that my daughters and I had just come from Canada and that the girls had asked to see the school. She smiled and asked me, "What would you like to know?" I asked my daughters if they had any questions for the teacher.

"How many instructors are there? How many subjects do you teach? Where do the textbooks come from? How far do the students have to walk to attend the school?" Lina peppered the teacher with her questions.

"I am the only instructor, and I teach all subjects. The Norwegian government donated the textbooks. The children walk 10 kilometers (6.2 miles) from home to school and back."

Lina went silent with astonishment and wonder.

Summer, who was six then, not to be undone or left out, also had some questions.

Her first question was, "Where is the gym?"

Her other question was about the shepherd herding cows nearby. He was a boy who looked like he was around ten years old.

She asked, "Why is this boy not in the class?"

The teacher knew English but didn't have an immediate answer for her. She smiled and looked to me for help. I turned to Summer and told her the entire field she saw behind the school was their gym, and the boy was an elementary school dropout who was working to support his family. Lina laughed, and Summer was content with my response.

I walked away from that site having learned an enormous lesson: no textbook or movie can teach children the meaning of sacrifice and what it's like not to have the luxuries they enjoy at home. A simple and unassuming stop resulted in a lesson I had never intended to teach my daughters.

The day we arrived at the Blue Nile Falls, the Ethiopian government started to divert the flow of the Blue Nile River to construct a giant dam to meet its energy needs.

The dam's primary purpose is to produce electricity to relieve Ethiopia's acute energy shortage and export electricity to neighboring countries. The dam will be the largest hydroelectric power plant in Africa and the seventh largest in the world when completed.

Because of the dam's size, the waterfall looked so tiny compared to the pictures I had shown my children before departing Canada.

My daughters asked, "Did we fly from Canada just to see this?"

It was a much smaller waterfall than the falls I showed them in their backyard in the Alberta Rocky Mountains. I had no answer other than telling them the water was being diverted for hydro.

"You should have checked that before you booked the flight!" they chastised me.

Dad was busted … that is the problem with raising your daughters to be intelligent and critical thinkers!

*

Since that trip, Lina has traveled to South Africa, Ghana, and Ethiopia to teach elementary and junior high school students math and how to read and write English. Every year, she spends a couple of hundred dollars to purchase and ship notebooks, pencils, and stationery to schools she previously visited. My daughters have traveled four additional times to Ethiopia to assist the Canadian Humanitarian Organization for International Relief. In addition, they are both involved in fundraising activities in Calgary to send money to Ethiopian children who have lost their parents to HIV/AIDS.

I'm proud that I raised two daughters who appreciate what Canada is offering them and who have the sympathy and generosity to help others. They are able to compare their lives to the lives of people who have less, personalize the issue, and take action. In particular, that they have chosen to support less fortunate people on the continent of my birth makes me happy.

Epilogue

You never really understand a person until you consider things from his point of view... Until you climb into his skin and walk around in it.

— Harper Lee, novelist, *To Kill a Mockingbird*

How did it all start, this crazy idea to write my memoir?

The time I devote to the Canadian Rocky Mountains has helped me develop a deep appreciation of the land I chose to be my home and a more comprehensive understanding of myself. It is therapeutic for me! Turning to hiking could not have been timed any better in my life, possibly because I was unknowingly building up to severe burnout in my late 40s.

Spending time in the Rockies has become as important to me as soccer was in my younger days. Perhaps more. The more time I spend in the mountains, the greater affinity I develop for them. Looking at these huge structures is humbling; I reflect on how big they are—how quiet, calm, and unmoving they are. The snow, the waterfalls, the trees are all so calm; they fill me with peace. Those giant rock structures tell me they need to be in harmony with me. Being in this nature makes me feel relaxed and rejuvenated. Grounded.

Perhaps I truly am a wild child deep down, and I can finally reconnect with that part of myself while roaming through the mountains. Or maybe I'm just reflecting on the stories I was told about my father and unconsciously mimicking his acts and lifestyle, such as his love for camping and the outdoors. Looking back, I feel like all the big life decisions I've made recently can be traced back to my childhood.

Two years after my divorce, my daughters moved to live with me full-time. While the custody and legal battles were steaming, my friends encouraged me to enlist an individual counselor for myself and a family therapist for the three of us. The family therapist was necessary as I was struggling to bond emotionally with my daughters. I simply lacked the communication skills to understand and support two teenage girls. Individual therapy was needed because I was carrying unresolved pain from my past.

The first time I understood my affinity to nature and the Rocky Mountains was when my therapist asked me, "When was the last time you felt completely calm and truly in the moment?" I thought for a few seconds and then remembered one moment during a trip to Tekarra Lodge in the Rockies. I was sitting in a deck chair on the banks of the Athabasca River in Jasper National Park. The sun was setting. I watched the stream of the river gently flowing. I admired the majestic Rocky Mountains, with their peaks covered in a soft layer of snow and the tall lines of trees glowing in the golden evening sun. I don't think I've ever been more at peace than at that moment.

Perhaps coming a close second is the hours I used to spend by the Red Sea at Mocha, watching gorgeous red, orange, and blue hues, which left me in awe as the sun descended toward the horizon. The ubiquitous sunshine provides twelve hours of life-giving light and sinks peacefully into the sea as if tucked in for the night.

Every time my head is full and I get overwhelmed, I think about that evening in Jasper and try to reclaim that sense of peace. Yeah, I know. I've changed. I can be calm and serene. Who knew?

I had always considered myself a true city boy, a business type—an office professional. Bragging about the number of rewards points I was collecting during business flights and about having been assigned a corner office. Handing out a fancy business card with a glorified title made me feel taller. Observing the breathtaking architecture of cities, enjoying a variety of restaurants, and playing computer games. I loved it. All of it.

But then something happened. I'm unsure what, when, or how, but something changed. *I* changed. This city man couldn't wait to leave the asphalt jungle and get lost in the great outdoors. Perhaps it started with the first trip with my daughters to Banff National Park, where I fell in love with the feeling of being so small at the foot of something so big and majestic. Something that wasn't manufactured but was created by Mother Nature. And during our time in the mountains, the thought suddenly hit me: *Why do we live in packed cities when there is so much beauty out there?*

During my trips to the mountains, I started to capture images using my cell phone to remind me of those moments when I returned home. Occasionally, I share those images on my social media. Two ladies, Meike and Mary, took notice of my captures. Both spotted my knack for photography—a skill I didn't know I had! They often encouraged me to take more pictures and even suggested investing in better equipment and some training. Meike asked if she could save my photos on her device as she liked them so much. I permitted her to use my photos, delighted that my pictures were so appreciated. Since then, she has shown me proof that my images now hang on her office and home walls.

Mary Noseworthy, the other friend, is a doctor of medicine and clinical assistant professor in the Department of Pediatrics at the University of Calgary. Mary is also a director at the Alberta Children's Hospital in the asthma clinic. She is a mother of four.

One Friday in late December 2019, I phoned Mary to ask if she would accompany me to the mountains.

She said, "Sure!"

She paused momentarily and said, "This would be strictly as friends."

"Of course! What else could it be?"

I picked her up the following morning at around 6. She hadn't had time to eat breakfast before I arrived, so she brought something for us to eat while driving.

The two-day plan included visiting a few frozen waterfalls between Banff and Jasper: Panther Falls, Athabasca Falls, and Sunwapta Falls. We also stopped at Lake Louise to visit Morant's Curve, an area of the Rockies where the train passes. We visited Maligne Canyon the second day, where six bridges displayed frozen water. The fifth of the six rewarded us with an epic view of the canyon's waterfall. The last stop on our way back to Calgary was Abraham Lake, the largest artificial lake in Alberta. The ice bubbles bloom under the lake like flowers, making for a stunning sight. We tried to focus on the lake and ignore the 90-km/hr (55-m/hr) wind we had to endure.

On this two-day trip, Mary asked about my childhood and early adult life. In those forty-eight hours we were together, I probably spoke about my life tales for twenty hours. Mary didn't mind at all and kept soaking it in while probing me for more. After hearing about several of my outlandish experiences at the end of day two, she said, "Adel, you should write a book!"

"I'm incapable of putting together a short email without making some grammar or spelling mistakes. Writing a book would be impossible!" I argued.

"Adel, you don't know it, but you're an excellent storyteller and have plenty of stories to share."

I highly regard Mary as a level-headed person. Not only did she encourage me to write my life story, but she was also instrumental in helping me to recover my father's military records from the British government. She constantly reminded me not to brush off the notion of writing my book, and when I began the process of writing, she consistently inquired about progress updates.

When visiting Yemen and Ethiopia with my daughters in 2010, they asked me to write my memoir. The idea didn't fully register until Mary raised the topic again ten years later. I didn't think my daughters' suggestion was convincing enough, as they were twelve and six years old. Plus, my headspace was all over the place then; it would have been impossible to focus on writing a book.

But several years later, after thinking about my daughters' and Mary's suggestions, I thought, "Yes, perhaps I do have a story to tell. And perhaps others can benefit from hearing my story." I began to collect my journals, my memories, and other documents I have kept over the years.

The Journals

When I embarked on writing my memoir, it was imperative that I give meaning to my life; explore my thoughts; see the progress I have made in how I view people, society, and the world; examine my interactions with people; and most importantly, reflect and touch on self-awareness. Introspection is one of the most important human skills to master to become a more compassionate and overall better person. A daily journal has always allowed me to have that introspection—even if it was just a taste—to reflect on who I was that particular day.

I needed the exact timeframe of when events happened. I have had many significant and profound interactions with people throughout my life. Keeping a journal helps me record those interactions. Reviewing them occasionally helps me remember and understand why those people remain so important to me long after the events have passed.

Progress is a critical component of any person's growth and improvement. I did not become the person I am today overnight. In the context of my important life goals and personal objectives, my journals help me see what's important to me. I record my thoughts on a particular day. Most are irrelevant, but there are inspirational and educational moments for me as I get older and reflect. Meaning in life is a subjective concept unique to each person. My journal tracks my dreams and aspirations and, through structure, allows me to figure out what is most important to me.

My journals have been sources of information for me for this and my first two books. Even though I presented a fraction of my life's events in my books, 90 percent of my story was based on my journals.

Once I finished extracting information from my journals—the ones from the first sixteen years of my life—I took them to Abraham Lake in Alberta and burned them in a campfire. Looking at the flame, I felt like I was burning everything that had happened to me. I felt freed—unshackled. It was my closure. Everything was solved. I was finally closing the door and locking it behind me on that part of my painful past.

*

My journals dating back to 1973 arrived, after much anticipation, in my mailbox in spring 2020 from Yemen and Ethiopia. The last batch came to me in June 2021. Many of the written records were lost with my journeys from Ethiopia to North Yemen, North Yemen to the US, back from the US to Yemen, and to Canada. Despite my moves across three continents, the deaths of many of the significant individuals from my childhood and early adult years, and other circumstances, I was, however, able to recover plenty of records thanks to those who kept them for me. My sister and my former in-laws kept my journals in Yemen and sent them to me from there. I'm also still amazed that my aunt, whom I lived with in Ethiopia when I was between ten and sixteen, kept my childhood journals all these years. I'm grateful that she did so and that she sent them to me when I started writing my memoir.

While I was filled with joy at seeing my early childhood handwriting, I had a considerable challenge. Due to the time that had passed without my reading, writing, and speaking Amharic (about forty-five years), I could not reread my childhood musings. I would recognize the letters and individual words but could not correctly comprehend what was written. When writing my journals, I had permanently altered names; in some cases, I wrote paragraphs mixing and matching sentences and words using Arabic, Amharic, and some English. The intent was that if the journals were found, the person reading them wouldn't be able to read all three languages. The likelihood of someone understanding them was slim to none during those days. I feared that someone would read them and know what I thought and said about the characters. As an adult, I was now a victim of my scheme!

When I began to go through my journals and plan out my memoir, I reached out to Betty, my childhood friend's daughter from Ethiopia, who was attending university in Winnipeg, Manitoba. I had half-siblings, cousins, and friends who could read the journals for me, and I would easily understand what was written if someone read them to me. But Betty Tilahun was suitable for this, as she was born decades after I left Ethiopia. She had no connection to the characters mentioned in my journals, so my private thoughts about relatives and friends would be contained.

The arrangement worked fine. I took pictures of the journals and sent them to her via email or text messages, and we set time aside during the evening hours so that she could read them to me. For the most part, she was engaged, as the stories she was reading were interesting, funny, and sad. She didn't mind spending the energy and time, nor did she get bored. Several weeks and months went on with such a routine: she read, and I took notes.

One evening, I phoned, ready to take notes.

Betty said, "Mr. Adel, I won't be able to read this journal section."

"Why?"

"It's a bit embarrassing for me to go through the details."

"What do you mean?"

"Well, you wrote about something I'm uncomfortable discussing."

I wasn't sure what was going on. I didn't think there should be any problems, as the section of the journal she was reading was written in 1982 while I was in North Yemen. There shouldn't have been anything to implicate anyone living in Ethiopia. I apologized and pressed her to explain to me.

She said, "You wrote a few pages, a long journal entry about the day you first watched a pornographic video."

The phone went dead silent.

I gathered myself and said, "I didn't know I had written on such a topic! My apologies. I wouldn't have sent it to you if I had known the content."

She said, "Not to worry. I can read other entries you sent me in the same email."

I didn't know what to say at that point. She had read something I had written almost forty years prior. I asked myself, *What did I write?*

While I was pondering, I was listening to her.

Then I heard her saying, "If I may ask? Do you mind if I ask you a question?"

"About what?"

"Thanks for understanding my position on the matter, but I have a question."

I said, "Shoot."

"After three pages of summary and analysis of the pornographic video, you said, 'That is not what I expected.' What were your expectations, if I may ask?"

I didn't have a response. I didn't even know I had written a three-page analysis!

That was the last of my journals she read for me.

*

After that conversation with Betty, I was afraid of what else might come out through my journals, so I ended the work with her. I turned my attention to my cousin, Sahle Mandefro, who lives in Atlanta, Georgia, US. He is one of my Aunt Emebet's children, and he was about eight years old when I left Ethiopia. (My Aunt Emebet is the woman who rescued me from living on the streets of Nazreth, Ethiopia, when I was ten years old. Sahle was a baby at that time.) My close relationship when I was a child was with his older brother, but Sahle and I developed a trusted relationship over time. What surprised me about Sahle was that he kept the letters I sent to the family from North Yemen to Ethiopia during the first few years I lived in Ta'izz and Hodeidah (1980-82).

Sahle took charge of reading the remaining journals and assisted me in translating them into English. Most of the content in Volumes Two and Three from my journal entries stems from his contributions.

After reading my journals, he made one comment that I thought was a good observation of my situation in my younger days: "If our mom hadn't come to rescue you at a tender age, it would have been impossible to put some structure or control over you. Luckily, her timing was unyielding!"

It is said it takes a village to raise a child; that is precisely what it took to raise me, and it was also necessary to have a group of people, including him, to complete my books.

Perhaps both Betty and Sahle enjoyed reading my journals more than my books!

Final Reflections

Volumes One and Two were released in 2022. At that time, Volume Three was well under way, but I needed a break. Working intensely on three books about my life was exhausting and Book One in particular brought my childhood trauma to the surface. I put Volume Three on hold for slightly more than a year and gave myself a chance to catch my breath. After all, this project was a marathon, not a sprint.

During the break, I reflected more. I looked back at my whole life—the first sixty-one years of it—and acknowledged that in spite of my struggles and traumas in my early days, despite experiencing racism in every country I have lived in, even though I was deprived of being raised by two parents in a typical family home, I have had a good life.

I have never turned to God and asked him to help me, but he has always been there, looking out for me.

What if my aunt hadn't rescued me from the streets? I likely would have died very young or been arrested for stealing food from markets.

What if my chance encounter with Bansser had never happened? I would have never connected with my father's side of my family and I perhaps would have never gone to Yemen.

What if the guards in the prison in Ethiopia hadn't had mercy on a young teenager? They would have tortured and killed me like they did so many others whom I was imprisoned with.

What if the Iraqi diplomat whose car I rear-ended hadn't come back and advocated for me? I would have rotted in that Yemeni prison for weeks, months, or longer.

What if I had never worked with John Rees in Yemen? I would have not had any connections to Calgary, and I may have immigrated to somewhere else in Canada or not at all.

All of these connection points allowed me to keep moving forward with my studies, my work, and my hobbies. None of these pivotal points are explainable to me except that God blesses a child who has nothing and who needs help. He sent all of these angels to me, to rescue me and look out for me. My life story is the result of the collective effort of humanity.

Afterword

It would be the simplest thing to say: my homeland is where I was born. But when you returned, you found nothing. What does that mean? It would be the simplest thing to say: my homeland is where I will die. But you could die anywhere or on the border between two places. What does that mean? After a while, the question will become more challenging. Why did you leave? Why did you go? For twenty years, you have been asking, why did they leave? Going is not a negation of the homeland, but it does turn the problem into a question. Do not write a history now. When you do that, you leave the past behind, and what is required is to call the past to account. Do not write a history except that of your wounds. Do not write a history except that of your exile. You are here—here, where you were born. And where longing will lead you to death. So, what is homeland?

— Mahmoud Darwish, Palestinian poet
and author

*I*t wasn't essential for me to gather scientific evidence to indicate that my experience facing sustained obstacles in life has benefited me with a greater propensity for resilience when dealing with subsequent stressful situations. I'm the product! Unequivocally, due to traumatic life events, I suffered from depression and anxiety, but I have displayed remarkable resilience. Over the years, I've gained the ability to regulate my emotions as a tool for protection and self-preservation. Today, I confess that fighting through a lifetime of misfortune has brought me better outcomes than a history without adversity would have.

What does it take to succeed when you leave behind everything you know and attempt to embrace a new way of life on a new continent? Everyone likes to be understood, respected, appreciated, and adequately characterized. Unfortunately, new residents to Canada and the US are often misunderstood, disrespected, or mislabeled due to inaccurate perceptions and assumptions by all parties.

Culture shock might better be rephrased as a culture clash.

Immigrants from all walks of life have common pains and gains.

The contrast in how the West views the settler versus how the immigrants picture themselves in the new home is starkly different. When we're understood, we celebrate. When we're respected/appreciated, we put on a festival. We cannot sleep due to our joy when we're lucky enough to be correctly characterized!

I'm grateful for my life in Canada. I enjoy freedoms I didn't have in Yemen and opportunities I wouldn't have in Ethiopia. To possess a Canadian passport is a privilege. That document makes me feel more potent and wealthier. Even if you have an empty stomach, that passport opens doors for travel, and the world is more welcoming to you. I have traveled far in the time between living on the dusty streets in Ethiopia as a youth. I'm nearing retirement after decades of work as a professional in a country that welcomed me so many years ago.

This is not a sociology or history book. I don't claim to be an expert on religion, history, or even culture. I'm sharing my life story so that others can reflect and learn about themselves through my reflections and experiences; I want to bring questions to readers' minds. One lesson I hope my readers will ponder is that two people don't have to have the same skin color, religion, ancestry, etc., in order to feel like brothers or sisters.

My memories, my childhood journal entries, and the lessons I learned from my schooling and all the books I've read have shaped my understanding and interpretation of my childhood. I have attempted to present my adult perspective of a varied, rewarding, and at times challenging life.

I've made it here from having nothing. Through hope, optimism, perseverance, and determination, my resilience is a testimonial to my silver lining.

Other Books in This Series

Volume One

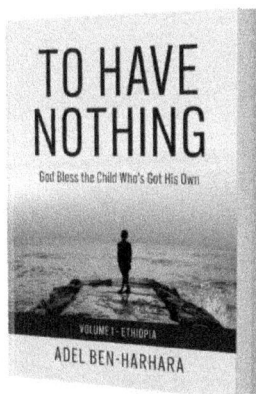

When life is defined and debated through sound bites and social media, who would want to hear a story about a boy who traversed multiple cultures, languages, religions, and geographical areas?

To Have Nothing, the first volume of Adel Ben-Harhara's three-volume memoir, delves into the voyage of a boy who was separated from his mother as a toddler and was essentially orphaned at the age of five when his father died. With his mother's inability to provide support, the boy was homeless, often left on the streets between the ages of eight and eleven. How did he survive?

The boy was born in Addis Ababa to a poverty-stricken, fifteen-year-old Ethiopian mother and a wealthy fifty-year-old businessman, a retired British soldier from the Middle East.

The boy received extensive religious teachings in Judaism, Islam, and Christianity as a child. As an adolescent Marxist in Ethiopia, he was imprisoned for taking part in a communist party youth movement. He barely avoided the death squad's bullets before moving to his ancestors' land: Yemen.

This is the story of that boy, an inspiring tale of perseverance and survival.

Volume Two

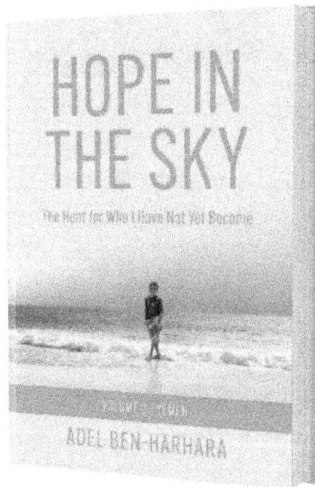

Hope in the Sky, the second volume of Adel Ben-Harhara's three-volume memoir, speaks about millions of Yemen's *Muwalladin* (foreign-born Yemenis) struggling for equal rights and citizenship. He was one young man who spent a dozen years in North Yemen, where he suffered from prejudice, discrimination, and the effects of civil war. He endured harsh treatment because he wore dark skin, was born in East Africa, and was unable to assimilate into an underdeveloped society living according to primitive cultural traditions. He stood firm and managed to depart his ancestors' land, not because he was tough, but because he had no choice.

What happened to one of the oldest nations on Earth, the cradle of Arab civilization, the home of the biblical Queen of Sheba, consort of King Solomon? With ties to the Semitic lands to its north and the cultures of the Horn of Africa across the Red Sea, Yemen is frozen in time and still practicing medieval traditions. Illiteracy and constant tribal conflicts serve as catalysts in suppressing development and modernization and in keeping the country and surrounding areas suspicious and threatening to the world.

Want to learn the inner workings of Yemeni life through the struggles of a sixteen-year-old boy who immigrated to his ancestors' land? Read on.

Acknowledgments

I am deeply thankful for the amazing support, belief, guidance, and flexibility that I received on my journey. The unwavering support of my caring supporters, the unwavering faith of my encouraging mentors, the invaluable wisdom of my experienced guides, and the unwavering adaptability of my accommodating companions – all of them have played a crucial role in helping me realize my full potential. The following are the names of individuals who were not included in the book dedication, equally important to my book success and my life.

Aalaa Alberdrani, Abera Lemma, Abinet Muluneh, Al & Shelagh Hawken, Al McGrath, Alexander Semaw, Ali Saeed, Ali Taher, Alibaba Zeaiter, Allan Dwyer, Amanda McGrath, Ameen Bahammam, Amy McClelland, Andrea Klassen, Andy Dragt, Anne Sorbie, Astrid Bordeville, Awadh Baobaid, Ayele Deneke, Azza Farid, Barb Young, Batoul Maklad, Belle Toren, Berhanu Kebede, Betty Tilahun, Bevereley Power, Bob Hallett, Brian Maxwell, Carol Walsh, Carolyn Kildare , Catherine Mitchel, Cathy Fun, Cathy Guo, Cheryl Dunn, Chris Skalr, Conrad Johnston, Dale-Lee Vezina, Dawn Crump, Deb Lentz, Debbie Whitney, Debra Chernesky, Denise Malmgren, Desalegn Seyoum, Don Dickinson, Doris Ross, Doug Warden, Ermias Mekonen, Fe Dimmangna, Ferdows Yusuf, Fisseha Gebremedhin, Gary & Cecilia Teare, Genet Hadgu, Geoff Hunter, Gergana Yankov, Gerry Miller, Haifa AlMaashi, Heather Matt, Heather Robertson, Heather Udchic, Helen Kokeshi, Ikram Awel, Irina Reznikova, James Ziegler, Jana Rade, Janet Croal, Janet Soukeroff, Janet Wayne,

Janine Shum, Jazmin Leigh, Jenn Parker, Jennifleur Lumley, Jody & Gerry Rabbi, John Cook, John Reese, John Wakoluk, Judy Funk, Judy Eliott, kahty Game, Karla Dawe- Paterson, Kate Dunn, Kathleen Warner, Kathy Adms, Kathy Ervin, Ken Chudleigh, Ken Ruller, Khamla Sirivath, Laura Davies, Laura Kowk, Lensa Mekonnen, Lina Palat, Liney Beltran, Lisa Lauchlan, Lorandonna Botter, Lorna Curran, Lucy Xu, Majed Al-Jefri, Marian Moise, Marie Martin, Marie-Josée Guérer, Mark Gershman, Mark Hansen, Mark Osterman, Mary Noseworthy, Matias Abebe, Matyas Feyissa, Meike Thomsen, Meron Mekonnen, Mesfin Genanaw, Mestewal Assefa, Mike Layton, Million Tafesse, Mohamed BaObeid, Mulitti Mosisa, Nessma Yousri, Nizar Bahumaid, Noelle Wilkinson, Omer Al-Hamadi, Rados Massey, Ramona Neyrinck, Raymon Feliz, Reagan Brown, Rhonda Wickett, Richard Wilson, Robert Christie, Romie Christie, Sabrina Samuelson, Sahle Mandefro, Sana Bagersh, Sami Al-Shatibi, Sandi Doiron, Sarah Lantry, Sharon MacDonald, Sherese Browntrouts, Sheryl Covey, Sheryl Page, Solanga Angulo, Solome Baraki, Sukhdeep Mann, Susan Johnston, Susan Meder, Susan Pendleton, Tigest Samuel, Tirsit Abay, Tracey & John Potter, Tracey L. Fillion, Trevor Penford, Trina Koops, Victoria Wilke, Wendy Frazier, Willa Wanke , YaLing Jiang, Yanita Gourkova, Yared Kidane, Yohannes Feyisa, Zeni Taye, Zina Corcoran Perry.

The Almaashi Family, The Bagarish Family, The Bahammam Family, The Bahumaid Family, The Banajah Family, The Baharon Family, The Bansser Family, The Hiking Community, The Samardzic Family, The Sakaf Family.

AGGUDO Coffee, Amhara TV, Arts TV, Calgary Public Library, EBC TV, EBS TV, Fana TV, Habasah Magazine, The Idaho State Library, Minber TV, The Running Community,

The Hiking Community, The Calgary Ethiopian Commynity, and The Calgary Yemeni Community.

Appendix One

In August 1992, Cecil D. Andrus, Governor of Idaho, wrote a letter to INS on my behalf asking them to review my case and consider allowing me to stay in the US. He explained that I was gainfully employed and that the library I was working for wanted to keep me on staff.

Sadly, Governor Andrus passed away in 2017 and so I am not able to obtain permission to print the letter verbatim here. However, I would like to acknowledge how much I appreciate his advocating for me in such a difficult time. It's amazing to me that the governor of the state would take the time to write on my behalf; he didn't even know me but he looked at the situation and decided to put his name behind such a request.

His support was a wonderful example of humanity.

Bibliography

"Mississippi Masala (1991) Starring Denzel Washington." YouTube,
    November 23, 2022. youtube.com/watch?v=jHQrw_s28qA. 1:28:17-1:28-
    39. Accessed April 12, 2024.

"Wikipedia: Battle of Madgala." Wikimedia Foundation. Last edited March 8,
    2024, 12:55. en.wikipedia.org/wiki/Battle_of_Magdala.

"Wikipedia: Black people and Mormonism." Wikimedia Foundation. Last
    edited March 19, 2024, 5:25.
    en.wikipedia.org/wiki/Black_people_and_Mormonism.

Allen, James. "As a Man Thinketh: The Secret Edition – Open Your Heart to
    the Real Power and Magic of Living Faith and Let the Heaven Be
    in You, Go Deep Inside Yourself and Back, Feel the Crazy and
    Divine Love and Live for Your Dreams." p.27. 2013. Lulu Press,
    Inc.

American History: From Revolution to Reconstruction. "John Fitzgerald
    Kennedy, Ich bin ein Berliner Speech." June 26, 1963.
    let.rug.nl/usa/presidents/john-fitzgerald-kennedy/ich-bin-ein-
    berliner-speech-1963.php.

Comic Strips Wiki. "Joe Btfsplk." Accessed February 11, 2024.
    comicstrips.fandom.com/wiki/Joe_Btfsplk.

John F. Kennedy Presidential Library and Museum. *Historic Speeches.*
    "Televised Address to the Nation on Civil Rights." June 11, 1963.
    jfklibrary.org/learn/about-jfk/historic-speeches/televised-address-
    to-the-nation-on-civil-rights.

Marathon Tours & Travel. "Abbott World Marathon Majors." Accessed April
    4, 2024. marathontours.com/abbott-world-marathon-
    majors#:~:text=At%20the%20end%20of%20the,Star%20journey
    %20more%20than%20once.

Marathon Tours & Travel. "BMW Berlin-Marathon." Accessed April 4, 2024.
    marathontours.com/races/bmw-berlin-marathon-382.

Merriam-Webster.com Dictionary, s.v. "Peter Principle." Accessed March 31,
    2024, merriam-webster.com/dictionary/Peter%20Principle.

Thought Catalog. "36 Of The Most Ridiculous 911 Calls In The History Of
    The Universe." Accessed April 4, 2024. thought.is/36-of-the-most-
    ridiculous-911-calls-in-the-history-of-the-universe/.

Endnotes

Introduction

[1] James Allen, "As a Man Thinketh: The Secret Edition – Open Your Heart to the Real Power and Magic of Living Faith and Let the Heaven Be in You, Go Deep Inside Yourself and Back, Feel the Crazy and Divine Love and Live for Your Dreams", p.27.

Major Life Events

[2] Volumes Two (Yemen) and Three (the US and Canada) are both divided into two parts, as I lived in the US between the two periods I lived in North Yemen, and then I moved to Canada.

III

[3] Throughout this book, I have used the word "nigger" in certain scenes. I recognize this word is offensive; I have chosen to use it to show the true character, mindset, and speaking patterns of the people I encountered. The use of this word does not reflect my values and attitudes nor those of my editors.

[4] John F. Kennedy Presidential Library and Museum, *Historic Speeches*, "Televised Address to the Nation on Civil Rights."

V

[5] Qat: leaves that Yemenis chew during social gatherings in the afternoons and during ceremonies. Qat is like chewing tobacco and dulls the senses.

Endnotes

VIII

6 "Peace be upon him" will be abbreviated in subsequent mentions as "pbuh".

7 Wikipedia; Wikipedia's "Black people and Mormonism": entry, Wikipedia's entry outlining the history of attitudes towards and the role of Black people in the Mormon church.

XI

8 Cecelia Ahern, Irish novelist.

9 American History: From Revolution to Reconstruction, "John Fitzgerald Kennedy, Ich bin ein Berliner Speech," June 26, 1963.

XII

10 Out of respect for her privacy, I have chosen not to include my ex-wife's name in this book.

XV

11 "Peter Principle: an observation: in a hierarchy employees tend to rise to the level of their incompetence," Source: Merriam-Webster.com Dictionary, s.v. "Peter Principle," accessed March 31, 2024, merriam-webster.com/dictionary/Peter%20Principle.

12 "Mississippi Masala (1991) Starring Denzel Washington."

XVI

13 Abebe Bikila was an Ethiopian marathon runner who won back-to-back Olympic marathon races. He was Ethiopia's first Olympic gold medalist, winning the marathon at the 1960 Summer Olympics in Rome while running barefoot. He then won the marathon at the 1964 Tokyo Olympics. He won both races in world record time.

14 Comic Strips Wiki, "Joe Btfsplk."

XIX

[15] Thought Catalog, "36 Of The Most Ridiculous 911 Calls In The History Of The Universe."

XXII

[16] Moshi: a town in Tanzania near the Kenya border.

XXIV

[17] Buff: a tube of lightweight, stretchy material that hikers, cyclists, runners, etc., wear around their heads to keep warm.

[18] Corral (or wave): a grouping of runners in a marathon. Not all runners can start the race at the same time, so runners are placed into corrals, or groups, and corral start times are staggered with the fastest runners being in the first corral to start and the slowest in the last.

[19] Marathon Tours & Travel, "Abbott World Marathon Majors."

[20] "The Battle of Magdala was the conclusion of the British Expedition to Abyssinia fought in April 1868 between British and Abyssinian forces at Magdala, 390 miles (630 km) from the Red Sea coast. The British were led by Robert Napier, while the Abyssinians were led by Emperor Tewodros II." Source: Wikipedia; Wikipedia's "Battle of Magdala" entry; Wikipedia's description of the Battle of Magdala.

[21] Marathon Tours & Travel, "BMW Berlin-Marathon."

Printed in the USA
CPSIA information can be obtained
at www.ICGtesting.com
JSHW082055030624
64162JS00003B/81